THE TRAGEDY OF

AMERICAN DIPLOMACY

William Appleman Williams

REVISED AND ENLARGED EDITION · A DELTA BOOK

A Delta Book
Published by
Dell Publishing Co., Inc.
750 Third Avenue
New York 17, New York
All Rights Reserved

This is a revision and enlargement of the 1959 edition published by the
World Publishing Company. It is published as a Delta Book by
arrangement with the original publisher.

Library of Congress catalog card number: 59–6655
Manufactured in the United States of America
Cover design by Fred Harsh
Book design by The Etheredges
Sixteenth Printing

AUTHOR'S PREFATORY NOTE

This paperback edition was set up and published from a manuscript
that emerged from a thorough reconsideration, revision and enlargement
of the book as originally published in 1959. This rewriting was done in
December, 1961.

For her suggestions bearing on that work, he wishes to thank Mrs.
Elizabeth Shepherd of the Dell Publishing Co.

FOR CORRINNE . . . . . FOR ALL THE REASONS

TABLE OF CONTENTS

I fancy a number of people all over the Western World still think of themselves as liberals, but are in essence no such thing. In their hearts they believe that their society won't (and shouldn't) change much, that Communism is the enemy absolute, and that the only tasks open to men of good will are to fight the Cold War with one hand and perform minor benevolent activities with the other. That is a tenable attitude, but it is one of people who have given up the intellectual struggle.

SIR CHARLES P. SNOW, 1957

This is a time for searching criticism, all right, but for criticism of the whole society.

JAMES RESTON, 1958

THE TRAGEDY OF AMERICAN DIPLOMACY

INTRODUCTION: HISTORY AND THE

We find genuine tragedy . . . only in that destruction which does not prematurely cut short development and success, but which, instead, grows out of success itself.

Breakdown and failure reveal the true nature of things. In failure, life's reality is not lost; on the contrary, here it makes itself wholly and decisively felt. There is no tragedy without transcendence.

This transformation may go the way of deliverance, where man rises to supreme reality through conquest of the tragic. Otherwise this transformation may go the way of decline into irresponsible aestheticism of the spectator: man distracted, drifting, falling off into nothingness.

KARL JASPERS, TRAGEDY IS NOT ENOUGH.

TRANSCENDENCE OF THE TRAGIC

The tragedy of American diplomacy is aptly symbolized, and defined for analysis and reflection, by the relations between the United States and Cuba from April 21, 1898 through April 21, 1961. The eruption of two wars involving the same two countries in precisely the same week provides a striking sense of classical form and even adds the tinge of eeriness so often associated with tragedy.

After three years of pressure culminating in an ultimatum, the United States declared war against Spain on April 21, 1898. The generally avowed objectives were to free Cuba from Spanish tyranny, to establish and underwrite the independence of the island, and to initiate and sustain its development toward political democracy and economic welfare.

During the subsequent 63 years, the United States exercised continuous, extensive influence in and over all aspects of Cuban affairs. And this influence and intervention produced some positive results. The advantages Cuba enjoyed as an American protectorate rather than a Spanish colony were significant and beneficial. Sugar production was modernized and increased. Some public utilities and other improvements associated with the basic sugar economy were gradually provided. And in the city of Havana, Americans and Cubans developed one of the business and entertainment centers of the Western Hemisphere.

As Cuba planted, harvested, refined, and sold more sugar,

it enjoyed slow and sporadic economic development. A modest number of Cubans improved their personal and group economic welfare. Furthermore, some of the forms and mechanisms of representative government were established and legalized, and some of the resulting institutions put out shallow roots into Cuban thought and culture. Reforms were instituted that helped stabilize Cuban politics and contributed to the elementary and routine kind of law and order necessary for moderately efficient economic activity. On rather widely separate occasions, small segments of the Cuban population participated in a consequential way in the process of representative government. And perhaps most important of all, the Cubans were encouraged—and exhorted—to define their future in terms of the democracy and prosperity so evident in the United States.

Yet when measured by the Cubans in the course of their own life-long daily experiences, or by outsiders concerned to discover and evaluate the results of American control, there was clearly a continuing, even increasing disparity between the actuality and the rhetoric. For the United States dominated the economic life of the island by controlling, directly or indirectly, the sugar industry, and by overtly and covertly preventing any dynamic modification of the island's one-crop economy. It defined clear and narrow limits on the island's political system and the men who dominated its operation. It tolerated the use of torture and terror, of fraud and farce, by those rulers. But it intervened with economic and diplomatic pressure and with force of arms, when Cubans threatened to transgress the economic and political restrictions set by American leaders.

That sad result was not caused by purposeful malice, callous indifference, or ruthless and predatory exploitation. American leaders were not evil men. They did not conceive and execute some dreadful conspiracy. Nor were they treacherous hypocrites. They believed deeply in the ideals they proclaimed, and their rhetoric as applied to the United States had substantial relation to the facts. And they did sincerely and rationally argue that their activities and policies would ultimately bring the same happy results in Cuba.

Precisely for those reasons, however, American diplomacy

contained the fundamental elements of tragedy. It held within itself, that is to say, several contradictory truths. Those truths, left to follow out their given logic without modification by men who understood that process and acted on their knowledge, would ultimately clash in a devastating upheaval and crisis.

There was first the truth of American power. Measured in relative or absolute terms, the United States had (and has) preponderant power in relation to Cuba, a power it has exercised vigorously and persistently.

There was secondly the truth that the use of that power failed to create in Cuba or in its relationship with America a reality that enjoyed any persuasive correlation with the ideals avowed as the objectives of the power. It generated neither a system analogous to the American political economy nor a society modeled on fundamental Cuban ideals and aspirations.

A third truth resulted from that deployment and use of American power. Gradually, but with increasing momentum, Cubans evolved a coalition of groups committed to important changes in their society. In turn, that objective implied significant modifications in Cuba's relations with the United States. Though this coalition included reformers and moderate conservatives, it drew most of its verve and drive from noncommunist radicals. Their dedication and courage in actively opposing the Batista regime sustained and strengthened the general movement, and ultimately won them recognition as the symbol and positions as the leaders of the campaign for a new and better Cuba.

The convergence and interaction of these three truths produced the Cuban crisis of 1959–1961. Rather than effecting a general and beneficent transformation of Cuban society during the years after 1898, American power and policy produced instead a Cuban and an American crisis that characterized and symbolized the underlying tragedy of all American diplomacy in the twentieth century. In Cuba, the half-century confrontation of the contrasting truths finally erupted in a militant social revolution conceived and designed to establish—*in fact and in the present*—the kind of Cuban society and development that American diplomacy had promised since 1898.

The Cuban Revolution of 1959–1960 was neither plotted,

planned, nor manufactured for export in the Soviet Union. Neither Russian troops nor Russian arms played any role in its success in deposing the Batista regime, or in establishing its authority throughout Cuba. Cuban communists discounted and opposed the revolution until after it had succeeded.

Once triumphant behind the leadership of Fidel Castro and the 26th of July Movement, the Cuban Revolution was conditioned by two factors: on the one hand, the internal politics of the Cuban revolutionary coalition; on the other, the dynamic effect of American power and policy upon that Cuban struggle. It is possible, though very improbable, that the radical wing of the Cuban coalition would have secured its ultimate control of the revolution even if American policy had been more tolerant, more imaginative, and more helpful. But American policy was none of those things. As a result, so creating the fourth truth and contributing to the tragedy, American policy interacted with the politics of the Cuban coalition in a way that strengthened the radicals. It probably also pushed them much further to the left than they had originally hoped or intended to go.

Two contradictory features characterized the early American response to the revolution. The surface pattern of formal (though noticeably cool and reserved) correctness was interpreted by many observers as a tactical approach to a final accommodation of American policy to the new circumstances. But beneath that veneer, and clearly discernible from the outset, there also existed a fundamental antagonism toward the revolution and its commitment to extensive but nondoctrinaire changes in the status quo.

Dominating American thinking and policy within a year, that antagonism presented itself in the rhetoric of anticommunism and the cold war. In turn, that ideology served both as justification for a hostile posture and as rallying-cry for strong measures. Undemocratic and arbitrary actions which on a much broader, more vicious level had been accepted and tolerated as routine under the Batista and earlier regimes were suddenly in a truly revolutionary situation advanced as proof that Cuba had become a Soviet puppet. And all Cuban moves toward controlling or nationalizing the powerful and extensive American property holdings in the island evoked similar outcries—and the first thoughts and discussions of retaliation.

In this respect, as in others, the American outlook on Cuba typified a general inability to comprehend and come to terms with two aspects of revolutions per se. Americans gained neither understanding nor perspective, for example, from the fact that during the American Revolution their own Founding Fathers arbitrarily confiscated British and colonial property. And they overlooked or discounted almost completely the economic and psychological needs of poor countries. Those requirements could be met only through extensive aid or through measures of nationalization.

Just as a good many early American fortunes, *and considerable capital for general development,* were obtained through confiscation and other arbitrary measures, so in the twentieth century the new, poor countries were prompted to employ similar devices. And neither the Americans in the 1770's (or the early 1800's), nor the Cubans in the 1960's, felt secure and confident about their respective independence until the economic power of their former overlords had been brought under control. But all of these considerations were conveniently evaded through the device of explaining everything as the diabolical work of Cuban communists and the Soviet Union.

When initially advanced, and for many months thereafter, the stereotype of Soviet influence or control was grossly at odds with the facts. Yet persistently and subtly advocated by official American leaders, and crudely merchandized as news or expert opinion by the mass media, it became the accepted picture and explanation of Cuban affairs. American policy based upon and derived from that mistaken view produced two grave and tragic consequences. In Cuba, American rhetoric and policy weakened the moderate elements in the revolutionary coalition and simultaneously strengthened the radicals. They also pushed those radicals further along their own revolutionary path and inclined them ever more toward a working alliance with Cuban communists. In the United States, such Cuban developments intensified the original antagonism, served as convenient if distorted proof for the a priori assertion of Soviet influence, and hardened the resolve to oppose the revolution. A momentum toward violence was thus established and sustained.

At first the United States used economic and political weapons designed to weaken and subvert the Castro Government. Then, after those measures had failed, the United States intervened by proxy on April 17, 1961, in an effort to overthrow and replace that government by force of arms. The counterrevolutionary forces that waded ashore in the Bay of Pigs were financed, armed, trained, and guided in their operation by private and official American leaders. This intervention occurred precisely 63 years after the United States had declared war on Spain to free Cuba. Despite official evasions and silences, the United States almost certainly used its own armed forces in a last, desperate, and unsuccessful effort to save the invasion. All such actions were blatant violations of the treaty system that the United States had with great solemnity established to govern international relations in the Western Hemisphere; they were also violations of American neutrality laws.

The main outlines of the tragedy are so clear that they prompted most Americans either to stand paralyzed by the totality of the debacle or to squirm and look away for a scapegoat. The central and miserable truth is that there would have been neither revolution nor abortive invasion if American policy had been successful within the framework of its own assumptions and logic.

Beyond paralysis or witch-hunting or an irrational resort to wholesale violence there may be two broad reactions to the difficulties and frustrations inherent in the tragedy of American foreign policy, which the Cuban example so classically symbolizes. The obvious and generally acceptable response is to inquire how the United States can more successfully act upon its traditional beliefs, assumptions, and logic: how, in short, its tremendous power can be used more efficiently and effectively. This is by no means an irrelevant issue. The techniques of power comprise an important, wholly legitimate question, and American diplomacy could undoubtedly benefit from additional maturity and sophistication in those matters. But it is more vital to ask whether or not the assumptions and logic behind that traditional diplomacy are inherently sound, and whether or not they contradict each other in practice. Whether or not, in short, a more efficient effort along established lines will do anything other than repeat the tragedy on a more majestic scale.

It is far more difficult to confront and explore this second issue. By its very nature, such an effort scrapes the marrow of our emotions and beliefs, and cuts just as deeply into the bone of our ideas. Even to accept the risk of discovering that we are not as perfect as we thought is an act of great courage. And to drive through to the finish of such an inquiry is an important act of individual maturity and national greatness.

Only a few Americans in a position to influence national policy have demonstrated that kind of bedrock courage in recent years. It is more customary for such spokesmen, even when they recognize and describe the difficulties, to call merely for more vigor and efficiency in the prosecution of traditional programs and policies. But Walter Lippmann, for example, has repeatedly and patiently explained the root causes of the crisis in American diplomacy, and has gone on to suggest cogent if often unpopular alternatives. And a few other commentators such as James Reston have written in a similar vein.

Another striking example has been provided by foreign service officer George Frost Kennan. At the end of World War II, Kennan played a key role in developing the containment policy toward the Soviet Union and other radical movements. That policy was predicated upon the assumption that, because of its great relative economic advantage and its absolute monopoly of atomic weapons, the United States was powerful enough to force the Soviet Union to change fundamentally its entire system. But within a decade, Kennan so modified that unrealistic estimate as to call repeatedly and with some eloquence for an end to the rigidity and single-track diplomacy that he had done so much to initiate.

It may be that President John Fitzgerald Kennedy will ultimately recognize that the crisis goes far beyond the strategy and tactics of power. His decisions which led to the failure in Cuba, for example, were apparently characterized by considerable ambivalence and anxiety about the nature and consequences of his actions. And later, in November 1961, he defined one central aspect of the crisis very bluntly. "We must face the fact that the United States is neither omnipotent nor omniscient, that we are only six per cent of the world's population, and we cannot right every wrong or reverse each adversity, and that therefore there cannot be an American solution for every world problem."

If there should finally evolve during the Kennedy era of

American politics a foreign policy that squared with that
candid statement of mid-twentieth century realities, it seems
probable that considerable credit will be due to Senator J.
William Fulbright. Beginning in the late 1950's, Fulbright
initiated a keen and sophisticated critical evaluation of American diplomacy from his position on the Senate Foreign Relations Committee. His talent for asking searching questions
and his ability to work through to relevant answers earned
him a reputation as one of the nation's most perceptive
leaders in foreign affairs.

In his vigorous and unqualified condemnation of the Cuban
invasion at a top-level meeting held before the initial landing,
for example, Fulbright revealed himself as a man of magnifi-
cent personal and political courage and as a man who grasped
the full dimensions of the tragedy of American diplomacy. He
flatly asserted that the proposed attack was morally, legally,
and practically a grave mistake. It was certain to cause a series
of incalculable but negative consequences whether or not it
succeeded in its immediate objective of initiating the overthrow of the Castro Government. Fulbright also questioned
the judgment of the proponents of the invasion in arguing
that Castro's Cuba posed a serious threat either to the military
security or to the vital national interests of the United States.
But even if that argument were granted, Fulbright insisted
that the means would subvert the ends of American diplomacy.
And that was his key insight into the general as well as the
immediate crisis.

Fulbright's powerful performance at the meeting on Cuba
can be more fully understood against the background of his
earlier analysis of the difficulties underlying American foreign
policy. Writing late in 1958, he advanced his central points
with unusual clarity and candor. "If there is a single factor
which more than any other explains the predicament in which
we now find ourselves, it is our readiness to use the spectre of
Soviet Communism as a cloak for the failure of our own leadership." Quite aware of Russia's challenge to American leadership, and in no way disposed to discount or evade that issue,
Fulbright nevertheless insisted that it was crucial "to ask ourselves some very searching questions." "We must stop thinking
about these problems in terms of a stereotyped view of the

world," he concluded. "We must abandon the clichés and reconsider all our assumptions."

A re-examination of the history of twentieth-century American foreign relations (and the relationship between foreign policy and the domestic economy) offers the most promising approach to such a reconsideration of our assumptions. First, we thereby confront directly what happened. We learn the ideas and the actions of the men who made or influenced policy, and the consequences of those events at home and abroad. Second, at the end of such a review of the past, we return to the present better informed. Finally, that increased knowledge and understanding may help us to muster the nerve to act in ways that can transform the tragedy into a new beginning.

For history is a way of learning, of getting closer to the truth. It is only by abandoning the clichés that we can even define the tragedy. When we have done that, we will no longer be merely acquiescing in the deadly inertia of the past. We will have taken the first and vital step in making history. Such a re-examination of history must be based upon a searching review of the way America has defined its own problems and objectives, and its relationship with the rest of the world. The reason for this is simple: realism goes nowhere unless it starts at home. Combined with a fresh look at Soviet behavior, such an understanding of American policy should help in the effort to outline new programs and policies designed to bring America's ideals and practical objectives closer to realization.

In the realm of ideas and ideals, American policy is guided by three conceptions. One is the warm, generous, humanitarian impulse to help other people solve their problems. A second is the principle of self-determination applied at the international level, which asserts the right of every society to establish its own goals or objectives, and to realize them internally through the means it decides are appropriate. These two ideas can be reconciled; indeed, they complement each other to an extensive degree. But the third idea entertained by many Americans is one which insists that other people cannot *really* solve their problems and improve their lives unless they go about it in the same way as the United States.

This feeling is not peculiar to Americans, for all other peoples reveal some degree of the same attitude toward the rest of the world. But the full scope and intensity of the American version is clearly revealed in the blunt remark of former Secretary of State Dean G. Acheson. He phrased it this way in explaining and defending the American program of foreign aid as it was being evolved shortly after the end of World War II: "We are willing to help people who believe the way we do, to continue to live the way they want to live."

This insistence that other people ought to copy America contradicts the humanitarian urge to help them and the idea that they have the right to make such key decisions for themselves. In some cases, the American way of doing things simply does not work for the other people. In another instance it may be satisfactory, but the other society may prefer to do it in a different way that produces equally good results—perhaps even better ones. But even if the American way were the *only* effective approach, the act of forcing it upon the other society —and economic and political pressure are forms of force— violates the idea of self-determination. It also angers the other society and makes it even less apt to accept the American suggestion on its own merits. Hence it is neither very effective nor very idealistic to try to help other people by insisting from the outset that they follow closely the lead and the example of the United States on all central and vital matters.

The same kind of difficulty arises in connection with the economic side of American foreign policy. The United States needs raw materials and other goods and services from foreign countries, just as it needs to sell some of its own goods and services to them. It might be able literally to isolate itself and survive, but that is not the issue. Not even the isolationists of the late 1920's and early 1930's advocated that kind of foreign policy. The vital question concerns instead the way in which America gets what it needs and exports what it wants to sell.

Most Americans consider that trade supplies the answer to this problem. But trade is defined as the exchange of goods and services between producers dealing with each other in as open a market as it is possible to create, and doing this without one of them being so beholden to the other that he cannot bargain in a meaningful and effective way. Trade is not defined by the transfer of goods and services under conditions established and controlled largely by one of the parties.

Here is a primary source of America's troubles in its economic relations with the rest of the world. For in expanding its own economic system throughout much of the world, America has made it very difficult for other nations to retain any economic independence. This is particularly true in connection with raw materials. Saudi Arabia, for example, is not an independent oil producer. Its oil fields are an integrated and controlled part of the American oil industry. But a very similar, if often less dramatic, kind of relationship also develops in manufacturing industries. This is the case in countries where established economic systems are outmoded or lethargic, as well as in the new, poor nations that are just beginning to industrialize. American corporations exercise very extensive authority, and even commanding power, in the political economy of such nations.

Unfortunately, there is an even more troublesome factor in the economic aspect of American foreign policy. That is the firm conviction, even dogmatic belief, that America's *domestic* well-being depends upon such sustained, ever-increasing overseas economic expansion. Here is a convergence of economic practice with intellectual analysis and emotional involvement that creates a very powerful and dangerous propensity to define the essentials of American welfare in terms of activities outside the United States.

It is dangerous for two reasons. First, it leads to an indifference toward, or a neglect of, internal developments which are nevertheless of primary importance. And second, this strong tendency to externalize the sources or causes of good things leads naturally enough to an even greater inclination to explain the lack of the good life by blaming it on foreign individuals, groups, and nations. This kind of externalizing evil serves not only to antagonize the outsiders, but further intensifies the American determination to make them over in the proper manner or simply push them out of the way.

The over-all result of these considerations is that America's humanitarian urge to assist other peoples is undercut—even subverted—by the way it goes about helping them. Other societies come to feel that American policy causes them to lose their economic, political, and even psychological independence. Writing in 1961 as a supporter of foreign aid, a citizen

of Pakistan provided dramatic and typical evidence of this
growing reaction. He spoke from a close study of the $1,234,400
that his nation had received from the United States between
1951 and June 30, 1960.

He first reviewed official American policy statements which
emphasize that such aid "is not something to be done, as a
Government enterprise, for its own sake or for the sake of
others. The U.S. Government is not a charitable institution. . . .
[Foreign aid] is only one of a number of instruments available
to carry out its foreign policy and to promote its national
interests abroad."* Granting that such an outlook was de-
fensible, if somewhat at variance with the more generally
advertised explanations of foreign aid, he raised two issues. He
asked whether it was good for Pakistan; and, if not, whether it
even achieved the desired results for the United States.

Concerning the inflow of American capital, he reached this
judgment: "It is essentially an extension of the marketing
activity of foreign manufacturers. Only in a very few fields,
such as cigarette manufacture and the soap industry, for example, are foreign firms engaged in activities which can be recognized as manufacturing proper. Here, their activities have
strangled local enterprise."

In the broader sense, he concluded that "the processes of
foreign aid have corrupted our freedom and paralyzed our
political will." Let us discount the extreme language on the
grounds that deep patriotic emotion and political interest
have pushed a vigorous intellectual analysis into the area of
exhortation. Even so, the central validity of the conclusion
remains unimpaired. That becomes apparent from the remarks
of Pakistan President Ayub during an interview with a correspondent of the Paris newspaper *Le Monde* in 1959. Asked
if his government was giving any consideration to requests for
assistance from other countries to balance American aid, he
offered a most revealing reply. "In the end the people will
oblige us to do so. We hope that we will not have to do so,
but it is a question of the instinct of self-preservation. One
cannot indefinitely resist the people's will."

---

* "Khusro," "The Burden of U.S. Aid," *Pakistan Today* (Fall, 1961); the
quotation is from *Technical Assistance: Final Report of the House Committee on Foreign Relations, December 3, 1957.*

As this episode reveals, the people in such countries come to feel that they are being harmed rather than helped. That inclines them to resort to political and economic retaliation, which only intensifies and further complicates a problem that is very complex at the outset. Thus the importance of trying to understand how the contradictions in American policy have developed. If that aspect of the problem can be resolved, perhaps then it will be possible to evolve a program for helping other people that is closer to American ideals and also more effective in practice.

But it is wise to avoid deluding ourselves even before we begin. "History writing," as Sir Lewis Namier has observed, "is not a visit of condolence." History is a mirror in which, if we are honest enough, we can see ourselves as we are as well as the way we would like to be. The misuse of history is the misuse of the mirror: if one uses it to see not only the good in the image, but to see the image as all good. As Oliver Cromwell spoke to England, so history speaks to all men: "I beseech you, in the bowels of Christ, consider that ye may be mistaken." The courage to accept that challenge is the precondition of winning even a chance to transform the tragedy into a new opportunity for great achievement.

THE TRAGEDY OF AMERICAN DIPLOMACY

CHAPTER ONE

A continuance of the present anarchy of our commerce will be a continuance of the unfavorable balance on it, which by draining us of our metals . . . [will bring our ruin]. In fact most of our political evils may be traced up to our commercial ones, and most of our moral to our political.

JAMES MADISON TO THOMAS JEFFERSON, 1786

Extend the sphere, and you take in a greater variety of parties and interests; you make it less probable that a majority of the whole will have a common motive to invade the rights of other citizens; or if such a common motive exists, it will be more difficult for all who feel it to discover their own strength, and to act in unison with each other.

JAMES MADISON, 1787

[Our success] furnishes a new proof of the falsehood of Montesquieu's doctrine, that a republic can be preserved only in a small territory. The reverse is the truth.

THOMAS JEFFERSON, 1801

We want our own markets for our manufactures and agricultural products; we want a foreign market for our surplus products. . . . We want a reciprocity which will give us foreign markets for our surplus products, and in turn that will open

IMPERIAL ANTICOLONIALISM

*our markets to foreigners for those products which they pro-
duce and which we do not.*

WILLIAM MC KINLEY, JANUARY 1895

*American factories are making more than the American people
can use; American soil is producing more than they can con-
sume. Fate has written our policy for us; the trade of the
world must and shall be ours.*

ALBERT J. BEVERIDGE, APRIL 1897

*It seems to be conceded that every year we shall be confronted
with an increasing surplus of manufactured goods for sale in
foreign markets if American operatives and artisans are to be
kept employed the year around. The enlargement of foreign
consumption of the products of our mills and workshops has,
therefore, become a serious problem of statesmanship as well
as of commerce.*

THE DEPARTMENT OF STATE, APRIL 1898

*Dependent solely upon local business we should have failed
years ago. We were forced to extend our markets and to seek
for export trade.*

JOHN D. ROCKEFELLER, 1899

In the field of trade and commerce, we shall be the keen com-

*petitors of the richest and greatest powers, and they need no
warning to be assured that in that struggle, we shall bring the
sweat to their brows.*

SECRETARY OF STATE JOHN HAY, 1899

*Even protectionist organs are for free trade in China, where
freedom is for the benefit of American manufacturers. Even
anti-Imperialists welcome an Imperial policy which contemplates no conquests but those of commerce.*

LONDON TIMES, 1900

America's traditional view of itself and the world is composed
of three basic ideas, or images. One maintains that the United
States was isolationist until world power was "thrust upon it,"
first to help Cuba, then twice to save the world for democracy,
and finally to prevent the Soviet Union from overwhelming
the world. Another holds that, except for a brief and rapidly
dispelled aberration at the turn of the century, America has
been anti-imperialist throughout its history. A third asserts that
a unique combination of economic power, intellectual and
practical genius, and moral rigor enables America to check the
enemies of peace and progress—and build a better world—
without erecting an empire in the process.

Not even Joseph Stalin maintained that America's record in
world affairs was exactly the reverse of this common view, and
for Americans to do so would be to mistake a candid and
searching re-examination of their own mythology for a tirade
of useless self-damnation. The classical ideas about American
foreign policy are not all wrong: the United States did come
to full, active involvement in international affairs by degrees;
it has been anti-imperialist in some respects at certain times;
and periodically it has consciously acknowledged various limitations on its power.

But those truisms do not offer much insight into, or much
guidance for understanding, the dynamic nature of American
foreign relations. It is both more accurate and more illuminating to realize that the successful revolution which began in

1775 and culminated in 1783 established the United States as a world power which sought and played a very active role in international affairs. The War of 1812 offers a revealing example of that strength. Although the United States suffered the embarrassment of having the Capitol in Washington burned, and failed in its grandiose objective of conquering Canada, it nevertheless fought the British Empire to a negotiated settlement that secured American ambitions west of the Mississippi. Spain recognized the meaning of that victory, and in 1819 conceded without a fight a huge strip of real estate extending from the Gulf of Mexico to the Pacific Ocean. And in the Monroe Doctrine of 1823, Americans boldly asserted their claim to predominance throughout the entire Western Hemisphere.

The vigorous expansionism manifested in the Monroe Doctrine was only the continuation and maturation of an attitude held by the Revolutionary generation. Americans thought of themselves as an empire at the very outset of their national existence—as part of the assertive self-consciousness which culminated in the American Revolution. Though at first it may seem surprising, when contrasted with the image of isolationism which has been accepted so long, in reality that early predominance of a pattern of empire thought is neither very strange nor very difficult to explain. Having matured in an age of empires as part of an empire, the colonists naturally saw themselves in the same light once they joined issue with the mother country.*

However natural, attractive, and exhilarating, such a commitment to empire nevertheless posed a serious dilemma for the Founding Fathers. Political theory of that age asserted the

---

* This early expansionist outlook, and its relation to classical and mercantilist thought, is discussed in the following studies: T. A. Bailey, "America's Emergence as a World Power: The Myth and the Verity," *Pacific Historical Review* (February, 1961); L. Baritz, "The Idea of the West," *American Historical Review* (April, 1961); A. B. Darling, *Our Rising Empire, 1763–1803* (New Haven: Yale University Press, 1940); R. W. Van Alstyne, *The Rising American Empire* (New York: Oxford University Press, 1960); C. Vevier, "American Continentalism: An Idea of Expansion, 1845–1910, *American Historical Review* (January, 1960); and W. A. Williams, *The Contours of American History* (New York: The World Publishing Company, 1961).

impossibility of reconciling democratic republicanism with a large state. Up to the time of the American Revolution at any rate, the British could remain ignorant of—or evade—that issue. Self-governing Englishmen never had to cope with the problem of integrating their conquests into their domestic social and political economy. Americans were not so fortunate, for any expansion they undertook immediately enlarged the mother country. Led by James Madison, they sought to resolve the contradiction between their drive for empire and their politics by developing a theory of their own which asserted that democratic republicanism could be improved and sustained by just such an imperial foreign policy.

Probably taking his cue from David Hume, an Englishman who attacked Montesquieu's argument that democracy was a system that could work only in small states, and from British mercantilists such as Francis Bacon, Thomas Mun, and James Steuart, Madison asserted that expansion was the key to preventing factions—themselves primarily the result of economic conflicts—from disrupting the fabric of society. Institutional checks and balances could help, and were therefore necessary, but they were not enough in and of themselves. Expansion was essential to mitigate economic clashes by providing an empire for exploitation and development, and to interpose long distances (and thus difficulties and delays in sustaining initial antagonisms) between one faction and the rest of the nation and the government itself.

Madison thus proposed, *as a guide to policy and action in his own time,* the same kind of an argument that the historian Frederick Jackson Turner formulated a century later when he advanced his frontier thesis, which explained America's democracy and prosperity as the result of such expansion. Madison's theory was shared (or borrowed) by many other American leaders of his time. Thomas Jefferson's thesis that democracy and prosperity depended upon a society of landholding and exporting freemen was a drastically simplified version of the same idea. Perhaps Edward Everett of Massachusetts most nearly captured the essence of the interpretation and argument in his judgment that expansion was the *"principle* of our institutions." In 1828–1829, Madison himself prophesied a major crisis would occur in about a century, when the continent had filled up and an industrial system had deprived most people of any truly productive property. His fears proved true sooner than he anticipated. For in the Crisis of the 1890's, when Americans *thought* that the continental frontier was gone, they advanced and accepted the argument that continued expansion in the form of overseas economic (and even territorial) empire provided the best, if not the only, way to sustain their freedom and prosperity.

The Crisis of the 1890's was a major turning point in American history. It marked the close of the age of Jacksonian Laissez Nous Faire, and provided the setting for the death scene of the individual entrepreneur as the dynamic figure in American economic life. At the same time, it marked the triumph of a new syndicalist system based upon, and characterized by, the corporation and similar large and highly organized groups throughout American society.

Initiated by the failures of the Philadelphia and Reading Railroad, and the National Cordage Company, early in the year, and symbolized by Industrial Black Friday of May 5, the Panic of 1893 quickly developed into a severe and double-cycle depression that lasted until 1898. "Never before," judged the *Commercial and Financial Chronicle* in August 1893, "has there been such a sudden and striking cessation of industrial activity. . . . Mills, factories, furnaces, mines nearly everywhere shut down in large numbers . . . and hundreds of thousands of men [were] thrown out of employment."

By the end of the first year, some 500 banks and 15,000 businesses had failed. One owner explained it very bluntly: "You have done business for nothing and still there has been no business." As for the farmers, railroad magnate James J. Hill reported on the basis of a survey throughout his empire that "very few of the farmers have any money, and the local banks are unable to help them." In mid-summer, 1894, there were 4,000,000 unemployed, and the editor of *Railroad Age* admitted that "never was human life held so cheap." Though the pathetic march of Coxey's Army, and the bitter failure of the Pullman Strike, became the symbols of the resulting unrest and violence, there were 30 other major strikes in progress at the time of more famous railroad crisis in Chicago.

Because of its dramatic and extensive nature, the Crisis of

the 1890's raised in many sections of American society the
specter of chaos and revolution. Conservatives and reformers
came to share the same conviction that something drastic had
to be done, not only to solve the immediate problem, but to
prevent the recurrence of such crises. That an expansionist
foreign policy would provide such relief and prevention rapidly became an integral and vital part of all but an infinitesi-
mal segment of such thinking about the general crisis. The
issue that in a few years developed into what in the 1950's
would have been called a Great Debate concerned *not* whether
such expansion should be pursued, but rather what *kind* of
expansion should be undertaken.

This broad support for expansion, and particularly overseas economic expansion, rested upon an agreement among
conservatives and liberals (even many radicals joined in for a
few years), and Democrats and Republicans, from all sections
and groups of the country. A strong majority agreed that
foreign policy could and should play an important—if not
crucial—part in recovering from the depression of the 1890's
and in forestalling future difficulties.

This consensus was based on two ideas. The first, held by
manufacturers, farmers, merchants, and most other specific
groups in the economy, explained the depression and social
unrest as the result of not having enough markets for their
specific product—be it steel, shoes, or sows. Hence each group
looked at foreign policy as a means of getting markets for
their merchandise or services. This attitude, and the resulting
agitation for vigorous action, was apparent during the dispute
in 1894–1896 with Great Britain over the boundary between
Venezuela and British Guiana.

The militant stand taken by President Grover Cleveland
and Secretary of State Richard Olney did upset bankers in
New York (along with some in Boston), but most industrial
and commercial leaders throughout the country backed the
assertion of American predominance in the Western Hemisphere. And a bit earlier, in a less well-known episode, businessmen such as William Rockefeller of Standard Oil had
urged the Cleveland Administration to intervene boldly in
the Brazilian Revolution of 1893. Determined to protect and
expand the trade with Brazil that was beginning to develop,

Cleveland deployed ships of the United States Navy in a way that helped defeat the rebels who were opposed to the pattern of unequal economic relations with America.

In both cases, Cleveland's action verified the striking prediction made in 1893 by the editors of the Omaha *Bee News*. Commenting upon his inauguration, they had welcomed Cleveland as one who could be relied upon "to promote as far as possible the 'Manifest Destiny' doctrine." Cleveland's handling of the American-conceived and executed revolution against Queen Liliuokalani in Hawaii (1893) followed the same pattern. While he withdrew the proposed treaty of annexation from consideration by the Senate, he did not carry through on restoring the Queen to power. Instead, he recognized the American-dominated Republic of Hawaii that was established on July 4, 1894, and maintained American naval forces in the islands. Indeed, and as subsequent events revealed, Cleveland can with much reason be viewed as the man who established, even before the Spanish-American War, the broad features of what ultimately became America's non-colonial but nevertheless imperial expansion in the twentieth century.

During the 1890's, meanwhile, many groups added their voices to the rising chorus for vigorous overseas economic expansion. Agreeing with labor leader Samuel Gompers that "the great storehouses are glutted," the sometimes radical farm leader "Sockless" Jerry Simpson argued that the "surplus must seek foreign markets." Flour millers agreed, as did the wool manufacturers, the large industrial leaders who organized the National Association of Manufacturers in 1895, and spokesmen for the National Live Stock Exchange. Editorials and articles in the *Scientific American, Engineering Magazine,* and *Iron Age* supported the same solution. And the *United States Investor* concluded that "an outlet for surplus stocks becomes an imperative necessity." Such agitation and pressure had become so general and insistent by the end of 1897 that the Department of State began to print and distribute its consular reports, which it described as being prepared "for the benefit of American industries seeking foreign outlets," on a daily schedule.

The second idea about expansion was much broader and took account of the particular outlook of all special interests.

It explained America's democracy and prosperity in the past as the result of expansion across the continent and, to a lesser degree, overseas into the markets of the world. Either implicitly or explicitly, depending on the form in which it was presented, the idea pointed to the practical conclusion that expansion was the way to stifle unrest, preserve democracy, and restore prosperity.

The generalization about the relationship between expansion, democracy, and prosperity became most well-known as the frontier thesis advanced by the historian Frederick Jackson Turner. Turner first presented his argument in a formal paper before the American Historical Association in December, 1893, but in 1896 he published a version of his interpretation for the general public in the *Atlantic Monthly*. "For really three centuries the dominant fact of American life has been expansion," he explained, and then went on to suggest that "the demands for a vigorous foreign policy, for an interoceanic canal, for a revival of our power upon the seas, and for the extension of American influence to outlying islands and adjoining countries, are indications that the movement will continue."

Although Turner's formulation of the argument that prosperity and representative government were tied causally to expansion became the most generally known version, the central idea was put forward with but minor variations by many other intellectuals during the same years. One such figure was Captain Alfred Thayer Mahan, who began his career as a naval strategist with antiexpansionist ideas. He first held that expansion would lead to centralized government and huge armaments, which would in turn promote wars, repression, and ultimately revolution. But his reading in mercantilist thought of the seventeenth and eighteenth centuries, and the economic difficulties and political unrest in the United States after 1888, combined to change his mind. Becoming a vigorous expansionist, he championed a big navy on the grounds that the United States had to move outward "to seek the welfare of the country." And though he often clothed his arguments in the rhetoric of Christianity and the White Man's Burden, Mahan essentially derived his proposals from what he termed "the importance of distant markets and the relation to them of our own immense powers of production."

Still another such expansionist intellectual was Brooks Adams, brother of the more famous Henry Adams and close friend of such political leaders as Theodore Roosevelt, Henry Cabot Lodge, and John Hay. Reasoning in terms that purported to be valid for all known civilizations, Adams insisted that expansion was the key to wealth and welfare and concluded that the United States would stagnate if it did not consolidate its position in Latin America and push on across the Pacific to make Asia an economic colony. And finally, such expansionism was also implicit in the writings of William Graham Sumner, an economist and sociologist who believed almost fanatically in the virtue and viability of the old order of laissez faire individualism.

These big ideas about expansion evoked responses from different ideological and political groups in the country. Turner's statement of the frontier thesis, for example, appealed to the wing of the reform movement which favored using antitrust laws and political reforms to preserve democracy and prosperity. Adams, on the other hand, had his largest following among other reformers who accepted the large corporation and the giant banks but wanted the national government to regulate and control them in behalf of the general welfare.

Sumner's role is more difficult to judge. For one thing, his influence was connected with that of Herbert Spencer, the British philosopher of laissez faire. For another, and unlike Turner and Adams, Sumner did not himself advocate an expansionist foreign policy. But one of his central ideas asserted that it was "the opening of the new continents and the great discoveries and inventions which have made this modern age. . . . The chief source of new power, however, has been the simplest of all, that is, an extension of population over new land." This explanation implied further expansion, just as his defense of laissez faire sanctioned such action as a natural right. In any event, Sumner's influence—whatever it amounted to—affected the more conservative section of American society which insisted that the principles and practices of laissez faire offered the best answers to all economic and social problems.

Those specific pressures and general ideas in favor of expansion rapidly gained strength after 1890. By 1895, many individuals and groups were stressing the importance of expansion as a way to solve domestic economic problems. The editors of *Harper's* magazine outlined the approach rather bluntly as early as 1893. "The United States will hold the key," they explained, "unlocking the gates to the commerce of the world, and closing them to war. If we have fighting to do, it will be fighting to keep the peace." Others saw expansion as a way to avoid labor unrest—or even revolution. "We are on the eve of a very dark night," warned businessman F. L. Stetson in 1894, "unless a return of commercial prosperity relieves popular discontent." A bit later, Senator William Frye was even more specific. "We must have the market [of China] or we shall have revolution."

As Frye's remark suggests, politicians responded very promptly to the growing interest in expansion. Some of them, like secretaries of state Gresham and Olney, and Theodore Roosevelt and Senator Lodge, were in some respects actually leading the agitation. "We have a record of conquest, colonization and expansion unequalled by any people in the Nineteenth Century," Lodge boasted in 1895. "We are not to be curbed now. . . . For the sake of our commercial supremacy in the Pacific we should control the Hawaiian islands and maintain our influence in Samoa." And at the other end of the political spectrum, Populist Jerry Simpson cried out in anguish that "we are driven from the markets of the world!" and threw his support behind the campaign for a big battleship Navy.

Senator Nelson Aldrich likewise demanded vigorous action in what he referred to as the "bitter contest" for "industrial supremacy" in the markets of the world. And in Wisconsin, the young Robert M. La Follette (who later became a critic of American expansion) opened his political career by calling in 1897 for a big Navy. He also suggested that Spain's island possessions throughout the world would provide excellent bases for the fleet. Not too surprisingly, La Follette judged that McKinley was headed in the right direction on foreign policy: "No man since Monroe has promised so much for the future wealth, safety and glory of this great republic." Still others, such as Woodrow Wilson, argued in the same years for expansion as a way to strengthen the executive branch of the government and thereby improve the general effectiveness of American politics. All in all, and as symbolized by the Republican Party's platform of 1896, the politicians concluded that "enlarged markets" would produce votes as well as profits.

Even the traditional policy of tariff protection was questioned and modified by Americans who saw reciprocity treaties as a way of getting into foreign markets. When it was organized in 1895, for example, the National Association of Manufacturers devoted over half its original program to the problems of expanding foreign markets. One of its specific proposals favored reciprocity treaties as a "practical method of extending our international commerce." And within a year the organization had established special commissions to push business expansion in Latin America and Asia. Its leaders also emphasized the role of such expansion in preventing labor unrest and in making it possible to obey the laws on child labor and yet earn a profit.

While he was president of the N.A.M. in 1897, Theodore C. Search summarized the general feeling within the business community. "Many of our manufacturers have outgrown or are outgrowing their home markets," he explained, "and the expansion of our foreign trade is their only promise of relief." Similar organizations, such as the Pan American Society and the American Asiatic Association, concentrated on promoting an expansionist foreign policy in one particular area. As the *Journal of Commerce* observed in 1897, more and more American economic leaders were fixing their eyes on "the industrial supremacy of the world." A growing number of bankers also began to consider overseas economic expansion as an attractive field for investment. Some favored direct loans to foreigners (which often strengthened those who were competing with American firms), while others preferred to finance the operations of companies in the United States. Such differences of opinion over strategy, and the antagonisms developed in competitive struggles, led to conflict within the financial community, and between the bankers and industrialists. Furthermore, the bankers suffered persistent difficulties in the years prior to World War I in raising enough capital to carry through their bigger projects. But the central point is that the financiers did support the general drive for overseas economic expansion.

From the outset, moreover, these economic organizations enjoyed close ties with leading politicians. The founding convention of the N.A.M. was keynoted, for example, by McKinley. He similarly pushed overseas economic expansion in his address at the opening of the Philadelphia Commercial Museum in 1897. And the N.A.M., no doubt encouraged by McKinley's appointment of Frank A. Vanderlip (Vice President of the National City Bank) as Assistant Secretary of the Treasury, maintained the liaison in its vigorous efforts to win such objectives as reform and enlargement of the consular service. As Theodore Search explained in a letter shortly after McKinley was inaugurated as President, "the manufacturers of the United States never were so deeply concerned in foreign trade as at the present time." And in a similar, and equally vigorous manner, the American Asiatic Association pressed its plans for expansion across the Pacific upon politicians and government bureaucrats.

Such general and active support for economic expansion is often neglected when considering the coming of the Spanish-American War. It is customary to explain the war as a crusade to save the Cubans or to interpret it in psychological terms as a release for national frustrations arising from the depression. But while it may be granted that economic leaders preferred not to go to war as long as they could attain their objectives without it, and although it may be useful to talk about Americans developing a national compulsion to punish Spain for mistreating Cuba, it is equally apparent that such interpretations do not take account of several key aspects of the coming of the war. For one thing, it is clear that various groups saw war with Spain over Cuba as a means to solve other problems. They reached that conclusion, moreover, at the end of a conscious exercise in considering alternatives— not in a blind and irrational outburst of patriotic or ideological fervor. Many agrarians viewed it as a way to monetize silver at home and thus pave the way for a general expansion of their exports to the sterling areas of the world. Some labor groups thought it would ease or resolve immediate economic difficulties. And many important businessmen, as contrasted with the editors of some business publications, came to support war for specific commercial purposes as well as for general economic reasons.

If there is any one key to understanding the coming of the war with Spain, it very probably lies in the growing conviction among top economic and political leaders that American military intervention was necessary in order to clean up the Cuban mess so that domestic *and other foreign policy* issues could be dealt with efficiently and effectively. It should be made clear, however, that in suggesting this explanation of the war there is no direct or implicit argument that other considerations were nonexistent or unimportant. Nor is it being hinted that the whole affair was the product of some conspiracy in high places. Consciousness of purpose is not conspiracy, even if those who are addicted to explaining everything in terms of irrational psychology often seem unable to distinguish between the two. There was consciousness of purpose in high places—as there should be, whatever one's individual judgment on either the goals or the means—but there was no conspiracy.

It likewise seems wise to emphasize the obvious, but nevertheless often overlooked, distinction between explicit economic motives and a more general economic estimate of the situation. Men have on occasion acted in certain ways because their pocketbook nerve prompted them to do so. They still do. Even historians have been known to change jobs (or their points of view) for more money, as well as for their egos, or for better research facilities. And the actions of some influential figures during the period leading up to the war with Spain can only be understood in that light. They wanted intervention to save and extend their property holdings. In a similar way, other men can and do act on the basis of an equally narrow political calculation. Some Americans wanted intervention on the grounds that it would save their personal and party political fortunes.

Yet it is also quite possible, and not at all unusual, for men to act on the basis of a broader, more inclusive organization and integration of information and desires. Sometimes such a conception of the world—or *Weltanschauung,* as it is more formally called—orders data in such a way that political, religious or cultural values are held to be the crucial factors. Thus some Americans undoubtedly supported war against Spain because according to their view of the world it was impossible to have peace or prosperity or good government in Cuba as long as it was ruled by Catholics.

To an extensive degree, however, American leaders of the 1890's entertained a *Weltanschauung* that organized data around economic criteria. They explained difficulties, and likewise advanced solutions and alternatives, by reference to economic phenomena. This did not make them economically motivated in the pocketbook sense, but it did lead them to believe that their objectives in the political and social realms could only be attained through economic means. To somewhat oversimplify the point to gain clarity, it can be summarized in this way.

Men like McKinley and other national leaders thought about America's problems and welfare in an inclusive, systematized way that emphasized economics. Wanting democracy and social peace, they argued that economic depression threatened those objectives, and concluded that overseas economic expansion provided a primary means of ending that danger. They did not want war per se, let alone war in order to increase their own personal fortunes. But their own conception of the world ultimately led them into war in order to solve the problems in the way that they considered necessary and best. These general remarks bearing on historical analysis and interpretation should be kept in mind throughout the book.

There are three central considerations to be evaluated and connected when explaining and interpreting the war against Spain. The first is that the basic policy of presidents Cleveland and McKinley was to secure the defeat of the revolution in Cuba and what they repeatedly and explicitly called "the pacification of the island" under Spanish rule. Both presidents wanted to get on with other domestic and foreign programs and policies; in particular, both were intensely concerned with vigorous overseas economic expansion into Latin America and Asia.

The outbreak of the Sino-Japanese War in 1894 upset Cleveland considerably, for example, and he formally warned the Congress and the country that the conflict "deserves our gravest consideration by reason of its disturbance of our growing commercial interests."* Cleveland not only repeated the same general theme in his message of December 2, 1895, but explicitly tied that problem to the outbreak of revolution in Cuba that was "deranging the commercial exchanges of the island, of which our country takes the predominant share." Shortly thereafter, in March and April 1896, Secretary of State Olney told the Spanish that the United States wanted to help "pacify the island."

Speaking with "candor," Olney explained Cleveland's "anxiety," and bluntly repeated the President's "earnest desire for the prompt and permanent pacification of that island." The United States wanted to avoid "a war of races" within the island, and sought "the non-interruption of extensive trade relations [and] . . . the prevention of that wholesale destruction of property on the island which . . . is utterly destroying American investments that should be of immense value, and is utterly impoverishing great numbers of American citizens."

After waiting eight months, Cleveland, on December 7, 1896, personally and publicly reiterated his desire for "the pacification of the island." America's concern, he bluntly pointed out, was "by no means of a wholly sentimental or philanthropic character."—"Our actual pecuniary interest in it is second only to that of the people and government of Spain." In the original draft of his message, Cleveland proposed to conclude with a warning strikingly reminiscent of the *Harper's* magazine remark of 1893 that "if we have fighting to do, it will be fighting to keep the peace." Cleveland originally put it this way: either Spain must end the rebellion promptly or "this government will be compelled to protect its own interests and those of its citizens, which are coincident with those of humanity and civilization generally, by resorting to such measures as will promptly restore to the Island the blessings of peace." He even added, again in the original draft, a deadline specified as "the coming of the New Year."†

The increasing vigor and militance (and even self-righteous-

---

* Perhaps it will be helpful to remind the reader that statesmen in general—and those of Cleveland's temperament in particular—do not resort to such phrases as "our gravest consideration" unless they are very serious.

† I am indebted to Professor Walter LeFeber of Cornell University for a copy of this first draft of Cleveland's message.

ness) of Cleveland's approach to Cuban affairs cannot be explained or understood in isolation. It has to be correlated with America's diplomacy in the Far East. Japan's attack on China had thrown open the lid of Pandora's Box of Imperialistic Rivalries, and American interests such as the American China Development Company (and other firms and banks) were caught and whipsawed in the resulting free-for-all between Japan, Russia, France, England, and Germany.

In the fall of 1896, however, China turned to the United States in an obvious and natural effort to protect its own position by aligning itself with a major power that had not indicated any significant interest in territorial concessions. At the same time they offered a railroad concession to Americans, a delegation of Chinese officials visited the United States. Received and entertained by public and private leaders, the Chinese clearly accomplished their initial objective of intensifying American interest in and concern over economic gains in Asia.

Cleveland's remarks on Cuba in the first draft of his December 1896 message would clearly seem to follow from that anticipated involvement in Asia—particularly since the President had called for the "gravest consideration" of that issue as early as 1894. But Cleveland had just been defeated by McKinley in the election of November 1896, and his position was obviously difficult. As a responsible politician, Cleveland no doubt realized that it would be unfair (and against tradition) to issue an ultimatum that would entrap his successor. He may even have been explicitly advised that McKinley had told Lodge that he "very naturally does not want to be obliged to go to war as soon as he comes in." Nor is it very likely that Cleveland judged it wise on second thought to go out of office as the man who gave the country a war as his farewell gift. In the message as delivered, therefore, he contented himself with the clear warning that "it can not be reasonably assumed that the hitherto expectant attitude of the United States will be indefinitely maintained."

Upon entering the White House, McKinley reiterated Cleveland's demand for prompt "pacification of the island." But in acting on that policy he began very quickly to squeeze Spain (and himself and the United States) into an ever more difficult position. To some extent, this pressure on Spain was prompted by the activity of various groups within the United States which insisted on more vigorous and dramatic action. This has led some historians to conclude that the pro-rebel newspaper campaign against Spain was primarily responsible for the war. Others have reduced the problem to a political issue, arguing that McKinley ultimately accepted war to sustain or save the influence and power of the Republican Party (and his position within it).

These interpretations which stress domestic pressure on the administration do define and raise the second principal consideration in any evaluation of the war. To put very simply the central point about the agitation of the public by the wild and irresponsible press campaign initiated and directed by William Randolph Hearst and Joseph Pulitzer: the newspapers never succeeded in whipping up any sustained hysteria for war until early in 1898—*if even then*. The evidence is overwhelming that the psychological Rubicon was not crossed until a few weeks after the sinking of the battleship *Maine* on February 15, 1898. Moreover, the argument that politics was the key to the war begs the real point about what provoked the political pressure.

Several other factors appear far more significant in explaining McKinley's increasing pressure on Spain. One of them is intimately connected with his continuation of Cleveland's policy of demanding prompt pacification. For along with other Americans, McKinley reacted against the very ruthlessness that the thinly veiled warnings from the United States encouraged Spain to employ. In insisting upon certain ends while prohibiting the use of forceful measures, McKinley was more the victim of his own irresponsibility than a puppet jerked about by the yellow press of Pulitzer and Hearst.

Furthermore, McKinley was being increasingly pressured by specific groups of avid expansionists. Some of those men were economic entrepreneurs acting on narrow interest-conscious motives. They wanted their property protected and their opportunities secured. That outlook was typified by Chauncey M. Depew of the New York Central Railroad, Alonzo B. Hepburn of the National City Bank, Edward F. Cragin of the Union League Club who had ties with the

Nicaraguan Canal Company and Standard Oil, Collis P. Huntington of the Southern Pacific Railroad, financier August Belmont, and John S. McCook of New York who was a railroad lawyer also active in organizing overseas economic ventures. Still another group was made up of broad-gauged expansionists like Roosevelt and Lodge, who saw a war with Spain as a way to bring empire to America by Caesarean section. "I have been hoping and working ardently," Roosevelt candidly admitted, "to bring about our interference in Cuba."

Finally, McKinley himself made it precisely clear in July 1897, that he was determined to finish up the Cuban crisis in order to proceed with other matters. This became apparent in the long instructions given his new minister to Spain (who was also a close friend). The document should also serve to correct once and for all the mistaken impression that McKinley drifted this way and that in response to whatever political winds were blowing. He knew quite well what he desired to accomplish. "The chronic condition of trouble . . . ," it was explained, "causes disturbance in the social and political condition of our own peoples. . . . A continuous irritation within our own borders injuriously affects the normal functions of business, and tends to delay the condition of prosperity to which this country is entitled."

Though it was not unique in the archives of diplomatic history, this assignment of responsibility for domestic welfare to a foreign power was a very striking and unequivocal example of that approach. It revealed beyond any possibility of misunderstanding the inner logic of all expansionist thought *whereby both opportunity and difficulty, good and evil, are externalized.* As Frederick Jackson Turner once acknowledged in a moment of deep insight, the frontier itself was "a gate of escape" from existing responsibilities; and when men began to act on the frontier thesis itself they merely sustained that pattern of defining issues in such a way that the solutions became progressively dependent upon external factors. Stated as directly as possible, the point is that none of the foreign powers involved—either in Cuba or in Asia—actually threatened the United States, nor did they have any inherent primary responsibility for what McKinley called "the prosperity to which this country is entitled." It was only the definition of American well-being primarily in terms of overseas economic expansion, a definition formulated by Americans, that led to the conclusion that the foreign nations had such obligations.

The related consideration concerning the way that McKinley and other influential Americans envisaged and anticipated the relationship between prosperity and social peace on the one hand, and foreign policy on the other hand, became increasingly clarified during the late summer and early fall of 1897. By August, for example, businessmen were generally convinced that recovery from the depression was being generated and sustained by overseas economic expansion. As a result, many of them began to change their earlier fears that intervention in Cuba would delay prosperity. Instead, they began to feel that it would be wise to remove that distraction so that the new frontier of exports could be given full attention.

In addition, many of those who had sympathized with or actively supported the rebels began to fear that a successful revolution would cause grave difficulties by bringing the lower class to power. McKinley was advised of this very explicitly by a correspondent who reported the growing anxiety that "the troublesome, adventurous, and non-responsible class" would control the island "causing chaos, injury, and loss beyond redemption."

Probably even more important in strengthening the inclination to intervene to pacify Cuba was the renewed outbreak of trouble in the Far East. Germany's seizure of Kiaochow on November 14, 1897, intensified existing fears that Japan and the European powers were going to divide China among themselves. Whether they defined the issue in narrow interest-conscious economic terms, or in a broader analysis that stressed the need of the American economic *system* to expand overseas, American leaders became very disturbed. Most of them looked to Asia, and to China in particular, as the great market which would absorb the surplus. It is beside the point that this did not happen; at issue is the nature of American thought and action at that time.

The influence of these events in the late summer and fall of 1897 was revealed in many striking episodes. In September, for example, Roosevelt discussed personally with McKinley a memorandum in which he advocated war in November, *and specifically recommended that "we take and retain the Philippines."* [Emphasis added.] In November, Senator Orville H. Platt and a member of the House of Representatives saw McKinley and added their advice that Manila was the key to the entire Asian crisis.* In January 1898, a petition from over 35 leading New York businessmen (many of whom had raised their voices—and pens—as early as May 1897) asked McKinley to intervene with "prompt and efficient measures" in Cuba to put an end to their "tremendous losses" and restore "a most valuable commercial field." And in February other entrepreneurs of the New York State Chamber of Commerce asked for similar action in Asia. Deeply concerned about the crisis in China and its effect upon "the privileges enjoyed under existing treaty rights by Americans," they "respectfully and earnestly" requested "the prompt and energetic defense" of such rights and "the preservation and protection of their important commercial interest in that Empire."

These activities clarify the third central aspect of the coming of the war: the McKinley Administration knew that an important and growing segment of the business community wanted prompt and effective action in Cuba and Asia. Until sometime in the latter part of March (or perhaps even the first week in April), McKinley undoubtedly wanted to end the Cuban affair without war. This seems quite clear despite his series of ultimatums to Spain that included a demand for independence (under American guidance) if the United States thought it necessary. But by the last 10 days in March (by which time Germany had secured a 99-year lease to Kiaochow with extensive economic concessions throughout the province of Shantung), the business community was ready to accept war.

A special emissary sent by McKinley to sound out the New York area reported that such key figures as John Jacob Astor, Thomas Fortune Ryan, William Rockefeller, Stuyvesant Fish, and spokesmen for the House of Morgan were "feeling mili-

---

* Here again I am indebted to Professor LeFeber, and to Professor Thomas McCormick of Ohio University, for sharing documents with me.

tant." Then Lodge advised McKinley on March 21, 1898, that Boston economic leaders had concluded that "one shock and then an end was better than a succession of spasms such as we must have if this war in Cuba went on." And four days later, the President received by telegram the following intelligence from a New York correspondent. "Big corporations here now believe we will have war. Believe all would welcome it as relief to suspense. . . . Don't think it necessary now mince matters."

Now the purpose of all this analysis is not to argue or suggest that McKinley went to war because important economic leaders told him to do so.* Neither is it to imply that the public clamor that arose after the sinking of the *Maine* was insignificant. The point is quite different. It is that American leaders went to war with Spain as part of, and as the consequence of, a general outlook which externalized the opportunity and the responsibility for America's domestic welfare; broadly in terms of vigorous overseas economic expansion into Latin America and Asia; and specifically in terms of Spain's inability to pacify Cuba by means (and within time limits) acceptable to the United States, and the separate but nevertheless related necessity of acting in Asia to prevent the exclusion of American interests from China.

This basic *Weltanschauung* underlying American diplomacy led directly to the great debate of 1898–1901 over the proper strategy and tactics of such expansion, a debate that was resolved by the promulgation of the famous Open Door Notes of 1899 and 1900. This national argument is usually interpreted as a battle between imperialists led by Roosevelt and Lodge and anti-imperialists led by William Jennings Bryan and Carl Schurz. It is far more accurate and illuminating, however, to view it as a three-cornered fight. The third group was a coalition of businessmen, intellectuals, and politicians who opposed traditional colonialism and advocated instead a policy of an open door through which America's preponder-

---

* It may be relevant to remind the reader that the United States did in fact start the war by blockading Cuban ports on April 22, 1898; and that the Congress dated its formal declaration of war as of April 21, 1898. Spain declared war on April 24, 1898.

ant economic strength would enter and dominate all underdeveloped areas of the world. This coalition won the debate,
and the Open Door Policy became the strategy of American
foreign policy for the next half-century.

Discounted in recent years as a futile and naive gesture
in a world of harsh reality, the Open Door Policy was in fact
a brilliant strategic stroke which led to the gradual extension
of American economic and political power throughout the
world. If it ultimately failed, it was not because it was foolish
or weak, but because it was so successful. The empire that
was built according to the strategy and tactics of the Open
Door Notes engendered the antagonisms created by all empires, and it is that opposition which has posed so many
difficulties for American diplomacy in the middle of the
twentieth century.

At the outset, it is true, the debate between imperialists and
anti-imperialists revolved around an actual issue—colonialism.
Touched off by the specific question of what to do with Cuba
and the Philippines, the battle raged over whether they should
be kept as traditional colonies or established as quasi-inde-
pendent nations under the benevolent supervision of the
United States. Though the differences were significant at the
beginning of the argument, it is nevertheless clear that they
were never absolute. The Open Door Notes took the fury out
of the fight. And within five years the issue was almost nonexistent. The anti-imperialists who missed that changing nature of the discussion were ultimately shocked and disillu-
sioned when Bryan became Secretary of State and began to
practice what they thought he condemned.

Such critics were mistaken in attacking Bryan as a back-
slider or a hypocrite. Bryan's foreign policy was not classical
colonialism, but neither was it anti-imperial. He had never
shirked his share of the white man's burden, though perhaps
he did shoulder a bit more of the ideological baggage than
the economic luggage. He was as eager for overseas markets as
any but the most extreme agrarian and industrial expansionists. As with most other farmers, labor leaders, and businessmen, economic logic accounts for much of Bryan's anticolonialism. Looking anxiously for markets abroad as a way of
improving conditions at home, all such men feared and op-

posed the competition of native labor. It was that consideration, as much as racism and Christian fundamentalism, that
prompted Bryan to assert that "the Filipinos cannot be citizens
without endangering our civilization."

Bryan's program for the Philippines symbolizes the kind of
imperial anticolonialism that he advocated. Once the Philippine insurrection was crushed, he proposed that the United
States should establish "a stable form of government" in the
islands and then "protect the Philippines from outside interference while they work out their destiny, just as we have
protected the republics of Central and South America, and
are, by the Monroe Doctrine, pledged to protect Cuba." Opposition spokesmen gleefully pointed out that this was the
substance of their own program.

Bryan also supported the kind of expansion favored by
such Democrats as Cleveland and Olney. "The best thing of
the kind I have ever heard," Cleveland had remarked of
Olney's famous assertion that the United States "is practically
sovereign on this continent, and its fiat is law upon the sub-
jects to which it confines its interposition." As for Hawaii,
Cleveland (and Bryan) wanted to control "the ports of a
country so near to Japan and China" without the bother and
responsibilities of formal annexation. Informal empire is
perhaps the most accurate description of such a program. Both
Cleveland and Bryan favored the overseas expansion of the
American economic system and the extension of American
authority throughout the world.

So, too, did such men as Roosevelt, Hay and Lodge. At
first, however, they stressed the acquisition of colonies, if not
in the traditional sense of colonialism, at least in the pattern
of administrative colonialism developed by Great Britain after
the Indian Mutiny of 1857. Thus the early arguments between
Roosevelt and Bryan were to some point. But the Roosevelt
imperialists soon modified that initial emphasis in their
argument. Part of this was due to their success in pushing
through the annexation of Hawaii on July 7, 1898, and to the
occupation of Puerto Rico later in the same month.

Even more significant, however, was the way that the rebellion of native Philippine nationalists against American
troops forced many anti-imperialists to retreat from their

blanket opposition to any territorial acquisitions. To be sure, some of them dwelt upon the obvious: the rebellion symbolized all the evils of empire and should be taken as a clear warning against imperialism. But others interpreted it to mean that the United States would have to take the islands if it was to secure a base for the economic struggle in China, and in their view such a base was absolutely essential. And others, like Bryan, argued that taking the islands was a lesser evil than continuing the war against Spain. Thus the logic of expansionism revealed its strange patterns: just as many had agreed to go to war to pacify Cuba, so in the end did others agree to acquire a colony in order to make peace.

Because it generated so much intense emotion and wild rhetoric, this debate between the Roosevelt and Bryan groups tended in subsequent years to create the mistaken notion that McKinley and his close advisors in the executive branch of the government were largely passive servants waiting patiently for outsiders to decide the issue. Such was not at all the case. After all, McKinley had discussed the importance of Manila to America's objectives in Asia at least as early as September 1897. And he ordered American troops (already staged in San Francisco) to sail for the Philippines even before he received direct, official confirmation of Dewey's victory at Manila Bay. Subsequent analyses and actions established McKinley and his close associates as vigorous participants in the debate itself, and further suggest that those men did much to work out the strategy of empire that was ultimately accepted by the country at large.

In particular, the long "Review of the World's Commerce," prepared by the State Department's Bureau of Foreign Commerce and dated April 25, 1898, made it apparent that the McKinley Administration understood quite clearly the basic features of the expansionist outlook advocated by Brooks Adams and other unofficial spokesmen. The central and common assumptions as phrased by the Department of State were that "the ability of the United States to compete successfully with the most advanced industrial nations in any part of the world, as well as with those nations in their home markets, can no longer be seriously questioned," and that "every year we shall be confronted with an increasing surplus of manu-

factured goods for sale in foreign markets if American operatives and artisans are to be kept employed the year around."

This meant very simply that "the enlargement of foreign
consumption of the products of our mills and workshops has,
therefore, become a serious problem of statesmanship." The
"zealous co-operation" of government officials acting under
"special instructions" to help private companies was naturally
necessary, and had already been undertaken. But the essence
of the problem was to devise a strategy that would prevent
other industrial powers from pre-empting the underdeveloped
areas of the world. "We ourselves have become a competitor
in the world-wide struggle for trade," the Department emphasized, and proceeded to define the regions of crucial importance.

China was of course given first attention: it "has, for many
years, been one of the most promising fields for American
enterprise, industry, and capital." Access to that market, "under conditions which would secure equality of opportunity
to the United States, would doubtless result in immense gains
to our manufacturers." Thus it was mandatory to prevent
Japan and the European powers from excluding the United
States: that was an "immediate and most important" objective.
But any similar partition of Africa raised "considerations of
an economic character of almost equal magnitude," as did any
drive by the nations of Europe to enlarge their economic
position in Latin America.

Feeling that "nowhere else" were such matters "of more
interest" than in China, and very worried about the "large
excesses above the demands of home consumption," Secretary
of State Day initiated, in June 1898, a special study of the
China situation. As such actions indicated, the McKinley
Administration was very pointedly and vigorously dealing
with the issue of overseas economic expansion without waiting
for a debate about imperialism, or for various Englishmen to
offer suggestions as to the proper strategy.

The Open Door Notes have often been attributed to British
influence, and it is true that English friends of Hay helped
draft the documents. But the policy was American.

All of the elements that went into the making of the Open
Door Policy converged within the McKinley Administration

as the President appointed his commission to make peace with Spain. Acting individually, and through groups such as the American Asiatic Association and the N.A.M., private economic operators pressured the government with their desires and recommendations. John Hay was appointed Secretary of State in the fall of 1898, and that gave the Adams-Lodge-Roosevelt group an additional means of influence for their ideas. And McKinley himself made it obvious that the administration already had the central idea of the final policy they were to evolve. For in his instructions to the peace commission of September 16, 1898, he specifically defined the broad issue as "the enlargement of American trade" in the Orient. Then, after discounting the necessity of acquiring "large territorial possessions" in order to win such trade, he explicitly used the phrase "the open door for ourselves" to describe the preferred strategy.

This is of course significant as well as striking, for the first of the Open Door Notes was not written until 1899. It remains so even after recalling that the central idea of obtaining "equality with all competing nations in the conditions of access to the markets" had provided the basis of American policy at the time of the International Conference on the Congo held in Berlin during the winter of 1884–85. For in that situation, as in Asia in 1897–99, the United States confronted rivals who already had spheres of influence or formal colonies. In any event, the point is not to provide some artificial birthday for the policy of the open door, but rather to indicate how the policy emerged from the interplay between private and public leaders.

Perhaps nothing illustrates this as neatly as the way that the arguments inside McKinley's peace commission brought out almost every shade of opinion. Even so, everyone agreed that the United States had at the very least to retain a port and a naval base. Three considerations seem to have convinced the administration to keep all the Philippines. For one thing, the crisis caused by the native rebellion was most easily—though by no means most successfully—resolved in that fashion. In another way, the serious inherent difficulties of keeping the main island of Luzon, or the key city of Manila, without disrupting the political economy of the remainder of the islands soon became apparent even to those who originally favored that kind of solution. And finally, the vigor of German and other expansionism in China exerted considerable influence on the thinking of the administration.

Though many of them felt that they had suffered a terrible defeat in the decision to retain the Philippines, the anti-imperialists actually won their domestic war over fundamental policy with the issuance of the Open Door Notes. Hay's dispatches of 1899 and 1900 distilled the conglomeration of motives, pressures, and theories into a classic strategy of noncolonial imperial expansion. Based on the assumption of what Brooks Adams called "America's economic supremacy," the policy of the open door was designed to clear the way and establish the conditions under which America's preponderant economic power would extend the American system throughout the world without the embarrassment and inefficiency of traditional colonialism. As Hay indicated with obvious anticipation and confidence in September 1899, the expectation was that "we shall bring the sweat to their brows."

Hay's first note of September 6, 1899, asserted the proposition that American entrepreneurs "shall enjoy perfect equality of treatment for their commerce and navigation" within all of China—*including the spheres of interest held by foreign powers*. That principle was soon extended to other underdeveloped areas. His second note of July 3, 1900, was designed to prevent other nations from extending the formal colonial system to China. That axiom was also applied to other regions in later years. Hay also circulated a third dispatch among the powers. Though rarely linked with the first two in discussions of the Open Door Notes, it was nevertheless an integral part of the general policy statement.* In that document, Hay made it plain that the United States considered loans to be an inherent part of commerce. The connection was always implicit, if not rather obvious. "It is impossible to separate these two forms of business activity," as one businessman remarked at the time, "since it is axiomatic

---

* My own knowledge of this note has been extended by the perceptive analysis of it prepared by Martin J. Sklar, a graduate student at the University of Wisconsin.

that trade follows the loan." The relationship was also and without any question in the minds of American policy-makers when the first notes were written, since such loans were being sought and discussed as early as 1897. Hay's purpose was to close every formal loophole through which America's competitors might seek to counter the strategy of the open door.

The Open Door Notes took the substance out of the debate between the imperialists and the anti-imperialists. The argument trailed on with the inertia characteristic of all such disagreements, but the nation recognized and accepted Hay's policy as a resolution of the original issue. Former Secretary of State John W. Foster summarized this point quite accurately in the *Independent* at the end of 1900. "Whatever difference of opinion may exist among American citizens respecting the policy of territorial expansion, all seem to be agreed upon the desirability of commercial expansion. In fact it has come to be a necessity to find new and enlarged markets for our agricultural and manufactured products. We cannot maintain our present industrial prosperity without them."

It took some years (and further discussion) to liquidate the colonial status of the territory seized during the war against Spain. It also required time to work out and institutionalize a division of authority and labor between economic and political leaders so that the strategy could be put into operation on a routine basis. And it was necessary to open the door into existing colonial empires as well as unclaimed territories. But the strategy had been set that was to last at least through the Potsdam Conference at the end of World War II, when President Harry S. Truman sought with considerable insistence to re-establish the open door for American economic and political influence in Eastern Europe and on the Asian mainland.

The Philadelphia *Press* was correct in its judgment at the time. "This new doctrine established for China is destined to be as important as the Monroe Doctrine has been for the Americas in the past century. It protects the present, it safeguards the future." Quite aware of the grand design, the Boston *Transcript* spelled it out in blunt accents. "We have an infinitely wider scope in the Chinese markets than we should have had with a 'sphere of influence' in competition with half a dozen other spheres." Many European commentators acknowledged that the strategy "hits us in our weak spot." Agreeing with the Boston analysis, a Berlin paper summed it up in one sentence: "The Americans regard, in a certain sense, all China as their sphere of interest."

Americans of that era and their European competitors were basically correct in their estimate of the Open Door Policy. It was neither an alien idea foisted off on America by the British nor a political gesture to the domestic crowd. Latter-day experts who dismissed the policy as irrelevant, misguided, or unsuccessful erred in two respects. They missed its deep roots in the American past and its importance at the time, and they failed to realize that the policy expressed the basic strategy and tactics of America's secular and imperial expansion in the twentieth century. When combined with the ideology of an industrial Manifest Destiny, the history of the Open Door Notes became the history of American foreign relations from 1900 to 1958.

The most dramatic confluence of these currents of ideological and economic expansion did not occur until the eve of American entry into World War I. For this reason, among others, it is often asserted that the United States did not take advantage of the Open Door Policy until after 1917, and some observers argue that the policy never led to the rise of an American empire. In evaluating the extent to which Americans carried through on the strategy of the Open Door Notes, there are two broad questions at issue with regard to statistics of overseas economic expansion, and they cannot be mixed up without confusing the analysis and the interpretation. One concerns the over-all importance of such expansion to the national economy. The answer to that depends less upon gross percentages than upon the role in the American economy of the industries which do depend in significant ways (including raw materials as well as markets) on foreign operations. Measured against total national product, for example, the export of American cars and trucks seems a minor matter. But it is not possible at one and the same time to call the automobile business the key industry in the economy and then dismiss the fact that approximately 15 per cent of its total sales in the 1920's were made in foreign markets.

The other major point concerns the role of such foreign enterprises and markets in the making of American foreign policy. This effect can be direct in terms of domestic political pressure, or indirect through the results of the American overseas economic activity on the foreign policy of other nations. In the broadest sense of gross statistics, moreover, the overseas economic expansion of the United States from 1897 to 1915 is more impressive than many people realize. Loans totaled over a billion dollars. Direct investments amounted to $2,652,300,000. While it is true that the nation also owed money abroad during the same period, that point is not too important to an understanding of American foreign policy. For the loans and the investments had a bearing on American foreign policy even though balance of payment computations reduce the net figure. Businessmen with interests in Mexico or Manchuria, for example, did not stop trying to influence American policy (or cease having an effect on Mexican or Asian attitudes) just because their investments or loans or sales were arithmetically canceled out by the debt incurred by other Americans in France.

Another misleading approach emphasizes the point that America's overseas economic expansion amounted to no more than 10 or 12 per cent of its national product during those years. But 10 per cent of any economic operation is a significant proportion; without it the enterprise may slide into bankruptcy. In that connection, the most recent studies by economists reveal that exports did indeed spark recovery from the depression of the 1890's. In any event, the businessmen and other economic groups *thought* the 10 per cent made a crucial difference, and many of them concluded that they could not get it in any way but through overseas expansion.*

Other considerations aside, the conviction of these groups would make the figure important if it were only one per cent. Or, to make the point even clearer (and historically accurate), it would still be significant if all an entrepreneur did was to pressure the government to support an effort that failed. In

---

* The best and most recent study of the importance of exports is I. Mintz, *American Exports During Business Cycles: 1879–1958. Occasional Paper 76* (New York: National Bureau of Economic Research, 1961).

that case the economic indicators would be negative, but the
relevance to foreign policy might be very high. Such was
precisely the case, for example, with the America-China Development Company. It ultimately disappeared from the
scene, but before it died it exerted an extensive influence on
American policy in Asia during the first decade of the twentieth century.

In another way, overseas economic operations which seem
small on paper may mean the difference between survival and
failure to a given firm. Faced by the near-monopoly control
over key raw materials exercised by the United States Steel
Corporation after 1903, Charles Schwab had to go to Chile to
get the ore supplies that were necessary to sustain the Bethle-
hem Steel Company. Schwab's investment was only 35 million dollars, but it played a vital role in his own affairs and
exercised a significant influence on Chilean-American relations. Or, to reverse the example, economic activity which
seems incidental judged by American standards is often fundamental to a weaker economy. This aspect of the problem
can be illustrated by the situation in Manchuria between 1897
and 1904, where approximately one-tenth of one per cent of
America's national product gave the Americans who were
involved a major role in the affairs of that region, and provoked them to agitate vigorously for official American support.
Their efforts were successful and led to crucial developments
in American foreign policy.

This facet of the Open Door Policy bears directly on the
argument that the open door did not actually create an
American empire. Leaving aside the question-begging approach which evades the issue by defining empire solely and
narrowly in terms of seventeenth- or nineteenth-century colonialism, the problem is not very difficult to resolve. When an
advanced industrial nation plays, or tries to play, a controlling
and one-sided role in the development of a weaker economy,
then the policy of the more powerful country can with accuracy and candor only be described as imperial.

The empire that results may well be informal in the sense
that the weaker country is not ruled on a day-to-day basis by
resident administrators, or increasingly populated by emigrants
from the advanced country, but it is nevertheless an empire.

The poorer and weaker nation makes its choices within limits set, either directly or indirectly, by the powerful society, and often does so by choosing between alternatives actually formulated by the outsider. And not only was the Open Door Policy designed to establish the conditions whereby the economic and political power of the United States could be deployed in that manner, it was exercised in that pattern in Asia, Latin America, and Africa. In Canada and Europe, too, for that matter.

Even the implicit dynamic of the policy worked to create the imperial relationship. Let it be assumed, for example, that American policy-makers were not at the time conscious of their superiority or of the expected consequences of that advantage. Then it could be argued that all they wanted was an open marketplace in the tradition of laissez faire; and that such a marketplace would reproduce a relatively pluralistic and balanced political economy in the poorer and weaker societies. But even under the most favorable circumstances, as in the United States during the nineteenth century, the competition of laissez faire produced giant entrepreneurs who dominated the little operators or squeezed them out of the marketplace.

In the case of the underdeveloped nations, furthermore, the conditions were anything but ideal for laissez faire, even in the short-run. For not only were the outside operators already giants both absolutely and relatively, but they worked with and through the most powerful elements in the weaker country. This served, as in Asia and Latin America, to create anything but a pluralistic and balanced society. In all respects, therefore, it seems accurate and fair to describe the strategy of the Open Door Notes as imperial in nature, and as leading to the rise of a modern American empire. That the empire had some positive features is not to be denied; its existence is the issue under discussion at this point.

It is impossible, in short, to judge the bearing of overseas economic expansion upon American diplomacy—and thus to judge the importance and efficacy of the Open Door Policy— in terms of gross statistics. The important factors are the relative significance of the activity and the way it is interpreted and acted upon by people and groups who at best are only vaguely symbolized by abstract aggregate statistics. And by these criteria there is no question about the great relevance for diplomacy of America's proposed and actual overseas economic expansion between 1893 and 1915—and throughout the rest of the twentieth century.

Still another interpretation which discounts the significance of the Open Door Policy is based upon America's failure to control Japanese and Russian activity in Asia. Though perhaps the strongest argument of its type, it nevertheless fails to establish its basic thesis. Three considerations undermine its conclusions: (1) the Open Door Policy was designed to secure and preserve access to China for American economic power, not to deny access to other nations; (2) America's difficulties with Russia and Japan between 1899 and 1918 stemmed from a failure of judgment concerning the execution of the policy, not from a flaw in the policy itself; and (3) the United States acted with considerable effectiveness between 1915 and 1918 to limit Japan's exploitation of America's earlier error.

In summation, the true nature and full significance of the Open Door Policy can only be grasped when its four essential feaures are fully understood.

First: it was neither a military strategy nor a traditional balance-of-power policy. *It was conceived and designed to win the victories without the wars.* In a truly perceptive and even noble sense, the makers of the Open Door Policy understood that war represented the failure of policy. Hence it is irrelevant to criticize the Open Door Policy for not emphasizing, or not producing, extensive military readiness.

Second: it was derived from the proposition that America's overwhelming economic power would cast the economy and the politics of the poorer, weaker, underdeveloped countries in a pro-American mold. American leaders assumed the opposition of one or many industrialized rivals. Over a period of two generations the policy failed because some of those competitors, among them Japan and Germany, chose to resort to force when they concluded (on solid grounds) that the Open Door Policy was working only too well; and because various groups inside the weaker countries such as China and Cuba decided that America's extensive influence in and upon their societies was harmful to their specific and general welfare.

Third (and clearly related to the second point): the policy was neither legalistic nor moralistic in the sense that those criticisms are usually offered. It was extremely hard-headed and practical. In some respects, at any rate, it was the most impressive intellectual achievement in the area of public policy since the generation of the Founding Fathers.

Fourth: unless and until it, and its underlying *Weltanschauung,* were modified to deal with its own consequences, the policy was certain to produce foreign policy crises that would become increasingly severe.

Once these factors are understood, it becomes useful to explore the way that ideological and moralistic elements became integrated with the fundamentally secular and economic nature of the Open Door Policy. The addition of those ingredients served to create a kind of expansionism that aimed at the marketplace of the mind and the polls as well as of the pocketbook.

CHAPTER TWO

That which is good for communities in America is good for the Armenians and Greeks and Mohammedans of Turkey.

THE AMERICAN BOARD OF FOREIGN MISSIONS, 1881

. . . a republic gradually but surely becoming the supreme moral factor in the world's progress and the accepted arbiter of the world's disputes.

WILLIAM JENNINGS BRYAN, 1900

If America is not to have free enterprise, then she can have freedom of no sort whatever.

WOODROW WILSON, 1912

Our industries have expanded to such a point that they will burst their jackets if they cannot find a free outlet to the markets of the world. . . . Our domestic markets no longer suffice. We need foreign markets.

WOODROW WILSON, 1912

The world must be made safe for democracy.

WOODROW WILSON, 1917

THE IMPERIALISM OF IDEALISM

Taken up by President Theodore Roosevelt and his successors, the philosophy and practice of secular empire that was embodied in the Open Door Notes became the central feature of American foreign policy in the twentieth century. American economic power gushed into some underdeveloped areas within a decade and into many others within a generation. It also seeped, then trickled, and finally flooded into the more developed nations and their colonies until, by 1939, America's economic expansion encompassed the globe. And by that time the regions where America's position was not extensively developed were precisely the areas in which the United States manifested a determination to retain and expand its exploratory operations—or to enter in force for the first time.

Throughout these same years, the rise of a new crusading spirit in American diplomacy contributed an outward thrust of its own and reinforced the secular expansion. This righteous enthusiasm was both secular, emphasizing political and social ideology, and religious, stressing the virtues (and necessities) of Protestant Christianity. In essence, this twentieth-century Manifest Destiny was identical with the earlier phenomenon of the same name.

Americans assumed a posture of moral and ideological superiority at an early date. Despite the persistence of the Puritan tradition, however, this assertiveness took predominantly secular forms. Supernatural authority was invoked to

explain and account for the steady enlargement of the United
States, but the justifications for expansion were generally based
on standards derived from this world. The phrase "Manifest
Destiny," for example, symbolized the assertion that God was
on America's side rather than the more modest claim that the
country had joined the legions of the Lord. As that logic
implied, the argument was that America was the "most progressive" society whose citizens made "proper use of the soil."
For these and similar reasons, it was added, the laws of "political gravitation" would bring many minor peoples into the
American system.

Though it had appeared as early as the eve of the American
Revolution, the assertion that the expansion of the United
States "extended the area of freedom" gained general currency after the War of 1812. President Andrew Jackson seems
to have coined the phrase, with his wildcatting intellectual
supporters making many variations. One of the more persuasive and popular, which won many converts during and after
the war with Mexico, stressed America's responsibility to extend its authority over "semi-barbarous people." By thus taking up the duty of "regeneration and civilization," America
could perform the noble work of teaching inferiors to ap-
preciate the blessings they already enjoyed but were inclined
to overlook. In turn, this would prepare them for the better
days to follow under America's benevolent leadership.

Near the end of the century, American missionaries and
domestic religious leaders began to impart a more theological
tone to this crusading fervor. This resulted in part from the
effort by the clergy to marry traditional Christianity with the
new doctrine of evolution and in that way adjust their
theology to the latest revelations, and also to sustain their
influence in the age of science. Josiah Strong was an innovator
of that kind. As a Congregationalist minister in whom the
frontier experience and outlook exercised an important influence, Strong concluded that the theory of evolution only
substantiated the doctrine of predestination. America had
been hand-picked by the Lord to lead the Anglo-Saxons in
transforming the world. "It would seem," he explained with
reference to the American Indians and other benighted peoples, "as if these inferior tribes were only precursors of a

superior race, voices in the wilderness crying: Prepare ye the way of the Lord."

Ever since New England ministers had accepted the challenge of saving the heathens of Hawaii, a crusade that began in the eighteenth century, American missionaries had been noticeably concerned about Asia—and in particular China. As the Reverend Hudson Taylor explained in 1894, there was "a great Niagara of souls passing into the dark in China." Though they never lost faith, a growing number of missionaries did get discouraged enough to question whether hell-fire sermons on the dangers of damnation were an approach sufficient unto the need. Some thought fondly of the sword of righteousness, and toyed with the idea of a "Society for the Diffusion of Cannon Balls." That kind of crusade was never organized, but the missionaries did begin in the 1890's to demand formal support and protection from the American Government.

This request, while never acted upon with the same vigor as those from business groups, did receive sympathetic and favorable consideration. For one thing, the religious stake in China was significant: America had over 500 missionaries in that country, and their schools claimed a total student body of nearly 17,000 Chinese. Many churches had also supported intervention in Cuba. But the most important factor was the way that the missionary movement began to evolve an approach that offered direct support to secular expansion.*

Missionaries had always tended to operate on an assumption quite similar to the frontier thesis. "Missionaries are an absolute necessity," explained the Reverend Henry Van Dyke of Princeton in 1896, "not only for the conversion of the heathen, but also, and much more, for the preservation of the Church. Christianity is a religion that will not keep." Religious leaders began to link the missionary movement with economic expansion in what the Reverend Francis E. Clark of the Christian Endeavor organization called "the widening of our empire." The Board of Foreign Missions also welcomed such expansion as "an ally."

---

* The best study of this development is P. A. Varg, *Missionaries, Chinese, and Diplomats* (Princeton: Princeton University Press, 1958).

Then, beginning in the mid-1890's, the missionaries began to change their basic strategy in a way that greatly encouraged such liaison with secular expansionists. Shifting from an emphasis on the horrors of hell to a concern with practical reform as the lever of conversion, they increasingly stressed the need to remake the underdeveloped societies. Naturally enough, they were to be reformed in the image of the United States. Such changes would lead to regeneration identified with Christianity and witnesses for the Lord would accordingly increase.

Not only did this program mesh with the idea of American secular influence (how else were the reforms to be initiated?), but it was very similar to the argument that American expansion was justified because it created more progressive societies. Missionaries came to sound more and more like political leaders, who were themselves submerging their domestic ideological differences at the water's edge in a general agreement on expansion as a reform movement.

The domestic reformer La Follette offers an excellent example of this convergence of economic and ideological expansion that took place across political lines. He approved taking the Philippines because it would enable America "to conquer [its] rightful share of that great market now opening [in China] for the world's commerce." Expansion was also justified because the United States had a "bounden *duty* to establish and *maintain* stable government" in the islands. Pointing out that from the beginning "the policy of this government has been to expand," La Follette justified it on the grounds that "it has *made men free.*" Thus, he concluded, "we can legally and morally reserve unto ourselves perpetual commercial advantages of priceless value to our foreign trade for all time to come" by taking the Philippines.*

Theodore Roosevelt's outlook reveals an even more signifi-

---

* Professor Charles Vevier was probably the first contemporary historian to explore this imperialism of the reformers. He did so in an unpublished thesis written at the University of Wisconsin in 1949. Others followed, e.g.: W. E. Leuchtenburg, "Progressivism and Imperialism . . . 1898–1916," *Mississippi Valley Historical Review* (June, 1952); and P. C. Kennedy, "La Follette's Imperialist Flirtation," *Pacific Historical Review* (May, 1960).

cant aspect of this progressive integration of secular and ideological expansionism. His concern for economic expansion was complemented by an urge to extend Anglo-Saxon ideas, practices, and virtues throughout the world. Just as his Square Deal program centered on the idea of responsible leaders using the national government to regulate and moderate industrial society at home, so did his international outlook revolve around the idea of American supremacy being used to define and promote the interests of "collective civilization."

Thus it was necessary, he warned in his Presidential Message of December 1901, to exercise restraint in dealing with the large corporations. "Business concerns which have the largest means at their disposal . . . take the lead in the strife for commercial supremacy among the nations of the world. America has only just begun to assume the commanding position in the international business world which we believe will more and more be hers. It is of the utmost importance that this position be not jeopardized, especially at a time when the overflowing abundance of our own natural resources and the skill, business energy, and mechanical aptitude of our people make foreign markets essential."

Roosevelt integrated that kind of expansion with ideological considerations and imperatives to create an all-inclusive logic and set of responsibilities which made peace itself the consequence of empire. In his mind, at any rate, it was America's "duty toward the people living in barbarism to see that they are freed from their chains, and we can free them only by destroying barbarism itself." Thus, he concluded, "peace cannot be had until the civilized nations have expanded in some shape over the barbarous nations."

The inherent requirements of economic expansion coincided with such religious, racist, and reformist drives to remake the world. The reason for this is not difficult to perceive. As they existed, the underdeveloped countries were poor, particularistic, and bound by traditions which handicapped business enterprise. They were not organized to link up with the modern industrial system in a practical and efficient manner. It was economically necessary to change them *in certain ways and to a limited degree* if the fruits of expansion were to be harvested. As with the missionaries, therefore, the economic and political leaders of the country decided that what was good for Americans was also good for foreigners. Humanitarian concern was thus reinforced by hard-headed economic requirements.

The administrations of Theodore Roosevelt understood this relationship between economic expansion and overseas reform, and explicitly integrated it into the strategy of the Open Door Policy. It was often commented upon in dispatches and policy statements concerning China and Latin America. In his famous Corollary to the Monroe Doctrine, for example, Roosevelt (who thought of the Open Door Policy as the Monroe Doctrine for Asia) stressed the need for reforms and asserted the right and the obligation of the United States to see that they were made—and honored.

It was in connection with the Algeciras Conference of 1905–06, however, that the relationship was most fully (and even brilliantly) explained and formally made a part of the Open Door Policy. Growing out of the imperial rivalry in Africa between Britain, France, and Germany, the Algeciras (or Moroccan) Conference proceeded on two levels. The dramatic battle concerned limiting German penetration to a minimum while giving it superficial concessions. In that battle the United States sided with England and France. But in another sense the conference offered the United States a chance to renew and reinforce its old drive of the 1880's for equal commercial rights in Africa. Roosevelt and Secretary of State Elihu Root used the strategy of the open door to wage both campaigns. Their policy instructions on the specific problems of organizing an international Moroccan police force, and on instituting financial reforms, revealed their full understanding of the nature and the extent of the interrelationship between reform and economic expansion.

After discussions with Roosevelt, Root reviewed the issue very thoroughly. Police reform was essential: it was "vital" to American "interests and no less so to the advantage of Morocco that the door, being open, should lead to something; that the outside world shall benefit by assured opportunities, and that the Moroccan people shall be made in a measure fit and able to profit by the advantages of the proposed reform." Fruitful economic intercourse depended upon "the existence of internal conditions favorable thereto." Those prerequisites included not only the "security of life and property," but establishing "equality of opportunities for trade with all natives."*

This need to enlarge the domestic market within Morocco, so that the open door would "lead to something," called for both negative and positive kinds of reform. Root defined the first as actions designed to remove conditions "which impair the freedom of salutary foreign intercourse with the native population." It was thus necessary to modify religious discrimination against non-Muslims; to establish the "orderly and certain administration of impartial justice" which guaranteed "vigorous punishment of crimes against persons and property;" to insure "exemption from erratic taxes and [similar] burdens" upon business enterprise; and to maintain an internal police force strong and efficient enough "to repress subversive disorder and preserve the public peace."

Root described the equally important positive kind of reform with similar clarity. In the most fundamental sense, Moroccan poverty and stagnation had to be ended. Economic development had to be initiated. There had to be enough of the kind of "improvement of the condition of the people that will enable them to profit by the opportunities of foreign trade." To avoid any misunderstanding, let Root's point be made more bluntly: even if their governments receive international loans, poor people cannot buy the goods and services exported by the richer industrial countries. No income, no purchases; no purchases, no trade; no trade, no prosperity in America and no "salutary" effects in the poorer country. Or so, at any rate, ran the logic and the fears of the open door strategy.

Root went on, in his handling of American policy during the conference, to stress the importance of securing access for American capital to the competition for public works construction. This was not only desirable as an economic opportunity in and of itself, but also represented one of the ways in

---

* Unlike many very important documents, this remarkable and extremely significant dispatch has been published. The citation is: Root to White, November 28, 1905: *Papers Relating to the Foreign Relations of the United States, 1905*, pp. 678–79.

which a minimum level of general development could be facil-
itated. Transportation and sanitation systems were as important as large loans or legal reforms in establishing the conditions for successful enterprise. Root was unequivocal about the
crucial element in arranging such financial reform: "the 'open
door' seems to be the sound policy to advocate."

At the end of the conference, the American representative
reported that the principle of "the open door in matters of
commerce" had been acknowledged, and thus the way had
been prepared for American participation in "the execution
of public works, or the future development of the great mineral
wealth of Africa." In the narrow sense, the Algeciras episode
offers illuminating perspective on newspaper stories about the
present-day activities in Africa of the Rockefeller and Kaiser
corporations (to name but two), and other reports on American
governmental loans for public works such as highways and
power installations.

The broader aspects of the analysis and policy statement
prepared by Roosevelt and Root are even more significant.
That document establishes once and for all the connection
between, and the convergence of, the drive for overseas economic expansion and the urge to reform other societies according to American and industrial standards. It likewise
removes any doubt about whether or not American leaders
were conscious of the relationship. And finally, it helps clarify
the nature and the dimensions of the tragedy of American
foreign policy that evolved out of the Open Door Policy.

On the one hand, of course, the positive features of the
reforms, including the general concern to initiate a minimum
of economic development, emerge very clearly. On the other
hand, it becomes apparent that the United States was opening
the door to serious and extensive unrest, as well as to potential economic development and political reform. Perhaps the
failure to understand this, or a not unrelated kind of persistent
wishful thinking that such unrest could somehow be avoided,
provides the final, irreducible explanation of America's difficulties in foreign affairs during the twentieth century. For
America's integrated reformist and economic expansion did
things that guaranteed trouble.

First: it undertook to initiate and sustain drastic, fundamental changes in other societies. The process of wrenching Morocco, or China, or Nicaragua out of their own neo-feudal, primarily agrarian condition into the industrial era involved harsh, painful alterations in an established way of life. Even under the best of circumstances, those consequences can only be mitigated. They cannot be entirely avoided.

Second: the United States identified itself as a primary cause of such changes. It thereby also defined itself as a principal source of the pain and unhappiness that followed. This is true, not only in connection with those groups in power which oppose the changes as they begin, but also for those who suffer from the consequences without means to oppose or moderate them, and even for others who generally approve of the new ways but despair of the costs and question the morality of outsiders interfering in such fundamental and extensive respects.

Third: the United States wanted to stop or stabilize such changes at a point favorable to American interests. This was at best naive. Even a most modest familiarity with history reveals that such alterations have wide and continuing consequences. It was at worst a knowing effort to slap a lid on dynamic development. That attempt can only be described as a selfish violation of the idea and ideal of self-determination, and even as an evasion of the moral obligation to accept the consequences of one's own actions.

Fourth: the effort to control and limit such subsequent changes according to American preferences served only to intensify opposition within the developing countries. The extent to which Algerian revolutionaries of the 1940's and 1950's revealed and illustrated all these points in their attitudes toward the United States offers a particularly relevant example of the tragic consequences of American reformist and economic expansion as it emerged during the Roosevelt administrations.

The integration of these elements was carried forward, and given classic expression in rhetoric, style, and substance, in the diplomacy of President Woodrow Wilson and Secretary of State Bryan. Both men were leaders of the secular American reform movement, and both brought to their conduct of foreign affairs a religious intensity and righteousness that was not apparent in earlier administrations and that has not been matched since their time. As Protestants imbued with a strong sense of Anglo-Saxon self-consciousness, they personified the assertive idealism that complemented and reinforced the economic drive for markets.

Bryan was a Fundamentalist in religious matters. Typified by the famous "Cross of Gold" speech which climaxed his nomination for the presidency in 1896, his sense of calling and mission infused all his political actions with a kind of hell-fire enthusiasm and determination. Those characteristics could be misleading, and in the Crisis of the 1890's prompted a good many Americans to view Bryan as a threat to social order. But as revealed even in the "Cross of Gold" speech (where he defined everybody as a businessman), as well as in his actions, he stood wholly within the reform tradition of capitalism. Bryan could himself joke about the misconception. Upon at least one occasion, when he visited the White House after his defeat in the election of 1904, he did so with considerable charm. President Roosevelt was one of those who had hurled all kinds of invective and wild charges at Bryan at one time or another during their political rivalry. As he arrived to make an invited call on the victor, Bryan revealed a kind of pleasant fatalism about such things. "Some people think I'm a terrible radical, but really I'm not so very dangerous after all."

As far as foreign affairs were concerned, Bryan's outlook was that of the Christian leader who concluded that his society needed overseas markets and was determined to find them. He fully intended, however, to do so in such a way that order and stability would be assured, a Christian peace secured and preserved, and the backward nations protected from rapacious foreigners while being led along the path of progress by the United States. Confident that Wilson was a man with the same goals, Bryan could without any reservations praise the President, in May 1914, as one who had "opened the doors of all the weaker countries to an invasion of American capital and American enterprise."

Candidly asserting America's "paramount influence in the Western Hemisphere," Bryan's objective was to "make absolutely sure our domination of the situation." Such moral and economic expansion, he explained in 1913, would "give our country such increased influence . . . that we could prevent revolutions, promote education, and advance stable and just government . . . we would in the end profit, negatively, by not having to incur expense in guarding our own and foreign interests there, and, positively, by the increase of trade."

While no less determined—his will won him more than one defeat—Wilson's idealism was that of the high church Presbyterian Calvinist who viewed himself and the United States as trustees of the world's welfare. The destiny of America was to be "the justest, the most progressive, the most honorable, the most enlightened Nation in the world." Small wonder, then, that when Wilson led the country into World War I he did so on the grounds that "the world must be made safe for democracy," or that he considered his own postwar program to be "the only possible" plan for peace which therefore "must prevail."

Wilson was both responsible and candid enough to admit that all was not perfect either in America or the rest of the world. But since he considered the philosophy of revolution to be "in fact radically evil and corrupting," he insisted that the only recourse was "a slow process of reform" led by trustees such as himself. At least, that is to say, *within* the United States. But America, just because it was the elect among the trustees of the world, had both a right and an obligation to use force "to do justice and assert the rights of mankind."

Wilson's imperialism of the spirit was well defined by his attitude toward the Philippines. The United States should grant independence to the Filipinos just as soon as American leadership had instructed them in the proper standards of national life, instilled in them the proper character, and established for them a stable and constitutional government. Such noble objectives justified—even demanded—the use of force. "When men take up arms to set other men free," he declared, "there is something sacred and holy in the warfare. I will not cry 'peace' as long as there is sin and wrong in the world."

But since Wilson's fundamental assumption about the nature of man was that he "lives not by what he does, but by what he thinks and hopes," this type of imperialism was, by the President's own standards, the most persuasive and extensive of any that could be devised. For in effect—and in practice—it subverted Wilson's support for the principle of self-deter-

mination. He asserted that other peoples were at liberty, and
had a right, to be free; but he judged whether or not they
chose freedom by his own standards. Or, as he put it during
the Mexican crisis, he would approve and recognize none but
"those who act in the interest of peace and honor, who protect
private rights, and respect the restraints of constitutional
provisions."

Both then and later, Wilson used American power to go
behind the forms of government to see if the substance squared
with his criteria, and if it did not, he deployed American power
in an attempt to force reality into correspondence with his
imagery and ideals. However one judges the ideals, and let it
be agreed they are of the highest, the fact remains that the
policy itself was the broadest kind of imperialism. Thus his
refusal to go along with American corporations that wanted to
recognize and sustain the regime of Victoriano Huerta during
the early phases of the Mexican Revolution is at most only
half the story. Wilson was perfectly willing to intervene vigorously, even to the brink of war, in order to force the Mexicans
to behave according to his standards. "I am going to teach the
South American republics," he explained to a British diplomat, "to elect good men."

These features of Wilson's conduct of foreign affairs have
understandably led many historians, including some of his
admirers, to characterize his diplomacy as "moral imperialism," "imperialism of the spirit," or "missionary diplomacy."
While accurate as far as it goes, that approach is seriously misleading because it ignores or neglects the extensive degree to
which Wilson advocated and supported overseas economic expansion. It also does Wilson an injustice. For he brought the
two themes together in a manner that surpassed even the
similar achievement of Roosevelt and Root.

The single most important insight into Wilson's propensity
and ability to fuse those two traditions very probably lies in
his Calvinistic *Weltanschauung*. Two of Calvin's central assumptions concerned the complementary nature of economics
and morality, and the responsibility of the trustee for combining them to produce the welfare of the community. He emphasized these very clearly and forcefully in his writings, and
tried to carry them out in actual practice. It is of course true

that Wilson was not Calvin (though upon occasion the President's actions provoked some of his critics to remark that there seemed to be some confusion in his own mind on that issue). Nor was he a disciple in the rigid and narrow theological or clerical sense. But he did make sense out of reality from the basic vantage point offered by Calvinism, and his consolidation of economics and ideas stemmed from that conception of the world. One of his remarks in 1912 captured that aspect of the working of his mind very neatly. "If America is not to have free enterprise," he asserted as an article of faith, "then she can have freedom of no sort whatever."

Granted this framework of Calvinism and capitalism, the consideration most directly pertinent in comprehending Wilson's handling of foreign policy is his commitment to the frontier thesis of Frederick Jackson Turner. They enjoyed a close personal and intellectual friendship while Turner was developing his thesis about American expansion and its prosperity and democracy as an advanced student at Johns Hopkins University. Wilson accepted the argument as the central explanation of American history. "All I ever wrote on the subject," he later remarked of Turner, "came from him." That was an exaggeration. Wilson shaped and used the intellectual tool of interpreting American politics from the perspective of the British parliamentary system on his own (and it was a stimulating approach). Even so, the frontier thesis was a crucial element in his thinking about the past and the present.

Wilson put it very directly as early as 1896 in explaining the Crisis of the 1890's. "The days of glad expansion are gone, our life grows tense and difficult." He read George Washington's Farewell Address in the same light. Wilson argued that Washington "would seem to have meant, 'I want you to discipline yourselves and . . . be good boys until you . . . are big enough to stand the competition . . . until you are big enough to go abroad in the world.' " Wilson clearly thought that by 1901 the United States had become a big boy: expansion was a "natural and wholesome impulse." And in a speech on "The Ideals of America" of December 26, 1901, which was remarkable for its close following of the frontier thesis, he projected the process indefinitely: "Who shall say," he asked rhetorically, "where it will end?"

With the publication the next year of his five-volume *History of the American People,* it became apparent that Wilson saw overseas economic expansion as the frontier to replace the continent that had been occupied. A section in Volume V (which reads like a close paraphrase of some essays written by Brooks Adams) recommended increased efficiency in government so that the United States "might command the economic fortunes of the world." Referring a bit later to the Philippines as "new frontiers," he concluded his analysis by stressing the need for markets—markets "to which diplomacy, and if need be power, must make an open way." In a series of lectures at Columbia University in April 1907, he was even more forthright. "Since trade ignores national boundaries and the manufacturer insists on having the world as a market, the flag of his nation must follow him, and the doors of the nations which are closed must be battered down." "Concessions obtained by financiers must be safeguarded," he continued, "by ministers of state, even if the sovereignty of unwilling nations be outraged in the process. Colonies must be obtained or planted, in order that no useful corner of the world may be overlooked or left unused. Peace itself becomes a matter of conference and international combinations." It was something of an anticlimax to learn that Wilson expected "many sharp struggles for foreign trade."

His persistent repetition of that warning serves to symbolize the extent to which Wilson's campaign for the presidential nomination and election in 1912 stressed overseas economic expansion. During January and February he reviewed the importance of a merchant marine, and bewailed the weaknesses of the banking system which handicapped American financiers in overseas competition. By August, when he won the nomination, he was ready with a general interpretation. The United States was an "expanding" nation. "Our industries have expanded to such a point that they will burst their jackets if they cannot find a free outlet to the markets of the world. . . . Our domestic markets no longer suffice. We need foreign markets." And also, he added, a major effort to educate the general public on the problem and its solution. Wilson was even more specific about the reason behind his sense of urgency at a campaign dinner for his supporters among the working class. (Not many day laborers could afford the prices, but their leaders attended.) "We have reached, in short, a critical point in the process of our prosperity. It has now become a question with us," he warned, "whether it shall continue or shall not continue." "We need foreign markets," he reiterated, because "our domestic market is too small." And as McKinley and Root before him, Wilson in 1912 unequivocally pointed to Germany as the most dangerous rival of the United States in that economic struggle.

Wilson's dramatic language about American prosperity turned out within a year to have been justified. The nation entered a recession at the end of 1913, and the downswing continued in 1914. Even before that unhappy development, or before he had to cope with the Mexican and Russian Revolutions, Wilson revealed the keen and sophisticated way in which he integrated crusading idealism and hard-headed economics. The situation in which he displayed such leadership was almost literally waiting for him as he moved into the White House in March 1913. Giant American bankers wanted a prompt if not immediate policy statement on their efforts (in conjunction with the Japanese and European financiers) to push through a large loan to China. Wilson's response has usually been interpreted as an abrupt and significant break with the whole tradition and practice of overseas economic expansion. That conclusion has been reached by an intellectual broad jump of prodigious proportions, taking off from the fact that Wilson did refuse to support the bankers in that one operation. But historical interpretation is not broad jumping. The fact itself is indisputable. The conclusion is indisputably wrong. In order to understand that apparent contradiction in Wilson's action, however, it is necessary to consider several factors that are seldom connected with it.*

It is essential first of all to review the difficulties that arose in putting the open door strategy into operation in Asia. Given the objective of winning the economic and political victory

---

* Martin J. Sklar has analyzed this episode in great detail; he has published a summary of his findings as "Woodrow Wilson and the Political Economy of Modern United States Liberalism," *Studies on the Left* (1960). While he reached similar conclusions quite independently, I have benefited since the first edition of this book appeared in 1959 from conversations with him and from reading the first draft of his Master's Thesis.

without the war (or wars), American leaders faced a difficult
task. There was no easy answer to their problems, and most
certainly no handbook of operations for them to follow. They
had to make difficult choices in innovating tactics, and to cope
with limitations and other troubles imposed by events at home
and in China. To avoid confusion in outlining such considerations (all of them cannot be summarized in one neat para-
graph), they will be numbered.

First: the natural and obvious tactic was to go it alone,
plunging ahead in China with the hope of rapidly establishing
extensive American influence. President William Howard Taft
tested this approach. "I regard the position at Peking as the
most important diplomatic position that I have to fill," he
explained in April 1909, "and it is necessary to send there a
man of business, force and perception." He followed through
by applying direct and personal pressure on the head of the
Chinese Government to secure participation by American
financiers (and industrialists) in a railroad development project in Hukuang Province. His objective was "a practical and
real application of the open door policy."

The United States never abandoned this ideal of direct
action. It was, and remained, the preferred method of exploiting the Open Door Policy in Asia. Other techniques were
seen as means to establish the preconditions for handling the
problem in that manner. But as Taft and other American
leaders discovered, there were two major difficulties involved
in pursuing that course of action. One was defined by the
simple (though perhaps to many surprising) fact that American
entrepreneurs were unable *on their own as capitalists* to accu-
mulate sufficient private capital to do the job alone.* The

---

* Historians have almost wholly neglected this extremely important
problem of capital shortage in twentieth century America. It is handled
indirectly in the studies of the Federal Reserve System, but its part in
private and official policy—and the relationship between them—has not
been explored in any significant or substantial investigations. Yet it
provides, as will appear below, a very important insight into American
diplomacy after the 1890's. For that matter, it can be shown that the
underlying solution evolved between 1913 and 1939—that of having the
government help directly and indirectly in accumulating capital for the
private sector—appeared very early (if not literally first) in connection
with overseas economic expansion.

other reason was more obvious. Such a blunt, bold move by the United States was sure to provoke, and did provoke, sharp and increasing opposition from Japan and other industrial nations. If persisted in, that confrontation would lead to war. Yet the policy itself was designed to avoid war. For both reasons, therefore, American policy-makers had at least to consider other tactics.

Second: it was possible to work wth the Russians, and thereby strengthen them against the Japanese. China (and probably Siberia as well) would then be developed in concert with the Tsar. The approach was not only conceivable, it was actually discussed. The Russians proposed the idea as early as the 1890's. They persistently repeated their overtures during the subsequent 15 years, but the McKinley, Roosevelt, and Taft administrations never explored them seriously. Secretary of State Hay did indicate some early interest, but Roosevelt (who supported the plan when first outlined) squashed the idea. The most promising exploration of it was undertaken by the financier-railroad magnate Edward Averell Harriman at the close of the Russo-Japanese War. Though plagued by many difficulties, he was making important progress toward a broad agreement with the Russians when he was stopped by the American Panic of 1907, and then by death in 1909. Harriman's close associate, Willard Straight, tried unsuccessfully to sustain the project at that time. The development of American-Russian economic relations did not affect foreign policy in a significant way until the end of the 1920's.*

Third: another approach, based on traditional balance-of-power maneuvers, was actually tried by President Roosevelt on the eve of, and during, the Russo-Japanese War. By en-

---

* On this matter see: E. H. Zabriskie, *American-Russian Rivalry in the Far East* (Philadelphia: University of Pennsylvania Press, 1946); W. A. Williams, *American-Russian Relations, 1781–1947* (New York: Rinehart and Co., 1952); and C. Vevier, *The United States and China, 1906–1913* (New Brunswick: Rutgers University Press, 1955). A convenient indication of business interest is provided by McKinley's Assistant Secretary of the Treasury, Frank A. Vanderlip, in his essay: *The American "Commercial Invasion" of Europe* (New York: Scribner's Magazine, 1902). Also see W. C. Askew, "Efforts to Improve Russo-American Relations Before The First World War: the John Hays Hammond Mission," *Slavic and East European Review* (December, 1952).

couraging and supporting Japan, which he took to be the
weaker as well as the more reliable power, he hoped to wear
down and cancel out both countries as opponents of American
predominance. It was expected that the result would be an
open field for American economic and political influence.
Several advisors warned Roosevelt that, even if the tactic was
sound, he should support Russia.* Appearances notwithstand-
ing, they cautioned the President, Japan was likely to be the
stronger power in a short war, and Russia the more likely to
co-operate. They were correct, and Japan proceeded to defeat
Russia and push American interests out of Manchuria.

Fourth: that failure prompted Washington to make a virtue
out of necessity and work with Japan. Policy-makers offered
two variations on that theme.

One group maintained that Washington should join Tokyo
in order to control and develop China as partners. Those men
argued from many motives. They had prejudices in favor of
Japan or against China, and took a somewhat fatalistic view
of Japan's power. Some were even willing, in the final showdown, to acquiesce in a broad measure of Japanese control
of China. Though they influenced policy, such men faced several handicaps in persuading other leaders to accept that tactic.
Japan provided increasing evidence that it would never be
satisfied with an equal relationship. And that only intensified
another difficulty: the majority of American policy-makers did
not really want a partnership—as indicated by their refusal
to consider working with Russia. The Open Door Policy, even
as originally conceived, anticipated a China strong enough to
resist partition by Japan and European powers and strong
enough to handle its responsibilities in connection with being
developed by American entrepreneurs, but not strong enough
to throw the foreign devils out. Giving Japan a free hand
under the name of partnership meant abandoning the very
policy that was supposed to be saved.

These factors strengthened the second group whose plan
for working with Tokyo was considerably more sophisticated.

---

* One such figure, Horace N. Allen, is the subject of an excellent
biography by F. H. Harrington, *God, Mammon and the Japanese* (Madison: University of Wisconsin Press, 1944).

Their plan was based on the idea of exploiting developing economic ties with Japan in order to win both a short-term and a long-term objective: in the short-run, to secure Japanese markets and also an indirect share of Japan's expansion on the Asian mainland; but, in the long-run, to use that economic involvement in Japan as a fulcrum upon which to rest America's political lever, which could then be used to control the extent of Japan's expansion. The essence of this plan was outlined by an American representative in China to Secretary of State Bryan in 1915, when Japan confronted Peking with its extensive Twenty-One Demands. "Our present commercial interests in Japan are greater than those in China, but the look ahead shows our interest to be a strong and independent China rather than one held in subjection by Japan." After a good many false starts and temporary setbacks, this approach was adopted by the United States and followed down to 1939, when the Administration of Franklin Delano Roosevelt made a strong effort to coerce Japan into retreating from China by using American economic influence over Japan's economy.

Fifth: Japan enjoyed many geographical advantages, and others of an economic and military nature that stemmed from its hierarchical social and political structure, which bedeviled and frustrated American efforts to put the Open Door Policy into action. In many respects, at any rate, it was not until the mid-1920's that the United States began to compete effectively in Asia.

The result of that handicap, and of the difficulty American entrepreneurs encountered in accumulating sufficient capital of their own, was to turn American policy-makers—both private economic leaders and elected or appointed officials— toward the idea and practice of joining international financial combines or consortia.* These organizations were similar to

---

* Since this subsequently raised a question of historical interpretation that claimed far more intellectual energy and time than it warranted, it may be useful to examine the issue. The great majority of American historians during the last 50 years has operated from the basis of the *Weltanschauung* of humanitarian laissez faire. Quite naturally (and, given their understanding of the assumptions of that outlook, quite logically), they have defined economics and politics as separate entities that operate or impinge upon each other in much the same fashion

the pools or gentlemen's agreements that developed in domestic economic affairs. Banking firms from several countries combined to share an opportunity in China (or another underdeveloped nation) on an agreed-upon percentage basis. Less capital was thereby required from each unit and, since deadly competition was avoided, the risk was decreased. That more than balanced the chance that any one unit could monopolize the field and the profit.

It should not be imagined, however, that American leaders abandoned their basic assumption when they took up the tactic of implementing the open door strategy through consortium agreements. Some were more patient than others, but all of them fully expected the economic power of the United States to dominate such arrangements, and thereby establish the nation's prodominant economic and political position. Indeed, Secretary of State Knox was so confident of his proposal of 1909 to neutralize the Manchurian railways (a maneuver he expected to reestablish American power in the region) that he did little to camouflage its rather blatant character. Not

---

as two billiard balls. As a result, they have forever been engaged in vehement, and sometimes bitter, arguments over which billiard ball—the red economic one or the white political one—caused the other one to move. They have sustained a long dispute over the question of whether it was the bankers who made foreign policy, or whether it was the politicians who made banking policy.

Yet the issue is itself a pseudo-problem. For, even by the axioms of laissez faire, economic actions were held to produce the general—including the political—welfare. Given conditions of representative government, the political leaders who won office would be those who acted on an internalized understanding of that fundamental truth. Hence they would not separate politics and economics in the way that later historians have done: they would instead hold that good economics was good policy.

Even during the heyday of laissez faire, in the nineteenth century, American politicians and entrepreneurs took for granted the interrelationship between, and the interpenetration of, business and politics. The most perceptive among them realized at the turn of the twentieth century, moreover, that the marketplace of laissez faire had to be managed in foreign affairs just as in domestic affairs if the free enterprise or capitalist system was itself to survive.

Thus both economic and political leaders viewed the tactic of consortia as natural and legitimate. Who acted first is beside the point. This is so, not only because individuals from both groups responded to the need in a similar way at the same time, but also because both groups acted in a reciprocal fashion. The consortium tactic represented a true consensus, not the result of the bankers controlling the White House—or vice versa.

unexpectedly, America's rivals turned it down out of hand.

Sixth: It soon became apparent, moreover, that the consortium tactic was in general less than successful from the American point of view. This harsh and disappointing reality was the product of a combination of factors which were not only interrelated, but whose effect on American participants in the consortia soon began to snowball into a serious crisis. Since there were a good many such elements in the situation, it may help to avoid confusion if they are enumerated formally.

A: the competitors of the United States feared its power. They broadly shared the American belief that over the long-run they were doomed to an inferior position.

B: thus they worked, both as private entrepreneurs and as governments, to combine inside the consortia against the United States. In the narrow, illustrative sense they used their power to outvote American participants.

C: these rivals soon realized, moreover, that American operators were having trouble accumulating capital. They responded in a natural way: they refused to facilitate the sale of American securities on their own exchanges.

D: Americans did not of course accept such opposition passively, and the result was a growing stagnation of the consortia.

E: this accelerated and intensified existing opposition to the consortia inside China. On the one hand, the Chinese Government became increasingly dissatisfied. On the other hand, Chinese critics of the consortia, who came to view them as symbols of outside domination, increased their agitation against the foreigners and also against their own government for negotiating such agreements.

F: as a result, independent economic entrepreneurs in several industrial nations began to compete with the consortia. The Chinese Government turned to them in exasperation with the consortia, and out of its fear that continued inaction would lead to revolution. They hoped that independent entrepreneurs could act effectively enough to dull the edge of the antiforeign unrest. In the United States, moreover, the independents began to argue that the consortium approach was the equivalent in overseas economic affairs of unfair competition at home.

G: finally, the consortium members had reluctantly con-

cluded that it was necessary to help China organize its own
governmental affairs before they could make any significant
profit on economic development projects. Such reorganization
loans, as they were called, were viewed unfavorably for three
main reasons. First: they involved less profit per se. Second:
they required some clear assurance from their own governments that China would be made to meet its obligations. And
third: that factor raised in turn the specter of more unrest in
China.

This long and admittedly rather complicated review of the
circumstances and conditions incident to implementing the
strategy of the Open Door Policy at the time of President Wilson's inauguration in March 1913, has had one main purpose.
The purpose has been to clarify the basic situation so that it
is possible to grasp the great significance of two crucial aspects
of Wilson's action. These can be stated very directly. President
Wilson, Secretary of State Bryan, and other top government
and private leaders understood the situation very accurately
and clearly. They were not wandering in the dark alleys of
ignorance and confusion. Wilson's decision not to support the
bankers (and the consortium) in pushing through the long-
pending reorganization loan was made on the basis of his
integration of reform and economic expansionism, and was
very consciously designed to cut free of the limitations and
dangers of the consortium tactic in order to reassert American
power and influence in China and Manchuria. When they
asked Wilson for a statement of policy, the American bankers
were edgy and anxious. For one thing, they wanted to know
where they stood with the new President. He was a Democrat
coming in after 16 years of Republican rule, and his periodic
vivid and righteous rhetoric about reform worried some businessmen. The bankers also felt that time was running out on
the specific reorganization loan. They wanted either to push
it through or get out of the affair.*

---

* It might be argued that the bankers were determined in any event
to leave the consortium, and in a clever maneuver used the President
to accomplish that objective. After careful evaluation, however, the evidence does not persuade me that the bankers were absolutely set on
withdrawal.

This tone of fish-or-cut-bait, which is apparent in the documents pertaining to the attitude of the bankers, can be misleading if it is interpreted too literally or narrowly. Wall Street was *not* on the verge of abandoning overseas economic expansion, either in general or in China per se. If their request on the reorganization loan was not met, they planned to (and did) turn to smaller industrial and developmental loans. The bankers needed and asked for two kinds of help, both of which were relevant to the reorganization loan. They wanted firm and formal government support in their dealings with China and other consortium members. And they sought the same kind of backing from the government in order to solve their problem of accumulating capital.

The turn to the government for help in corralling capital was known, explained, and documented by a good many people at the time. One State Department official, for example, admitted ruefully that it was impossible "for us alone to float any very large international loan." The clearest public exposition of this factor was provided, however, by Willard Straight. After his long tenure as advisor to Harriman, during which time Straight also served periodically in the Far Eastern Division of the Department of State, he went to work for the House of Morgan (which took the lead in consortium affairs). In a series of articles and speeches during 1912, 1913, and 1914, Straight candidly described the problem in great detail. His point of departure was the proposition that firms engaged in overseas economic expansion were "national assets;" "representatives of our country, trustees for its trade and of its reputation."

He usually began by explaining the difference between borrowing from the public, by selling bonds and other securities, and obtaining the funds from other banks through commercial loans. Commercial loans could not provide enough money. After all, the banks participating in the consortium were the giants of the American financial community. Hence the bankers had to go to "the public." "It is not the bankers who provide the money to finance a foreign loan," Straight remarked bluntly, it comes instead from bonds "sold to the public." As the bankers had learned through experience, "the American investor is not willing to buy Chinese bonds unless

he believes that the American Government will protect him
by all possible diplomatic means."

Thus the issue was "whether our Government will back us
up." "If the American public," Straight summarized, "is to be
educated to the point of financing the sale of our materials
abroad—and that is the question of foreign trade and foreign
loans—the American Government must make some statement
which will reassure the public and give them the thought and
the belief that in case of default or in case of difficulty . . .
the Government will act as the advocate of the public . . . and
see that the American investor gets what is his due."

Beginning with the Wilson Administration, and continuing
in a steadily increasing manner, the Government of the United
States proceeded to provide what Straight and the bankers
asked—and considerably more. Tax monies collected from individual citizens came to be used to provide private corporations with loans and other subsidies for overseas expansion,
to create the power to protect those activities, and even to
create reserve funds with which to make cash guarantees against
losses. The bankers lost in their effort to secure that line of
policy by one hard push in March 1913, but the final program
as it existed in 1962 far exceeded their original objectives.

Wilson was quite willing, even eager, to help the bankers
and other entrepreneurs engaged in overseas economic expansion. But he was perceptive enough to realize that the Open
Door Policy had to be reasserted and upheld outside the framework of the consortia, and in a way that would strengthen
America's position in the underdeveloped countries. That
meant in the narrow sense, as Secretary of State Bryan phrased
it, that Wilson refused to back the bankers in the reorganization loan because "the American group . . . could not have a
controlling voice" in the operation.

For that matter, Bryan provided the best general explanation of Wilson's decision. Significantly, it was offered as a
public statement. "The President believed that a different
policy was more consistent with the American position, and
that it would in the long run be more advantageous to our
commerce . . . I may say that American interests will be protected everywhere. . . . The President in his policies as thus
far announced has laid even a broader foundation for the

extension of our trade throughout the Orient. He is cultivating
the friendship of the people across the Pacific. . . . The President's policy contemplates the formulation of an environment
which will encourage the growth of all that is good. . . . So, the
government, while it cannot trade, can give to trade an environment in which it can develop, and that is the duty of our
government to do."

Or, as Wilson said in a memorandum to Bryan, the basic
objective was "the maintenance of the policy of an open door
to the world." This explicit and heavy emphasis on long-run
objectives explains why the President's refusal to support the
bankers in the reorganization loan is so misleading if it is
interpreted as a change in basic policy. There is really no
reason to do that, moreover, because even the published documents leave no doubt about Wilson's vigorous support for
economic expansion. Bryan reported, for example, that the
cabinet expressed full agreement on "a strong declaration
favorable to the extension of our commerce in the Orient."
And Wilson's own dispatch explaining his action is even more
explicit. He was "earnestly desirous of promoting the most
extended and intimate trade relationship" with China. Americans "certainly wish to participate, and participate very generously, in the opening to the Chinese and to the use of the
world the almost untouched and perhaps unrivaled resources
of China." He closed with a sober promise to "urge and support" such expansion, and to provide American entrepreneurs
with "the banking and other financial facilities which they
now lack and without which they are at a serious disadvantage."

Finally, Wilson's critical words to and about the bankers
in his public reply to their request must be evaluated in the
context of these other factors. The verbal wrist-slapping was
a gesture quite in keeping with Wilson's reformist outlook,
and also an obvious maneuver to win favor with the progressives in both parties. A more important consideration may well
have been the way that it served to enhance America's image
in the eyes of the Chinese. Here was the President of the
United States accepting a point made by foreign critics. In no
way was the criticism insincere (nor is this analysis meant to
imply that such was the case in a subtle way), but it did not

mean the end of official support for the bankers, or for general overseas economic expansion. It merely symbolized a more sophisticated approach to those objectives. The reformer as expansionist would be more successful than the conservative as expansionist.

Any doubts concerning Wilson's basic position were removed by subsequent events. After "very satisfactory" conversations with Bryan, Straight reported to a meeting of bankers and other entrepreneurs that the Secretary of State was most cooperative. "No one could have been more ready to support [us] and to telegraph Peking, and urge measures on the part of the Chinese Government." Even more revealing, perhaps, was the relationship between the Wilson Administration and the National Council of Foreign Trade. Secretary Bryan and Secretary of Commerce William Redfield were the major speakers during the first day of the council's national convention in May, 1914.

This date is significant, for it specifies the policy of the Wilson Administration at a time when it was clear that America was suffering a serious economic downturn, yet at an hour prior to the outbreak of World War I. Secretary Redfield, who had been president of the American Manufacturers Export Association and a vigorous advocate of overseas economic expansion before Wilson called him to the crusade for the New Freedom, led off with a broad outline of government policy. He assured the corporation leaders that "because we are strong, we are going out, you and I, into the markets of the world to get our share." A bit later, in 1915, Redfield revealed even more clearly why he was so vehement about overseas economic expansion. Speaking again to businessmen, he emphasized that "it is a noble work that we are engaged in. It carries with it so much of hope, so much of growth, so much of power, such a promise of prosperity . . . [It is] the pendulum . . . [that] controls the whole movement of the mechanism."

Secretary Bryan spoke next. First he reminded the audience that President Wilson had already made it clear that it was official policy to "open the doors of all the weaker countries to an invasion of American capital and enterprise." Having made that point, Bryan referred to an engaging custom of one such country as a way of convincing the businessmen of his deep concern for their welfare. "In Spanish-speaking countries," he reminded them, "hospitality is expressed by a phrase, 'My house is your house.'. . . I can say, not merely in courtesy —but as a fact—my Department is your department; the ambassadors, the ministers, and the consuls are all yours. It is their business to look after your interests and to guard your rights."

On the next day the convention left its downtown quarters for a special meeting in the East Room of the White House. President Wilson had seen fit to take time from his more official duties to address the delegates. His purpose was to assure them that he gave full and active support to a mutual campaign to effect "the righteous conquest of foreign markets." Perhaps it was because some in his audience seemed startled by that candid statement of policy, but in any event Wilson went on to emphasize the point by remarking that such an objective was "one of the things we hold nearest to our heart."

As in earlier periods, the question of whether or not American leaders acted from personal economic motives is beside the point. Indeed, such an approach raises false questions. Without any doubt, the businessmen acted on an economic calculus, and it is sophistry to camouflage the obvious as the complex. It is far more important that many of the businessmen and politicians were thinking about American foreign policy in terms of the functioning of the economic *system,* and that they saw overseas economic expansion as the key element in such security and welfare.

In most respects, furthermore, the Wilson Administration agreed with the businessmen about the best means to facilitate such overseas economic expansion. One section of the Federal Reserve Act, for example, had just that purpose. Wilson's tariff commission also concentrated on enlarging and securing markets for surplus production. An even more dramatic step was taken with the passage of the Webb-Pomerene Act. This law developed out of the consensus on the need to improve America's weapons in the battle for supremacy in world markets, a concern heightened by the realization that the postwar struggle would be even tougher. It repealed the antitrust laws at the water's edge, thus providing a bipartisan American answer to foreign cartels. Another law, the Edge Act, extended the provisions of the Federal Reserve Act which encouraged American financial operations overseas. Wilson also reactivated the old American banking consortium as the chosen instrument of American open door expansion in the Far East. Such moves took on added significance in the context of the Bolshevik Revolution in Russia in November 1917 (after which event Wilson undertook to extend the open door to Russia), but it is vital to realize that these acts represented a consensus between the Wilson Administration and the business community which had been apparent as early as 1912.

An understanding of this consensus, and of the related convergence of the reformist and economic drives for expansion, offers a key insight into America's entry into World War I. Most Americans shared Wilson's nationalistic outlook. None but a handful of citizens quarreled with his assertion that it was the destiny of the United States to become the "justest, the most progressive, the most honorable, the most enlightened Nation in the world." Indeed, a sizable plurality thought, if they did not assume, that the destiny was being realized in their own time. In the early months of the war, therefore, it was quite natural for them to feel, along with Wilson, that America had neither reason nor necessity to enter the conflict.

But, and again in agreement with Wilson, most Americans wanted the Allies to win, and they were willing to help bring about that result. Whatever the faults and sins of England and France, they were better than autocratic Germany. America could work with them toward a peaceful, prosperous, and moral world, whereas such would be impossible if Germany won. This attitude, and the actions which it prompted, led Wilson and America into a position where they had either to abandon their determination and destiny to lead the world or go to war.

The early economic decisions made by businessmen and the Wilson Administration committed the American economic system to the Allied war effort. That did not, in itself, make it inevitable that America's nonbelligerent alignment with the Allies would involve America in the war on their side; but it did make it extremely difficult for Wilson to achieve his objectives in any other way.

The American economy was in a depression when the war erupted. Financier J. Pierpont Morgan described the situation in an accurate and straightforward manner. "The war opened during a period of hard times that had continued in America for over a year. Business throughout the country was depressed, farm prices were deflated, unemployment was serious, the heavy industries were working far below capacity [and] bank clearings were off." Vanderlip's comment was more elliptical: "The country was not in a prosperous situation."

The first economic shocks of the conflict subjected the system to even more difficulties. The stock market and the cotton exchange were closed on July 31, 1914, and did not reopen for public trading for many, many months. "We were looking after our own troubles," Vanderlip later explained, and "bankers in general were not considering technical matters of neutrality." Instead, Vanderlip went on, "we had the idea very much of keeping up our foreign trade throughout the world." In making that effort, it was not very surprising that American entrepreneurs concentrated on reopening their connections with the Allies, who together with their colonies had purchased 77 per cent of American exports in 1913—and with whom the majority of American bankers had their closest connections.

But in restoring America's foreign trade by tying it to England and France (and by expanding old connections with such nations as Russia), rather than by insisting upon economic neutrality, Wilson and American businessmen tied themselves to a prosperity based on the Allied war program. Wilson developed no other plan to end the depression, and hence this way of dealing with the problem exerted a subtle but persuasive influence on later decisions.

Economic ties to the Allies also reinforced the bias of Wilson's ideology and morality toward defining German naval warfare as the most important diplomatic issue of the war. Wilson denounced submarine warfare on moral and humanitarian grounds, whereas he opposed British trade restrictions on legal and historical precedents. And the fact that Wilson launched no crusade against the Allied food blockade of Germany, which had equally devastating moral and humanitarian consequences, dramatized this double standard.

This ability to make such fine moral discriminations forced Wilson into an extremely difficult situation. He hoped to remain a nonbelligerent until a stalemate developed and then step in as the arbiter of the settlement and as the architect of a world organization to establish and maintain peace. But by seeming to foreshadow the defeat of England and France, the success of submarine warfare also threatened his ability to lead the world to permanent peace. Wilson resolved his difficulties (and apparently eased his troubled conscience) by defining the situation as similar to the case of the Philippines. America was justified in using force "to do justice and assert the rights of mankind." To that end, war against Germany would be prosecuted until it established "a government we can trust."

By the time of World War I, therefore, the basic dilemma of American foreign policy was clearly defined. Its generous humanitarianism prompted it to improve the lot of less fortunate peoples, but that side of its diplomacy was undercut by two other aspects of its policy. On the one hand, it defined helping people in terms of making them more like Americans. This subverted its ideal of self-determination. On the other hand, it asserted and acted upon the necessity of overseas economic expansion for its own material prosperity. But by defining such expansion in terms of markets for American exports, and control of raw materials for American industry, the ability of other peoples to develop and act upon their own patterns of development was further undercut.

Those unfortunate aspects of American foreign policy were summarized rather well by an American reformer who at one time had shared the attitude of Roosevelt and Wilson. He even agreed that entry into World War I was necessary. But he broke with Roosevelt and Wilson over the very points which undercut the ideal, and the practice, of self-determination. Perhaps his judgment is too harsh, yet it offers an important insight into Wilson's failure and into America's difficulties at mid-century. For that reason, but not as a final verdict either on Wilson or the United States, it deserves consideration.

Looking back across the years, Raymond Robins reflected on the origins of the crisis in American diplomacy in these words: "Wilson was a great man but he had one basic fault. He was willing to do anything for people except get off their backs and let them live their own lives. He would never let go until they forced him to and then it was too late. He never seemed to understand there's a big difference between trying to save people and trying to help them. With luck you can help 'em— but they always save themselves."

One of the most helpful aspects of that estimate of Wilson and his diplomacy lies in the suggestion that it offers about American entry into the war and America's response to the revolutions which occurred during and at the end of that conflict. For given entry into the war on the grounds that "the world must be made safe for democracy," the crucial questions become those about the definition of democracy and the means to insure its security. Having answered those questions, it may then be possible to determine and understand the reasons why the effort did not succeed.

CHAPTER THREE

I am proposing, as it were, that the nations should with one accord adopt the doctrine of President Monroe as the doctrine of the world. . . .

I am proposing that all nations henceforth avoid entangling alliances. . . .

I am proposing government by the consent of the governed . . . freedom of the seas . . . and that moderation of armaments which makes of armies and navies a power for order. . . .

These are American principles, American policies. We could stand for no others. And they are also the principles and policies of forward-looking men and women everywhere, of every modern nation, of every enlightened community. They are the principles of mankind and must prevail.

WOODROW WILSON, JANUARY, 1917

The Peace which we propose must be a people's peace . . . guaranteeing to each nation freedom for economic and cultural development. Such a peace can only be concluded by the direct and courageous struggle of the revolutionary masses against all imperialist plans and aggressive designs.

Overthrow those robbers and enslavers of your country. . . . Let them no longer violate your hearths! You must yourselves

THE RISING TIDE OF REVOLUTION

be masters in your own land! You yourselves must arrange
your life as you see fit! You have the right to do this, for your
fate is in your own hands!

PRESIDENT WILSON [*remarked that*]. . . . *There was certainly*
a latent force behind Bolshevism which attracted as much
sympathy as its more brutal aspects caused general disgust.
There was throughout the world a feeling of revolt against
the large vested interests which influenced the world both in
the economic and in the political sphere. The way to cure
this domination was, in his opinion, constant discussion and
a slow process of reform; but the world at large had grown
impatient of delay.

The question now arose whether we ought to include in the
new terms of the armistice other problems, such as that of
Poland.

PRESIDENT WILSON *suggested it might be unwise to discuss a*
proposal of this sort on its individual merits, since it formed

*part of the much larger question of . . . how to meet the social
danger of Bolshevism.*

FROM THE MINUTES OF THE MEETING OF THE SUPREME
WAR COUNCIL IN PARIS, JANUARY, 1919

Woodrow Wilson's attempt to use America's great power to
make the world safe for democracy, and to establish an international order to maintain that security, was an essentially
conservative effort. His definition of democracy, his emphasis
on preserving that particular society, and the means he proposed to accomplish the task were rooted in the nineteenth-
century liberal conception of the world. And his view of
human nature, his political theory and action, and his idea
that the United States would take over the international role
that Great Britain had played between 1815 and 1915 further
characterized him as a man of that outlook and tradition.
Wilson was confident that the principles and procedures of
nineteenth-century liberalism were just and sound; he felt,
therefore, that the basic problem was to establish a framework
in which they could produce the well-being of all concerned.

Wilson's reservations about the existing state of affairs did
not include any doubts concerning the fundamental structure
of society. He did realize that the rise of the large corporation,
and similar organized groups in the political economy, called
for some changes in the *Weltanschauung* of nineteenth-century
liberalism. There were three broad approaches that could be
followed. One answer was to evolve a new philosophy and
program to fit the facts of advanced industrial society. Another involved extensive and probably somewhat ruthless
government intervention to recreate the political economy of
the individual entrepreneur.

But either of those proposals involved drastic action, and
Wilson had no intention of embarking upon such a course.
"We shall deal with an economic system as it is and as it may
be modified," he announced as he entered the White House in
1913, "not as it might be if we had a clean sheet of paper
to write on." That strong antipathy to fundamental change

limited Wilson to the third alternative. He accepted the corporation and similar groups and tried somehow or other to modify and adapt, and thereby sustain, his nineteenth-century liberalism in a situation in which the individual had actually lost much of his power to initiate, or even control, affairs that affected him immediately and fundamentally.

Despite the series of specific and general revolutions that occurred throughout the world between his election in 1912 and his death in 1924, Wilson never seriously altered his conception of the world. As indicated in an article in the *Atlantic Monthly,* he was still looking at the end of his life for "The Road Away From Revolution." But the impact of these revolutions provoked many Americans formerly in agreement with him to modify their outlook. A majority of those who left Wilson's position emphasized the need for America to oppose the revolutions with more determination, and to continue its independent expansion with greater vigor. Only a few argued that it was wiser to accept the revolutions and to modify or change America's traditional conception of the world. Taken together, however, those who disagreed with Wilson were more numerous than those who continued to support him. In the end, therefore, Wilson's crusade was defeated by revolutions overseas and by the domestic American response to these upheavals.

At the hour of its entry into the war, however, America broadly shared the assumptions of Wilson's liberalism and responded to his definition of America's war aims. Though it admitted that there were exceptions in reality, American liberalism was a philosophy derived from the axiom and belief that a harmony of interests actually existed and could be secured. Such an underlying community of interest was held to eventuate in community well-being if it was not distorted or thwarted. As a consequence of their ideological childhood within the tradition of natural law, their enormous natural resources, and the absence of any serious opponents in the New World, Americans had followed the line of least resistance in developing their political economy. Founded on a simple (if not crude) concept of natural law, its theory was as neat a circle as ever was drawn freehand. Conflicts of interest were asserted to be mere appearances, or the result of misguided action by others, because the doctrine of a harmony of interests defined them in that fashion. Hence intervention in the social process was necessary and justified only to remove the obstacles placed there by others who did not understand or honor the truth.

Though negative in form, such intervention became very positive in practice, for the theory defined every opponent of the United States as being misadvised about the nature of the world. In a way that John Locke had tended to do in his own philosophical writings which provided the master text for liberalism, Americans became very prone to define such rivals as unnatural men. They were thus beyond the pale and almost, if not wholly, beyond redemption. Reinforced by an expansionist, or frontier, interpretation of history that explained nationalistic expansion as a necessary and justified part of natural law, the theory was further supported by ethnic and religious prejudices. The final result was that domestic problems became international problems, for it was necessary to remove the restrictions upon America's natural right to resolve its domestic difficulties by natural expansion.

This outlook was literally an all-encompassing conception of the world. Americans could not only conquer nature, but they could put their self-interest to work to produce the well-being and the harmony of the world. Their theory not only held that they could do such things; it asserted the natural necessity of such action. Any other course violated natural law and thus subverted the harmony of interests. Throughout the twentieth century, and particularly after World War I, the thesis was advanced with great force by various American experts in casuistry. But the logic of the theory itself led most Americans to the conclusions in complete innocence. They were neither hypocrites nor sophists; they simply accepted and believed the idea that American expansion naturally improved the world—as well as being necessary for their own democracy and prosperity.

Turning from these general characteristics of American liberalism, it is helpful to outline the more specific nature of the society which Wilson and other Americans had in mind when they asserted that the world must be made safe for democracy. Supported by an examination of the means proposed to accomplish that task, such a review will provide considerable insight into the international and domestic opposition which developed between 1917 and 1920. There are several ways to approach this task of definition, but one of the most fruitful is to consider American liberalism from the vantage point of its outlook on key issues: economics, politics, social questions such as race, color, and religion, and the international phenomena of nationalism, colonialism, and imperialism.

As defined by Wilson and other Americans, the economic aspect of democracy was based on the classical liberal assumption of a society composed of free, independent, and enlightened individuals who acted in their own self-interest as producers and consumers. For the consumer, price was the criterion of self-interest. For the producer, it was profit—or the wage contract that the worker negotiated with the owner. Since all of these indicators could be measured in money, the interplay of the various self-interests in the market place produced an automatic and perpetual functioning of the system. Hence the profit motive, if allowed to operate freely through the individual, produced the maximum benefit for the community as well as the welfare of the individual.

Given a natural system of this character, the government had neither cause nor justification to intervene in economic affairs except for a few well-defined purposes. Almost all were negative in nature: protecting the validity of the money, or measuring, system; maintaining order; enforcing the definition of economic malpractices; and clearing out any remnants of mercantilism. Its one positive responsibility was nevertheless vitally important to the functioning of the system: the protection and extension of the market in which the principle of free competition could operate. As with mercantilism, classical liberal economics led to an expansionist foreign policy.*

In most cases, therefore, the liberal state maintained and

---

* Liberalism's intervention in domestic affairs should not, however, be misconceived as another similarity with mercantilism. Mercantilists intervened on the assumption that there was *not* any natural harmony of interests, and that men had therefore to create such harmony as there was by conscious, rational effort. The liberal, in contrast, intervened to establish conditions under which competition would—through the power of Adam Smith's famous Hidden Hand—allow the natural harmony of interests to assert itself. The distinction is crucial.

extended the practice of colonialism. In others, it modified the
pattern of expansion into what British historians have called
"informal empire" or "free-trade imperialism," where the
liberal state relied upon its industrial and general economic
power to structure and control weaker or less developed nations.* Local or native peoples often ruled, but they did so
within limits (and rules) defined by their economic ties with
the imperial power. As far as the weaker country was concerned, this meant in practice that one segment of society
ruled. When this pattern of events was called democracy, as it
often was, the rest of the population tended to conclude that
democracy was not what it wanted. For this reason, as well
as in consequence of the more obvious economic results of
the policy, such peoples were inclined to respond to radical
leadership that offered them a greater share in running affairs,
as well as a more general distribution of wealth.

Wilson's original program was designed to perform the
domestic and international functions of the liberal state. As
with Theodore Roosevelt before him, however, Wilson was
confronted by the fact that free competition worked to restrict
free competition. As implied by its very name, the system of
natural law tended to establish a balance among the powerful
or cunning survivors of competition. It was impractical, if
not impossible, to destroy the successful competitors. And
neither Wilson nor the majority of Americans even considered
substituting a different system. To cope with the domestic side
of the dilemma, Wilson moved toward a modification of the
classical liberal position. He accepted the existence of certain
large groups, particularly the corporation and the labor union,
and attempted to fit them into traditional liberal economic
and social theory.

While at first glance this may seem to offer a rational and
perceptive solution, even a modest amount of reflection reveals
at least two fundamental weaknesses. In the first place, the
result of equating the organized and institutionalized group
with the individual is to create a kind of syndicalism in which

---

* Here see: H. S. Ferns, "Britain's Informal Empire in Argentina, 1806–
1914," *Past and Present* (1953); and J. Gallagher and R. Robinson, "The
Imperialism of Free Trade," *The Economic History Review* (1953).

the groups (or blocs) compete with each other. The individual, unless he is one of the very few to attain a position of great power or high authority within such blocs, has almost no role in the formulation of alternatives, and only moderate and occasional influence in choosing between programs or policies developed by the top leaders. The second weakness concerns the way in which this ostensible solution promotes discouragement, disillusionment, and finally apathy or a particularly narrow and selfish kind of cynicism, as the discrepancy between the theory and the reality becomes increasingly apparent.*

Despite such handicaps of that outlook, of which he was not totally unaware, Wilson nevertheless transferred his approach to domestic affairs to the problems of foreign policy. His conception of the League of Nations, for example, was clearly evolved in that fashion. And for Wilson, as for his predecessors and successors, the Open Door Policy was America's version of the liberal policy of informal empire or free-trade imperialism. None of them had the slightest idea of organizing the co-operative, planned, balanced economic development of world resources. Wilson aimed to use American power, inside and outside the League of Nations, merely to order the world so that such classical competition could proceed in peace. If this could be done, he was confident that American economic power could take care of the United States —and of the world.

Wilson's political ideas and objectives were equally traditional. Based on the same principle of natural law which underwrote liberal economic theory, liberal political theory asserted that each individual participated in the process of decision-making on the basis of his own self-interest. Given the existence of natural political freedoms, such as those of speech and association, the individual's exercise of his positive freedom to participate in the political process would lead to

---

* For further discussion of this development see, *The Contours of American History* (New York: World Publishing Co., 1961). The best known (but nevertheless unsuccessful) attempt to squeeze such syndicalism into the framework of liberalism is J. K. Galbraith, *American Capitalism. The Theory of Countervailing Power* (Boston: Harper & Bros., 1952).

democratic decisions. The theory asserted, in short, that the enjoyment and exercise of natural political rights assured the individual of his share of power.

More than was the case in economic matters, however, Americans were aware of the discrepancy between this theory of political liberalism and the reality of their political experience. For a generation before entering World War I they had grappled, through the instrument of the bipartisan Progressive movement, with the imbalance created by the impact of consolidated economic power on the political process. They grew ever more aware that such economic power exercised disproportionate political influence—directly by organized pressure on elected representatives and indirectly by the broad political and social consequences of economic decisions. As one American of the time expressed it, "the dollar votes more times than the man." Some Americans, probably Wilson among them, ultimately sensed that the Mexican Revolution was in part a violent protest against a similar discrepancy ·between theory and reality. This experience helped them understand a bit more the general revolt against political liberalism and was a restraining factor in their response to the challenge, but it did not lead them to formulate and act upon a new conception of democracy.

This reluctance to embark upon a thoroughgoing re-examination of the existing order was the result of many factors. Some of them were negative. By comparison with the depression years of the 1890's, for example, the period after 1900 seemed bright and rosy. In addition, the war intensified the general psychological propensity to go along with the existing order despite its weaknesses and failures. A more important consideration, and one that was positive in character, was the renewed confidence that came with recovery from the depression.

Reforms such as the initiative and the referendum, the direct election of senators, and numerous antitrust prosecutions encouraged the belief that classical liberalism could be modified to work under new conditions. And the convergence of the reformist and economic expansionism generated enthusiasm for America's mission in the world. The frontier interpretation of American history, having been modernized to fit an industrial society, was once again becoming an article of faith—just as its agrarian version had done in the 1830's and 1840's. Americans increasingly considered themselves once more on the move to "extend the area of freedom."

But this new enthusiasm in the United States developed at a time when classical liberalism was coming under heavy criticism in much of the world. Thus there were many doubts about the *kind* of freedom that America was extending, as well as about the morality of doing so. In addition to questions about the economic effects of such overseas expansion, there was also skepticism about some of its political and social characteristics. An increasing number of foreigners was aware, for example, that political and social democracy in the United States were largely limited to white Anglo-Saxons.

When transferred to the world scene, those color and ethnic restrictions became even more apparent. Democracy tended in practice to be replaced by an outlook summarized in the familiar phrase about the white man's burden. That approach was based on the quite different thesis that colored people were somehow never ready for democracy and self-government. It was possible, of course, to defend various limitations on democracy and representative government on logical as well as historical and practical grounds. Indeed, a very great deal of intellectual and emotional energy was invested in that effort by Americans, as well as by Europeans with colonial empires to defend.

Such arguments were not very strong, however, because political democracy had begun, even in the white Western countries, as a process in which only a small segment of the adult population participated. Colored peoples pointed out, quite plausibly, that their societies were already structured for such a form of democracy. And when, as was the case with American liberalism, it was further implied, if not vehemently asserted, that democracy *really* worked only for white, Anglo-Saxon, Protestant Christians, the appeal of democracy suffered even more. For this argument led rather rapidly to the conclusion that even at best democracy meant little more than the modification of colonialism in the direction of less harsh protectorates or open-door imperialism.

For these reasons, American liberalism's definition of democracy as it pertained to self-determination and colonialism lost much of its democratic content once it moved beyond Western Europe. Colonial societies began to realize that America's anticolonialism neither implied nor offered freedom from extensive and intensive foreign influence. Whatever the evidence that Wilson ever entertained any idea of actually trying to limit such absentee authority to its absolute minimum of voluntary respect and emulation, and such data is neither extensive nor convincing, it is clear that he never developed or pushed such a program.

At best, Wilson's actions were in keeping with the principles of a moralistic and paternalistic open-door imperialism. At worst, he intervened with force in the affairs of other nations. America's verbal support for the principle of self-determination became in practice the reordering of national boundaries in Europe on the basis of ethnic and linguistic criteria. Though it had considerable relevance for Western Europe, this principle and practice of nationality had less meaning in Eastern Europe—and still less throughout the rest of the world. But it was not even applied to many areas. Japan was treated as an inferior, for example, and the colonial empires were hardly touched. They were most certainly not broken up into independent states according to the principle of self-determination. And even though some improvements did result from the mandate system where it was applied, that approach was characterized by minimum changes in the existing pattern of colonialism.

Taken seriously, a commitment to the principle of self-determination means a policy of standing aside for peoples to make their own choices, economic as well as political and cultural. It is based on a willingness to live and let live—a broad tolerance for other peoples' preferences and a willingness, if the opportunity is offered, to help them achieve their own goals in their own fashion. It is the philosophy of an integrated personality, and it might be defined as the foreign policy of a mature society.* Though it avowed this principle, the actions

---

* It could of course be maintained with considerable power that the philosophy of self-determination actually leads, if followed rigorously, to pacifism, and to anarchism practiced within small communities. Both Wilson and the Bolsheviks declined to pursue the logic that far.

of America in the realm of foreign affairs did not follow this pattern. Hence it was not surprising, as Wilson's actions became apparent, that many peoples of the world felt misled by Wilson's slogans about self-determination. It was one thing to shape one's own culture, but quite another to be pushed aside while others haggled over ethnic statistics and then drew lines on a map.

As suggested by many of his actions in Mexico, and by his call for war without quarter until Germany erected a government that "we can trust," Wilson's liberal practice was not in keeping with his liberal principles. This became even more apparent as he began to reveal his ideals about a League of Nations. That program amounted to a direct and almost literal application of the principles of America's domestic liberalism to the world at large. The League of Nations became the state, and its function was to maintain order and enforce the rules of the game at the international level. Given such security, the national pursuit of self-interest would, according to the doctrine of a harmony of interests, produce peace and prosperity throughout the world.

Beyond that point, however, the attempt to formulate an international system on the principles of such liberalism encountered a difficult issue. It was simple to say that the League corresponded to the state, but it was not at all easy to specify the power structure of the international state. The logical answer defined it as a Parliament of Man, but that did not answer the question; it only asked it in a different way. It was still necessary to specify such mundane but vital things as the nature of the franchise and the institutional structure of the government. Wilson answered such questions by combining his concept of America's supremacy with the political theory of classical liberalism. Every nation could vote, but nothing could be done without the prior existence of a concert of power (or harmony of interests) among the big nations. That was as weighted a franchise as ever proposed under the name of liberalism, particularly since Wilson assumed that America (in association with Great Britain) would lead the concert of major powers.

Considered on its own merits, the idea of a concert of power among the strongest nations had much to recommend it on the grounds that it assigned responsibility to those with the

ability to make basic decisions. But when judged against the
rhetoric and principles of classical liberalism it was quite
clearly a contradiction in terms. For by the key tenet of
liberalism, namely the existence of a harmony of interests,
it was possible to produce the general welfare only under conditions of free competition. Yet by establishing an oligopoly
of power, and formalizing it in an unconditional guarantee of
"the territorial integrity and existing political independence"
of the nations admitted to the League (on criteria prescribed
by the oligopoly itself), Wilson's proposal destroyed the possibility of free competition. And it was precisely on this point
that the League of Nations was attacked by some American
liberals themselves, as well as by radicals and conservatives in
the United States and throughout the world.

Both at home and abroad, the radicals made the most fundamental criticism because they also challenged all of Wilson's
definitions of liberal democracy. Their assault was supported,
particularly in the early years of the revolutionary upsurge
throughout the world, by a heretical movement within liberalism itself which strengthened the radicals by weakening Wilson's position. Left-wing liberalism developed from the same
philosophy of natural law which classical liberalism cited as
the sanction for its own program. But while they accepted the
doctrine of a natural harmony of interests, the heretical liberals went on to raise the question as to why the existing
society did not correspond to the ideal society. In reply, they
argued that certain institutions, particularly that of private
property in its large, concentrated, and consolidated forms,
prevented the natural harmony from emerging from the free
interplay of individuals pursuing their self-interest. That analysis led the heretics to the conclusion that it was necessary
to make structural changes in the existing society before the
workings of natural law could produce the general welfare.
In sharp contrast, Wilson (and the conservatives) would support nothing more than a "slow process of reform" in which
they saw no need, and most certainly had no intention, of
shaking the foundations of the status quo. Hence the heretics
proposed many measures, particularly in economic, social, and
international matters, which approximated some of those advanced by the radicals. But the heretic liberals were drastic

reformers, not revolutionaries. This was a vital distinction, for in time it led the heretics to oppose the radicals as vigorously as did the classical liberals or even the conservatives.

For their part, the radicals started from a fundamentally different premise. They denied the existence—save perhaps in some mythical past—of a natural harmony of interests. They held that conflict was the essence of life and that it would never end short of death. Yet they also argued that each broad conflict within society was resolved on a higher level and thus produced a better life in the new society. And, in some of their most free-wheeling arguments and prophecies, they asserted that later conflicts would be nonviolent and would concern ideas and broad cultural issues. Men would dispute the best means of becoming more human, not the distribution of wealth and power. In its own way, therefore, the radical theory promised a society not too different from the one prophesied by the heretical liberals on the quite different basis of a harmony of interests inherent in natural law. But the radicals not only thought it necessary to go further in changing society, they also accepted revolution as a justifiable and honorable method.

In economic matters, for example, they denied the validity of the liberals' market economy. They judged it neither fair nor truly efficient. They advocated instead the idea of planned production for use and welfare. To accomplish this, they proposed that the government should take title to resources and direct the production of goods and services for all the society on an equitable basis. Such economic decisions would not only facilitate development in other areas of life, they would also become the stuff of politics, and in that fashion politics would once again become relevant and meaningful to each citizen. This mode of production and distribution would not only make work itself meaningful to the individual and the group, but would end the struggle for raw existence and hence free men for personal and cultural development.

Radicals made no discrimination as to which men would enjoy such fruits of the revolution, except that they excluded those who fought to retain their privileges of the past. They handled the question of religion in two ways. In the broadest sense they secularized it, converting it into a faith in the ability of man to realize his full potential in this world. More immediately, either they attacked it as a façade for privilege and power or interpreted its idealism as support for their program. As for color or ethnic origins, they denied the validity of such criteria as the basis of any decision, an attitude that enabled them to avoid Wilson's contradiction between self-determination and nationality and the exclusiveness of his Protestant Christianity and Anglo-Saxonism. In this way, radicals appealed to all men across all existing—or proposed—boundaries.

Their approach to self-determination gave the radicals a double-edged weapon against colonialism and the less overt forms of imperial expansion such as the Open Door Policy. For by asserting the right of self-determination, they identified themselves with anticolonialism, which was the lowest common denominator of nationalism, yet also aligned themselves with the more developed and specific expressions of nationalism. Thus they offered leadership to those who wished to end formal colonialism, as well as to others who sought to assert their full sovereignty against spheres of influence and similar restrictions established under the Open Door Policy.

In the broadest sense, therefore, the radicals offered the peoples of the world an explanation of their existing hardships, a program to end such difficulties and build a better world, and leadership in that common effort. This radical assault on classical liberalism and conservatism was a direct challenge to Wilson and to the United States. And through the communist victory of November 1917, in Russia, all those separate revolutions—in economics, politics, social values, and international affairs—seemed to become institutionalized in a nation of tremendous potential.

Though obviously of great importance to an understanding of American diplomacy in the twentieth century, the Bolshevik Revolution and the subsequent rise of the Soviet Union as a thermonuclear power can nevertheless be overemphasized to the point of creating serious errors of analysis and interpretation. Indeed, that very preoccupation (and the warped perspective that it created) does a great deal to explain many otherwise perplexing actions by American leaders. It helps tremendously, for example, to account for the near-panic manifested by otherwise perceptive, intelligent, and sober men when Castro sustained his power in Cuba.* And in a broader sense, it offers considerable insight into the way that American leaders persistently interpreted political and social unrest throughout the world as a consequence of the Bolshevik Revolution, and also into the way that they steadily expanded the nation's commitments beyond a rational calculation (even by the axioms of their expansionist *Weltanschauung*) of the country's resources.

This myopic and self-defeating preoccupation with the Bolshevik Revolution existed long before the Soviet Union orbited a man in space. Fundamentally, and from the outset, American leaders were for many, many years more afraid of

---

* Perhaps the most striking example of this is provided by Adolf A. Berle, Jr. Berle, prior to the Cuban Revolution, was one of the most astute and rigorous minds seeking to resolve the tragedy of American diplomacy in a creative manner. For that matter, his analyses of the domestic political economy continue to exhibit those exceptional characteristics. But Castro so provoked and frightened Berle that he was unable (along with others) even to interpret the Cuban crisis within the limits of his formerly sophisticated expansionism.

Before the Cuban Revolution, for example, I had the good fortune to hear Berle expound for two hours in an exceedingly brilliant manner on the dangerous consequences of America's expansion within the strategy of the Open Door Policy. He spoke knowingly and candidly about the way that the expansion of corporations into Latin America influenced the politics of those countries, and of the manner in which they returned an unfair share of their gross profits to the United States—and thereby intensified tensions even further. He concluded his analysis with a remark so simple and eloquent, as well as true, that it visibly and deeply affected the twenty-odd men and women who heard it: "Either we build a true and brilliant community in the Western Hemisphere—or we go under."

Now the central point of all this should not be misunderstood. Let the whole issue of expansionism stand moot. What remains, and what can not be rationalized away, is the inability of Berle to act on his own aphorism. For the Cuban Revolution offered the United States an almost unique opportunity to get on with the work of building a community in the Western Hemisphere. Yet Berle very soon interpreted that revolution as part of a conspiracy by the Soviet Union to spread communism. Neither Berle nor the others of the large group he symbolizes made any serious or sustained effort to jump in, *even within the assumptions of their expansionist outlook,* and help the moderate elements begin that work—which would in turn have given them a very strong position within the revolutionary coalition. A more saddening example of the unhappy consequences of reading world history since 1917 in terms of the Bolshevik Revolution would be very difficult to find.

the implicit and indirect challenge of the revolution than they were of the actual power of the Soviet Union. Communist Russia never posed a direct and significant danger to the vital national interests of the United States, let alone to its existence as a state, until—at the earliest—the period between 1949 and 1952. Up to that time, at any rate, it had neither the power nor the freedom of maneuver at home to initiate such action.

It is essential to remember, in this connection, that American leaders expected Hitler to conquer Russia in six weeks; and that they were not only well informed about the serious and extensive damage suffered by the Soviet Union during World War II, but expected to benefit from that relative and absolute weakness of Russia. From 1917 to 1950, the United States had, *and knew it had,* a preponderance of power as compared to the Soviet Union. It is very probable, moreover, that the United States sustained that position for at least five more years. All the talk after 1955 about the balance shifting to Russia has to be interpreted in the light of the avowed American objective of restoring the situation as of 1939 or 1941. An inability to do that short of war does not mean that the balance has actually shifted. It means only that the epoch of Western superiority has ended in a stand-off. What happens in the future has yet to be determined. No analysis or interpretation of American-Soviet relations can be taken seriously unless it is based on a recognition and acknowledgment of those elementary truths.*

It thus seems clear that the great majority of American leaders were—like President Wilson—concerned so deeply with the Bolshevik Revolution because at bottom they were so uneasy about what Wilson called the "general feeling of revolt" against the existing order, and about the increasing intensity of that dissatisfaction. From this it follows that the Bolshevik Revolution was only the symbol of all the revolutions that grew out of that discontent. And that is perhaps the crucial insight into the tragedy of American diplomacy.

---

* These considerations should be kept in mind, or reviewed, when the reader reaches Chapters Six and Seven. One might add that it was the collapse of the illusions encouraged by the awareness of this power that led ultimately to the emotional intensity of American feeling against Russia.

Those other specific and general revolutions would have continued and come to their climaxes even if the Bolsheviks had never seized power in Russia. They were revolutions that had been fed and sustained by the policies of the West itself for more than a century. American policy was fundamentally no more than a sophisticated version of those same policies.

The underlying nature of the tragedy is defined by the confrontation between those two elements, not just or primarily by the conflict between the United States and the Soviet Union. The tragedy was of course dramatized, and unquestionably made more intense, by the way that American leaders reduced all such revolutions to the Bolshevik Revolution. Indeed, their behavior could be offered as a textbook example of the reductionist fallacy. Or, to use a metaphor from daily life, they blinded themselves at the outset of their search for an answer to the "general feeling of revolt" that disturbed them so much.

It is vital to realize, therefore, that the radical and revolutionary impact was not limited—even between 1917 and 1921 —to events in Russia. On the European scene, communists came to power in Hungary and showed strength in Germany;* and the heretical liberals attacked the status quo in England and other countries. The Arab Revolution in the Middle East, while it was predominantly anticolonial and nationalistic and was led by liberals and conservatives, nevertheless represented the international elements of the broad radical movement. A similar pattern emerged in the Far East. Chinese revolutionaries, some of whom did look to Russia for advice and leadership, asserted their rapport with the radical challenge—on domestic as well as international issues. And Japanese conservatives (and liberals), who asserted their nationalistic and ethnic equality with the West, pre-empted certain radical policies as weapons for their own purposes. All of these developments, considered individually and en masse, posed serious problems for American leadership at the end of World War I.

---

* The reader should remember that the army of the Soviet Union had nothing to do with this communist revolution in Hungary at the end of World War I. As will be seen, it was the West, under the leadership of President Wilson and Herbert Hoover, which intervened to overturn the earlier communist revolution.

Confronted directly by the opposition overseas, Wilson faced still other difficulties. His original hope to establish a concert of power with Great Britain and France was weakened by their initial opposition to certain of his proposals. The revolutionary ferment in Europe, Asia, and the Middle East only intensified the determination of the imperial powers to retain and strengthen their existing empires. A similar reaction occurred in America, and Wilson's coalition for the crusade to make the world safe for democracy disintegrated into a great internal struggle over what policy would enable America to assert its power most effectively in dealing with Japanese and European competitors and the wave of revolutions engulfing the world.

Wilson's personal dilemma symbolized the broader difficulties faced by classical liberalism. According to the basic principles of natural law, he should have accepted the revolutions as competing units which would contribute their share to a broader and deeper harmony of interests. But his expansionist philosophy of history, his Calvinism, and his nationalism—which also were integral parts of his liberalism—prompted him to oppose the revolutions as barricades on America's road to domestic well-being and world leadership. The tragedy was defined by his attempt to resolve the dilemma by preserving and extending democracy through a policy of open-door expansion.

His approach satisfied neither his own followers nor the foreigners who looked to America (and to Wilson in particular) for a creative alternative to the revolutionaries. Instead, it left the battleground to the conservatives and the radicals. By attempting to achieve security through the traditional policy of the open door, America's conservatives emphasized the weakest aspects of Wilson's own program. And the liberals, having failed to offer a positive and effective alternative of their own, had in the end no place to go but into a bipartisan alignment with the conservatives.

CHAPTER FOUR

I. A GREAT DEBATE OVER THE TACTICS OF EMPIRE

It is wrong, perhaps, to say that Hughes stole Wilson's thunder,
for Wilson himself had stolen Hay's.

A. WHITNEY GRISWOLD, 1938

I want for my part to go in and accept what is offered us, the
leadership of the world. A leadership of what sort, my fellow
citizens? . . . a liberating power . . .

Article X is the heart of the enterprise. . . . [It] says that every
member of the League, and that means every great fighting
power in the world, . . . solemnly engages to respect and pre-
serve as against external aggression the territorial integrity
and existing political independence of the other members of
the League. If you do that, you have absolutely stopped am-
bitious and aggressive war.

WOODROW WILSON, 1919

If perpetual, [Article X] would be an attempt to preserve for
all time unchanged the distribution of power and territory
made in accordance with the views and exigencies of the Allies
in this present juncture of affairs. It would necessarily be futile.
. . . It would not only be futile; it would be mischievous.

THE LEGEND OF ISOLATIONISM

Change and growth are the law of life, and no generation can impose its will in regard to the growth of nations and the distribution of power, upon succeeding generations.

ELIHU ROOT, 1919

We are a great moral asset of Christian civilization. . . . How did we get there? By our own efforts. Nobody led us, nobody guided us, nobody controlled us. . . .

I would keep America as she has been—not isolated, not prevent her from joining other nations for these great purposes— but I wish her to be master of her own fate. . . .

HENRY CABOT LODGE, 1919

You must either give them independence, recognize their rights as nations to live their own lives and to set up their own form of government, or you must deny them these things by force. . . . You must respect not territorial boundaries, not territorial integrity, but you must respect and preserve the sentiments and passions for justice and for freedom which God in his infinite wisdom has planted so deep in the human heart that no form of tyranny however brutal, no persecution however prolonged can wholly uproot and kill. Respect nationality, respect justice, respect freedom, and you may have some hope of peace. . . .

*But your treaty does not mean peace—far, very far from it.
If we are to judge the future by the past it means war.*

WILLIAM E. BORAH, 1919

Though they did not do so at the time, Americans have come
to think of the 1920's as the nation's Lost Weekend in international affairs, as a period when the United States disregarded its world responsibilities by getting inebriated on the
homemade gin of isolationism. Natural though it may be to
take that view, looking back at the era through the smoke
and debris of World War II with a vision distorted by a decade
of cold war, such an outlook nevertheless produces serious
misconceptions about American diplomacy. It not only de-
forms the history of the decade from 1919 to 1930, but it
also twists the story of American entry into World War II
and warps the record of the cold war.

Reconsidered, the postwar era appears as a crucial period
during which American leaders debated, formulated, and put
into operation their basic policy in response to the broad
revolutionary movements which erupted between 1910 and
1919. Approached in that fashion, the great debate over the
League of Nations appears less as a fight over accepting or
rejecting one document and one organization, or as a personal
struggle between Senator Henry Cabot Lodge and President
Wilson, and more as a broad argument over how America
should sustain and extend its power and authority in a world
of revolutions.

Though often defined and interpreted as an argument over
strategy, or the broad plan for achieving basic objectives, the
fight over the League of Nations was in reality a conflict over
tactics, or the means of implementing the strategic program.
A vast majority of American leaders, both private and official
(and of both parties), accepted the Open Door Policy as the
strategy of the United States in foreign affairs. That was not
at issue.

Wilson and his supporters advocated joining the League of
Nations on the grounds that its system of collective security

to preserve the fundamental features of the status quo offered the best method of keeping the world safe for the Open Door Policy. Given that framework, American power consolidated behind the integrated program of reformist and economic expansion would produce the perpetual welfare of the United States and the world. The bulk of Wilson's opponents accepted every essential point in that argument except the unequivocal involvement in a system of collective security which was in their view charged and committed by Article X of the League Covenant to a course of action that was—in Root's words—both futile and mischievous. They argued, in short, that Wilson's tactics would subvert the strategy.

Only a small, even tiny, minority maintained that the strategy itself was either inherently wrong, or that it had been rendered obsolete by the upsurge of revolutions throughout the world. Such men automatically opposed the tactics proposed by Wilson and his other critics. They disagreed among themselves over the kind of strategy that should be adopted to insure the security and welfare of the United States. Some wanted to align America more openly and actively with the revolutionary ferment in the world. Others were more conservative, but thought that the best strategy was to concentrate on affairs at home and let the example of a successful America win international influence and authority for the nation.* Whatever those differences, the minority as a group nevertheless insisted that the nation had to re-evaluate its role in the world and develop policies relevant to the new circumstances. And they had enough votes in the Senate to insure Wilson's defeat on the League of Nations.

Thus the end result of the great debate was neither a bold new strategy nor approval for Wilson's tactical proposal for implementing the existing one. The consensus that emerged was based on an agreement to push American overseas political and economic expansion, and on a further decision to

---

* These conservatives—a minority within a minority—are the only men to whom the term *isolationist* can be applied with any relevance or accuracy. The term is thus extremely misleading when generalized even to all those who voted against the League Treaty, let alone the policy-makers of the interwar years. Its use has thus crippled American thought about foreign policy for 40 years.

avoid the policy of collective security on the grounds that it might easily weaken the United States, both defensively and offensively, by tying it to various features of the status quo that were sure to disappear—and others that ought to be altered by America itself. The key to understanding American diplomacy of the 1920's is the realization that it was based on this coming of age of the Open Door Policy. It represented, indeed, a synthesis of the Open Door Notes, the Monroe Doctrine, and Washington's Farewell Address. By preserving and using its independence of action, America would employ its great economic power and ideological attractiveness through the means of the Open Door Policy to apply the principles of the Monroe Doctrine to the entire world. Woodrow Wilson and Herbert Hoover both agreed that this was the "road away from revolution."

Often presented as classic antagonists, Wilson and Hoover actually complemented each other in their common effort to preserve the world of classical liberalism.* Wilson's greater human appeal made him a more successful politician and gave him more insight into certain aspects of the revolutionary ferment throughout the world. But Hoover thought more incisively about the basic problems of saving liberalism in an age of corporations and labor unions (even if he did not solve those issues), and also understood the dangers of an a priori commitment to the principle and practice of collective security.

Hoover unquestionably grasped the central weakness of Article X. It was seldom necessary for dealing with small conflicts; and, where the case was marginal, the collective security approach initiated a momentum that could easily turn it into a major crisis. When applied to one of two major powers involved in a conflict over vital national interests it would not resolve fundamental issues. Either the nation judged the aggressor would retreat only to emerge more antagonistic and dangerous or it would fight. To this extent, at least, and despite his personal aloofness, Hoover understood

---

* Readers who find this so unusual an interpretation as to be dismissed at the outset are referred to Hoover's recent volume, *The Ordeal of Woodrow Wilson* (now in McGraw Hill paperback edition). It is a moving tribute to Wilson, and also a very illuminating review of American foreign policy at the end of World War I.

the principle of self-determination better than Wilson.

For such reasons, coupled with his far better understanding of the American economy, and its interrelationships with the world, Hoover placed less emphasis than Wilson on the political aspects of foreign policy. He felt that the right kind of politics would evolve from sound economics, and that it was more important to avoid serious political mistakes than to strive for brilliant political victories.* Hoover therefore concentrated, both while he was Secretary of Commerce (1921–1929) and President (1929–1933), on the more prosaic—but no less vital—job of building the kind of a *system* of overseas economic expansion envisaged by the strategy of the Open Door Policy. He wanted working agreements with the advanced industrial nations: they were to accommodate their differences peacefully so that they could stand together in the face of the revolutionary challenges of the age. On the other hand, and while he most certainly wanted to limit and control that ferment throughout the world, Hoover viewed the poor and underdeveloped societies as "the crippled countries" that should be helped by the United States.

During the crisis defined by communist triumphs in Russia and Hungary, and the revolutionary activity elsewhere in the world, Wilson and Hoover worked together very effectively. Both men grasped the fundamentals of America's dilemma. They realized, in different but overlapping ways, the broad challenge of the revolutions against the liberal world. They saw that the assault had grown out of the failure of liberalism to realize its theory and ideals, and hence understood the need to make it work in the United States as well as elsewhere. They agreed, moreover, that peace was a necessary prerequisite for this to be accomplished. At that point, however, the problem became very difficult. Policies had to be formulated to deal with each aspect of the crisis, yet all such policies had to be co-ordinated in one general outlook and program. Otherwise, American diplomacy would ultimately fail and leave the United States in a negative and weakened position.

Naturally enough, the issue of what to do about the communist victories in Russia and Hungary was of immediate

---

* Even if this propensity be called conservative, the conservatism involved is temperamental and not ideological.

importance. Hoover has provided a classic statement of this
fact: "Communist Russia was a specter which wandered into
the Peace Conference almost daily." The crisis completely disrupted Wilson's original peace program, making it necessary
to delay the work of reforming the world under American
leadership as part of sustaining America's own democracy
and prosperity. First priority had to be given, at least temporarily, to the problem of checking the revolutions. That specific
phase of the crisis was generalized, though not in communist form, by similar upheavals in the Middle East and Asia,
where anticolonialism and nationalism challenged the existing
order. But the noncommunist revolutions served to intensify
rather than mitigate the differences among the victorious
Allies. England and France, for example, opposed some of
Wilson's suggestions concerning Germany and colonial territories. And Japan, though formally allied with the Western
powers in Europe, was busy in Asia trying to exploit the
anticolonial and nationalist revolutions for its own imperialist
purposes. Yet all three powers shared Wilson's opposition to
the communist revolutions, and their help was necessary if the
liberal coalition was to be effective.

Though it sometimes appeared vague, even irresolute and
contradictory, Wilson did develop a general program to cope
with the complex crisis. His objective was to structure the
peace settlement so that America could provide the intellectual, moral, economic, and military power and leadership to
reinvigorate and sustain the liberal way of life throughout the
world. So strengthened, liberalism would effectively undercut,
and ultimately defeat, its revolutionary and radical antagonists.

True to the logic of his frontier-expansionist outlook, Wilson concluded that the victory abroad would insure domestic
American welfare. That would make it possible to embark
upon his desired "slow process of reform," which was to be
based upon "some sort of partnership" between capital and
labor, with the government playing the multiple roles of
agent for each broad group within society and mediator between all of them. American diplomacy was thus the instrument of domestic well-being, and to this end Wilson proposed
and acted upon two key ideas. He insisted upon Article X of
the League of Nations Covenant, which secured the "terri-

torial integrity and existing political independence" of member states (Russia was excluded), and he sought to halt further revolutionary gains.

Wilson actively opposed the communist revolutions in Russia and Hungary. To do so he resorted to force, the manipulation of food supplies, and economic and military aid to counter-revolutionary groups. In Hungary, for example, Wilson collaborated closely with Hoover in employing the American Food Relief Mission to unseat the radical government of Bela Kun by denying needed supplies to that country as long as the communists stayed in power. This American intervention to overthrow a locally established communist government in Hungary offers more than just an illuminating parallel with the Russian intervention in Hungary in 1956. Of course, the Russians were directly ruthless. Yet it is self-righteous to argue that the American use of food to accomplish the same kind of objective was somehow more moral or civilized. Furthermore, the American action in 1919 may well have influenced the vigorous and very serious debate among Russian leaders before their decision to intervene with the Red Army in 1956.

In Russia, moreover, the United States used guns as well as the control of food and other economic supplies in its support of anti-Bolshevik forces A great many efforts have been made, particularly during the years of the cold war, to prove that the United States did not intervene in Russia to overthrow the Bolshevik Revolution. Only a few of them have been based on extensive research and argued with any degree of sophistication. And even those have not been convincing because the evidence does not bear out the contention.*

The key to understanding and interpreting American intervention in Russia was supplied by Wilson himself. He did so while arguing against Winston Churchill, who advocated ruthless armed assault on the Bolsheviks, in a meeting of the

---

* The best efforts to establish this view are by B. M. Unterberger, *America's Siberian Expedition, 1918–1920* (Durham: Duke University Press, 1956); and G. F. Kennan, *Soviet-American Relations, 1917–1920* (Princeton: Princeton University Press, 2 vols., 1956, 1958). For a contrary view see: R. D. Warth, *The Allies and the Russian Revolution* (Durham: Duke University Press, 1954); and this writer's *American-Russian Relations, 1781–1947*.

Big Five at the Paris Peace Conference on February 14, 1919.
In reply to Churchill's powerful rhetoric, the President put it
all in two sentences: *"President Wilson . . .* himself felt guilty
in that the United States had in Russia insufficient forces, but
it was not possible to increase them. It was certainly a cruel
dilemma."

Since it was Wilson himself who said in January 1918,
that policy toward Russia was "the acid test" of Allied and
American intentions, it does not seem unreasonable to suggest that the President knew he was failing his own examination question. Wilson and his advisors first attempted from
November 1917 through the spring of 1918 to resolve the
"cruel dilemma" by aiding anti-Bolshevik forces short of
committing American troops. They realized that open armed
intervention would very probably strengthen the Bolsheviks
by enabling them to play upon the normal patriotic feelings
of all Russians. As should be obvious, that policy did *not* mean
that the Wilson Administration approved of the Bolsheviks,
and it did *not* mean that the United States refrained from
intervention.

Two developments changed the situation, and that early
strategy, by the early summer of 1918. First, the Bolsheviks
were still in power, and Wilson was clearly interested in seeing
them overthrown. He had by that time ignored several overtures from Moscow. Second, Japan was intervening in Siberia,
and that was viewed by Wilson as a danger to the Open Door
Policy throughout Asia, *including Siberia*. Wilson considered
it "essential" to maintain the open door strategy by checking
the Japanese maneuver. The resulting policy was a bit complex, perhaps, but by no means so complicated or shrouded
in mystery as to be impervious to research and analysis. The
United States intervened against the Bolsheviks with troops
and aid to anti-Bolshevik Russians, and it did so in a fashion
designed to thwart Japan's ambitions in Siberia, Manchuria,
and Northern China. Those who try to defend American
action by denying the anti-Bolshevik side of it might be more
effective in their general purpose, as well as more accurate,
if they would defend the policy as a rather sophisticated attempt to accomplish an extremely difficult task.

Several factors combined to limit the extent and the effectiveness of American intervention. At first, the war against Germany claimed priority. Then, after the armistice, opponents of intervention in Russia (such as Senators William E. Borah and Hiram S. Johnson) blocked more vigorous action by threatening a Congressional investigation. Wilson told his subordinates to overcome that opposition by "the utmost frankness" in describing the situation and the objectives to Senate leaders. His assistants replied that the critics were holding the high ground: "Senator Johnson is demanding that troops be withdrawn from Archangel, and there is considerable support of his position on the ground that our men are being killed and no one knows why they are still there." In addition, American troops in Russia made it clear that they were against the policy. Some of them refused to fight. And finally, the anti-Bolshevik forces offered poor and uninspiring leadership in Russia. The cruel dilemma was finally resolved by the Bolsheviks who won the Russian civil war.*

While Wilson handicapped himself in his efforts to block Japan by refusing to work directly and vigorously either with China or the Russians, he did stabilize the situation after Japan's first penetration into Manchuria and Siberia. His persistent opposition, manifested by the American forces and his efforts to reorganize and use the banking consortium to keep the Japanese from taking over the Chinese Eastern Railway, did prevent Tokyo from consolidating its initial gains.

Finally, Wilson opposed both traditional colonialism and revolutionary nationalism, seeking a compromise in the mandate system, under which the Open Door Policy would be used to reform the political and economic life of the areas according to American interests. And in all of this program, he vigorously asserted (though he was not able to maintain) the predominance of American power and leadership. Granted

---

* Wilson was more successful in Poland. As in Hungary, Hoover and the President collaborated to use American control of food supplies to bring conservatives to power. The conservatives were then given arms and money during their efforts to extend Poland's boundaries eastward into Russia, and into the Baltic States.

its essentially conservative character, for it was a program designed to preserve the existing order in the face of broad revolutionary challenges, Wilson's program was about as comprehensive an approach as anyone could have devised.

Along with Herbert Hoover, who helped Wilson formulate and put it into operation, such men as Elihu Root, Charles Evans Hughes, and Henry L. Stimson initially supported the program and its policies. Had they continued to do so, the League of Nations Treaty would have passed the Senate, for the influence of these men would have been sufficient to override the opposition. Hence it is vital to understand the reasons that led these key leaders to leave Wilson and join other opponents of the treaty.

Political and personal motives no doubt influenced all of Wilson's opponents, but the basic sources of their opposition can be found in their conception of America and its role in the world. For the group led by Hoover, Hughes, and Stimson, one factor seems crucial. They had more insight into the structure and functioning of industrial society and thus grasped the weaknesses of classical liberalism more thoroughly than Wilson. As men who knew the market as well as the library, they were aware that the liberal system in practice did not function according to its theory. That knowledge led them to propose a more concrete program for the future.

With Wilson, they accepted the principles of natural law, but they knew from experience that the individual was no longer free to act in accordance with this theory. The individual had become part of a larger group. Realizing that, they had more specific ideas about how to define and structure what Wilson vaguely referred to as "some sort of partnership" between capital and labor.

Hoover provided the most advanced intellectual leadership within this group. He analyzed America's mature industrial system as an intrinsically corporate society composed of, and organized on the basis of, three primary units—capital (including agriculture), labor, and the government. The objective was to establish a pattern in which, despite their differences and short-run conflicts, those groups would work together to create the conditions under which the natural harmony of interests would manifest itself. Hoover even predicted four ways in which the effort to create such a corporate society might fail: large business interests could take over and produce fascism; labor could win out and turn to socialism; the government bureaucracy could itself become dominant and create a kind of ad hoc and aimless tyranny; or the government would become in practice the marketplace in which the other units scrambled for power and profit, an alternative that Hoover quite accurately called capitalistic syndicalism.*

Transferred to the international scene, Hoover's analysis pointed to the necessity of defining and establishing a similar community with Germany, Japan, and Italy, as well as with England and France. Secretary of State Hughes explicitly called for such a "community of ideals, interests, and purposes." That kind of community would not only strengthen each country individually, but would, being led by the United States, be capable of controlling the revolutionary challenge to the existing order. While Hoover was the central figure in this group opposing Wilson over Article X, the others understood the approach, accepted its central features, and worked in their own ways to put it into operation.

These men understood that the American economy was an interrelated and interdependent *system,* rather than a random conglomeration of individual operations mysteriously unified by the abstract functioning of the marketplace. This knowledge, which most of them had gained as practicing entrepreneurs or as corporation lawyers before they entered politics, was the source of their differences with Wilson and of their own foreign policy. Since they thought about economic and political affairs as an interlocking system, they had far more

---

* Perhaps the most striking evidence of Hoover's long thought about these problems comes from his early books on mining engineering. See, for example, the discussion of the injustices of corporations and other capitalists, and of the rights and legitimate expectations of labor, in these items: *Principles of Mining Valuation, Organization, and Administration* (1909); "The Training of the Mining Engineer," *Science* (November, 1904); "Economics of a Boom," *The Mining Magazine* (May, 1912). Also consult, where available (it is unfortunately something of a rare item), his *American Individualism* (New York: Doubleday, Page, and Co., 1923). This approach to Hoover is developed in more detail in this writer's *Contours of American History.* One of the nicest introductory essays to Hoover was prepared by a graduate student at the University of Wisconsin, Robert E. Treacy, as a seminar paper entitled "Herbert Hoover to 1920."

in common with mercantilists than with the advocates and philosophers of laissez faire. They were not mercantilists: mercantilism was a *Weltanschauung* of the seventeenth and eighteenth centuries. The term is used for the purpose of offering an analogy that may help clarify their efforts to transform the existing private enterprise syndicalism into a truly corporate capitalism.

Two similarities to mercantilism are important for understanding the outlook and activities of such men as Hoover and Hughes. One concerns the active role of government in promoting the interal organization and stability of the economic system. Hoover and others such as Bernard Baruch and Owen D. Young gave considerable attention to the problem of rationalizing the domestic economy through such institutions as trade associations and by establishing the practice and habit of close co-operation between government and business. Of itself, this was nothing new. Theodore Roosevelt and Herbert Croly of the Progressive movement favored it, and Woodrow Wilson practiced the same kind of collaboration during World War I. But Hoover and Baruch did a great deal to develop, extend, and popularize the idea through the 1920's.

The second aspect of their political economy that bore similarities to mercantilism affected foreign policy even more directly. For in thinking of economic activity in terms of the system, while at the same time keeping their basic capitalistic concept of economic life, such men as Hoover, Hughes, and Stimson emphasized that the overseas economic expansion of the system was *necessary* for continued prosperity. Corporation and banking leaders agreed. The result was a vitally important integration of thought: political and economic leaders came to share the same idea about the relationship between domestic and foreign policy. Overseas economic expansion became an integral part of the domestic expansion of the system itself, rather than the interest or concern merely of certain segments of the system. This did not conflict with the average citizen's understanding of America's greatness and prosperity, for the frontier thesis explained the nation's democracy and well-being in terms of just such expansion.

For these reasons, which were reinforced by the fact that most of them had less of the crusading temperament than

Wilson, men such as Hoover and Hughes stressed the importance of extending America's economic empire. So, too, did most businessmen. Many economic leaders, such as Thomas Lamont of the House of Morgan, originally favored Wilson's program for peace, thinking it a good plan to stabilize world conditions and prepare the way for American expansion. But the majority of corporation leaders and bankers lost their early enthusiasm for Wilson's approach, some because they came to agree with Hoover's criticism of the League Covenant and others because they were anxious to get to work "in the frontier countries" and hence wanted to stop wasting time in an apparently endless, and profitless, argument.

Frank Vanderlip caught the spirit of that growing impatience in his remark (and concern) about what he called "the war after the war." He had organized the American International Corporation in 1914 for the specific purpose of opening up the poor, underdeveloped countries. In similar rhetoric, the *Wall Street Journal* emphasized its concern with the "stupendous trade battle" then developing. Another man with the same ideas—and fears—was Silas H. Strawn of Montgomery, Ward & Co. He flatly asserted that the United States "must expand;" a failure to do so "would result in such intense competition as to precipitate an economic panic in this country the like of which has never been seen." And John Hays Hammond warned the N.A.M. of the same danger. "It is obvious . . . that we must either curtail the capacity of our factories . . . or we must depend upon the exploitation of foreign countries for the relief of our congested home markets." All such economic spokesmen, as well as the majority of the political figures who opposed Wilson, stressed such expansion of the American economic system, as well as the enlargement of their own particular operations. But they were less immediately concerned with the political and ideological aspects of that imperial growth. They generally assumed that those features of the American system would develop more or less automatically as a consequence of economic progress; or, if not, that such affairs were the concern and responsibility of the politicians.

Two other groups also opposed Wilson over the issue of Article X. Each did so, however, for different reasons. The vigorous empire men, led by Senator Henry Cabot Lodge and

Theodore Roosevelt, defined America's role as the new—and better—British Empire. At home, they called for an aristocratic elite to control labor and capital within the framework of an industrialized concept of *noblesse oblige*. Overseas, they proposed to use America's power to implement the Open Door Policy and build a modern industrial empire. "Let us make it our policy," advised Lodge, "that what we shall do and when we shall do it shall be determined by us." Some businessmen shared his view. Edward A. Filene, who was at one time national director of the Chamber of Commerce, thought that the United States was "in the exact position of a man of peace in a frontier community. It is our duty to advocate and to stand ready to join an International Vigilance Committee." He assured America that it could, "*in no way, write a better insurance policy for its future material prosperity.*" In their own way, such politicians and businessmen agreed with Bismarck's classic phrase: "If there is to be a revolution, we would rather make it than suffer it." This outlook led them to support the Hoover group once Wilson was defeated on the League issue.

At the other extreme was an even smaller group of men who were almost doctrinaire laissez-faire liberals in domestic affairs and antiempire men in foreign policy. Led by Senator William E. Borah, they made many perceptive criticisms of existing policy, but their specific policy suggestions did not appeal to many Americans. Their domestic proposals, based as they were on an almost pure theory of competition, had but little relevance to a mature and complex industrial society. Hence they attracted little support from urban or rural businessmen and almost none from organized labor. Each of those groups wanted to regulate or control competition in its particular behalf. The men around Borah suffered from similar weaknesses in foreign affairs, for in criticizing America's imperial expansion they opposed the general feeling that such expansion was economically necessary as well as ideologically and morally just.

In an ironic way, moreover, the Borah group undercut its own position by aligning itself with the Lodge and Hoover groups to defeat Wilson's League treaty. For in this fashion they inadvertently strengthened the impression that America was not (and need not become) involved politically by such economic expansion. Hence it was difficult for Borah and similar critics to attract much organized and effective support for their own program. They were often misunderstood, furthermore, as a result of their opposition to Wilson. These weaknesses and misimpressions tend to obscure the fact that their criticism was insightful and fundamental, that they were by no means as naive about international politics as their critics charge, and that they had a strangely "modern" attitude toward aid to underdeveloped nations.

The argument advanced by Borah and other antiempire spokesmen was based on the proposition that America neither could nor should undertake to make or keep the world safe for democracy. They maintained that the idea was unrealistic because it neglected the different cultural traditions of most of the rest of the world and because of the power that some or all of those nations could bring to bear against the United States. And even if it were possible to build such an empire, they concluded, the effort violated the spirit of democracy itself. Borah provided a classic summary of these two arguments in one of his speeches attacking the proposal to clamp a lid on the revolutionary ferment in China after 1917. "Four hundred million people imbued with the spirt of independence and of national integrity are in the end invincible. There is no power which can master them or hold them in subjection. Warships and Gatling guns and dead students may mislead some but the forces which determine the action of empires and great nations lie deeper."

Borah and others also relied on this assumption in making their assessment of events in Europe, Latin America, and Asia, and in proposing modifications of American policy. Johnson, for example, concluded that the story of American loans to Latin American countries was "a sordid tale, at once grotesque and tragic." Concluding that his investigation of the facts had "stripped some of the hypocrisy" away from the usual accounts of the policy, he pointed out that American money was used to "maintain dictators in power," and that it was "party to the suppression of every natural right of citizens of South American Republics." Johnson quickly added that citizens at home also suffered. Some were subject to "shameful, and even infamous, exploitation" by the bankers who sold the securities. And everyone lost because of the bitter reaction against the United States.

Representative Fiorello La Guardia and Senators La Follette and Borah joined Johnson's attack. Borah condemned the "drumhead diplomacy" of Wilson and Bryan in Central America, and denied that the Monroe Doctrine gave the United States any right to intervene throughout the hemisphere in that manner. Just as he opposed the narrow policy of many business interests in China, Borah also used his influence to block the oil companies and other groups that wanted vigorous intervention against the government of the Mexican Revolution. He played a significant role in the appointment of Dwight Morrow as Ambassador to Mexico, and supported Morrow's ultimately successful efforts to halt the deterioration of relations and to negotiate an interim settlement of the oil and other property issues.

As that action suggests, Borah and the other anti-imperialists were more than critics. They offered many positive suggestions. Borah was particularly active, for example, in urging the government to take the lead in the economic reconstruction of Europe, and in reaching some agreement on limiting armaments in the Pacific. La Guardia, Johnson, and La Follette all supported the recognition of Russia for economic reasons as well as on the grounds that such action was in keeping with the principle of self-determination. Borah agreed with those arguments concerning the recognition of Russia, and added others that were even more perceptive. He concluded that a rapprochement with the Soviet Union was "the key to a restored Europe, to a peaceful Europe." In addition, he thought that the United States could play a crucial role in creating the circumstances in which there could "emerge a freer, a more relaxed, a more democratic Russia." Finally, and perhaps most striking of all, Borah offered a keen analysis of the importance of Russia to America's general security. His estimate of the strategic and power factors was considerably more astute than the supposed realism of most of the critics who dismissed him as an isolationist.

Borah warned in 1923 that American policy—"a narrow-visioned, intolerant policy"—was helping to push Russia and Germany together. That was "not at all desirable," and he urged the government to recognize the Soviets as a move to weaken that relationship. A bit later, after Japan had again indicated its determination to expand on the mainland of Asia, Borah offered a very direct warning: unless the United States moved to prevent it, Russia would be forced to come to terms with Japan. "I feel more strongly than ever," Borah wrote Secretary of State Stimson in 1932, "that our relationship with Russia ought to undergo a change. I am satisfied that by proper steps taken upon the part of our government any close relationship between Russia and Japan could be avoided."* Dramatic as they are, Borah's observations on the interaction between the United States, Russia, Germany, and Japan were only conclusions drawn from his basic insight into the broader issue. His remark of 1925 on the consequences of American policy toward Russia was indeed prophetic: "So long as you have a hundred and fifty million people outlawed in a sense, it necessarily follows that you cannot have peace."

Toward underdeveloped and poor countries, Borah and others like him manifested a complex and somewhat contradictory attitude. Men like La Follette and Borah were of course concerned and sympathetic with the problems of poverty and independence. But they did not in the last analysis believe that a nation or a people could be given freedom and prosperity by outsiders. They were very skeptical of the argument that democracy could be exported along with surplus commodities and manufactured goods or created by foreign loans. That conclusion was an integral part of their knowledge of, and judgment on, European colonialism and America's own imperial expansion. They were all opposed, as La Follette put it, "to the dollar diplomacy which has reduced our State Department from its high place as a kindly intermediary of defenseless nations, into a trading outpost for Wall Street interests, aiming to exploit those who should be our friends."

As a result, Borah and the others preferred to deal with other nations on a strict, even narrow, economic basis, leaving

---

* Borah's analysis was borne out, not only by Russia's open bid for a nonaggression treaty with China and the United States, but also by its decision, after that overture was declined, to sign with the Japanese. American policy of the years 1904–1912 was thus repeated with the identical results.

them alone and free to use their wealth as they saw fit. Clearly enough, they underestimated the importance per se of a minimum, and improving, level of economic welfare, and of the relationship between that foundation and the development of political and cultural maturity. And they discounted—no doubt because they generalized American experience to other nations—the great difficulties that underdeveloped countries faced in starting and sustaining such improvement on their own. Yet they were willing to help nations weakened by war or catastrophe or nations just getting started in their own development. Perhaps this explains their preference, when pushed to the wall (as in the case of Liberia in the 1920's), for outright grants of assistance over government loans or private investment.

Of all Americans, the group around Borah most clearly understood the principle and practice of self-determination in foreign affairs. For that reason, as well as other aspects of Borah's criticism, President Wilson singled out Borah as his most important critic—as the man who might turn out to be right. In his own time, however, Borah enjoyed little praise and almost no support. He served as spokesman for various small groups which sought to change policy toward Russia, China, and Latin America, but at most—with the possible exception of Russia—these groups exercised a minor influence on American foreign policy. Borah himself became stereotyped as a naive, irresponsible, and wrong-headed gadfly. But a generation later, in the midst of a cold war, those who like their history with a twist of irony might find it illuminating to compare his speeches and letters between 1917 and 1935 with the most recent policy proposals advanced by later "realists" who had ignored or deplored his earlier actions.*

Opposed by the powerful coalition of Hoover, Root, Lodge, and Borah, and unwilling to compromise over Article X, Presi-

---

* The orthodox view of Borah can be reviewed in R. Ferrell, *Peace in Their Time* (New Haven: Yale University Press, 1952). The most recent biography is M. C. McKenna, *Borah* (Ann Arbor: University of Michigan Press, 1961). A stimulating article is O. S. Pinckney, "William E. Borah: Critic of American Foreign Policy," *Studies on The Left* (1960). The best volume of Borah's own remarks is *American Problems. A Selection of Speeches and Prophecies by William E. Borah* (New York: Duffield & Co., 1924); but it is unfortunately rather hard to find.

dent Wilson lost his battle for the League of Nations Covenant. But most of his opponents shared Wilson's conception of America as the leader of the world, and they turned quickly from the tactical skirmish with him to the work of putting the strategy into operation through the policy of the open door.

II. THE INTERNATIONALIZATION OF BUSINESS

We are seeking to establish a Pax Americana *maintained not by arms but by mutual respect and good will and the tranquilizing processes of reason. . . .*

When we have a clear sense of our own interests, we are just as inflexible as others.

CHARLES EVANS HUGHES, 1924

We must finance our exports by loaning foreigners the wherewith-all to pay for them. . . . Without such loans we would have the spectacle of our neighbors famishing for goods which were rotting in our warehouses as unusable surplus.

JOHN FOSTER DULLES, 1928

We must find a profitable market for our surpluses.

HERBERT HOOVER, 1928

Our investments and trade relations are such that it is almost impossible to conceive of any conflict anywhere on earth which would not affect us injuriously.

CALVIN COOLIDGE, 1928

The present is a time of great unrest and disquiet throughout the world, and it is to the interest of all governments to try to maintain order and stability.

HENRY L. STIMSON, 1932

Confronted by revolutionary opposition throughout much of the world, plagued by conflicts with and among their recent Allies, and disturbed by the continued antagonism between the victors and the defeated, American policy-makers concluded that peace was the *sine qua non* of any effort to implement the strategy of the Open Door Policy. Without stability and peace, there could be no economic expansion, which all of them considered the dynamic element in producing America's well-being. In the view of these men, at any rate, most of the troubles they faced in the 1920's had either been caused by World War I or had been intensified by that disruption of law and order. It later became fashionable among historians and other commentators to criticize leaders like Hoover and Hughes (as well as Borah) on the grounds that they were naive, or that they trusted Germany and Japan too much on too little evidence. Much of that criticism resulted from interpreting the 1920's in a very narrow, relativistic manner. Men who had to fight Germany and Japan (and who thought they might well have to fight Russia) concluded that anyone must have been blind or misguided not to see what would happen if those countries were not blocked by the threat—or the use—of force. That judgment was further strengthened by the effect of World War II on attitudes toward force: having come to use force without limit in international affairs, and in many respects to take that approach for granted, such critics tended to define realism in foreign affairs largely in terms of such an acceptance of force.

Whatever its merits as a general approach to foreign policy, that point of view produces serious misconceptions about American policy-makers of the 1920's. In the first place, those men were not naive about power. All of them had broad experience in economic and legal affairs, which are hardly unrelated to conflicts of power, and had also participated in the American war effort. None of them were pacifists. It is true that they preferred not to employ force. Neither did they take its use casually or cynically. But those characteristics may be signs of their maturity instead of symptoms of their naiveté.

In the broader sense, men like Hoover and Hughes understood the crucial point about the strategy of the Open Door Policy that their critics overlooked: *it was designed to win the objectives without recourse to war*. These critics might with more relevance (and perhaps even profit) examine the objectives instead of continuing to condemn the reluctance to resort

to force. It is one thing to say that the objectives of American
foreign policy in the twentieth century could not have been
achieved without resorting to force. That is a straightforward,
cogent line of argument. But contrary to the apparent belief
of many people who follow that interpretation overtly or implicitly, it does not prove two other things. It does not prove
that any nation which resisted (or resists) those objectives was
(or is) evil, and therefore to blame for subsequent conflict or
violence. And it most certainly does not prove that men were
naive because they were inclined either to abandon or modify
those objectives, or postpone the victory, rather than use force.
Finally, the leaders of the 1920's were hardly naive in seeing
a correlation between war and social unrest culminating in
revolutions, or between war and the restriction of democracy
even in the United States.

American leaders concluded that the best way to reconcile
the necessary expansion of the American economic system with
the necessity of peace was by working out a general concert of
policy between the United States, Great Britain, France, Germany, and Japan based on the acceptance of the Open Door
Policy by all those powers. Such a de facto entente in behalf
of a "community of ideals, interests, and purposes" was designed to operate on three levels. The nations would compromise their differences and stand firm against the Soviet Union
and other revolutionary movements. Thus aligned, they would
direct and set limits on the development of colonial, mandated,
and other nonindustrialized areas. Finally, America's economic
predominance would enable it to guide the operation while at
the same time strengthening and extending its own open-door
empire.

In this fashion, economic expansion became both a means
and an end for American policy-makers. Defined as a goal
because of its vital importance to the continued success of the
domestic economic system, it was also considered a means to
build the empire of peace and prosperity which would secure
the world for continued expansion in the years to come. One
of the most striking features of American diplomacy of the
1920's was the extent to which all policy-makers expressed
this in their public, as well as private, remarks. President
Harding urged Americans to "operate aggressively" and *"go*

on to the peaceful commercial conquest of the world" in order
to avoid social conflict at home. Though by no means gre-
garious, President Coolidge was not backward about expressing his similar view of America's role in the world. Feeling
it was "perfectly obvious" that if any action was "wrong . . .
within the confines of the United States, it is equally wrong
outside our borders," Coolidge asserted that "the one great
duty that stands out requires us to use our enormous powers
to trim the balance of the world." It was in keeping with that
outlook, moreover, that Secretary of State Hughes explained
that "the preponderant thought among us undoubtedly is that
our influence would not be increased by pooling it" in an
organization such as the League of Nations.

Less traditional in their conceptions of empire than Coolidge, Hughes and Hoover explicitly sought to eliminate "the
old imperialistic trappings." In a crisis, they agreed with Coolidge: interventions undertaken "to discourage revolutions"
were not war "any more than a policeman on the street is making war on passers-by." But Hoover and Hughes concentrated
on *preventing* revolutions by the expansion of American economic power. Anxious to locate "the antidote to Bolshevism,"
Hughes understandably viewed "the tendency to have revolutions" as a "regrettable condition" of world affairs. He also
emphasized the importance of controlling key raw materials.
And he reacted promptly to a warning from his departmental
advisors that "the vast increase in the surpluses of manufactured goods . . . must find a market, if at all, outside the United
States." Hence he gave first priority to the problem of establishing and maintaining peace in order to "deal with the
economic verities." Striving for an American-led community
of interests with other industrial nations, it was natural for
him to conclude that "it is self-determination which makes for
wars and places obstacles in the way of all plans for keeping
the peace."

Stimson shared this concern with "peace and order." At
home, he thought that the "richer and more intelligent" citizens should manage affairs. Extending that hypothesis to the
world, he defined America as the elite of the international community. As for the white man's burden, he believed "in assuming it." His basic strategy called for the expansion of

"big, high-class American business" throughout the world and for political intervention of the subtle and behind-the-scenes variety that would not arouse the antagonism of the natives or the American public. According to Stimson, such a foreign policy would ultimately bring inferior peoples into step with America's standards and practices. His vigorous and extensive conception of America's role in the world led Stimson to feel more at home with Franklin Delano Roosevelt than with Herbert Hoover, but during the 1920's he shared with Hughes and Hoover a broad area of agreement.

Though officially no more than Secretary of Commerce from 1921 to 1928, Hoover demanded, and received, an unofficial veto over foreign policy as a condition of entering the cabinet. Armed with this authority, he exercised great influence in foreign affairs. Highly disturbed by the "spread of revolution over one-third of the world," he developed a program designed to halt the "drift toward socialism." Hoover's basic proposition was simple: the American system was "the *only* safe avenue of human progress." Concluding that the world was "passing from a period of extreme individualistic action into a period of associational activities," he sought to organize the new system within a capitalistic framework that protected political democracy. He approached the problem by defining labor and capital as "both producers . . . not classes." As such, they had "great areas of mutual interest," the most important of which was the continued existence of corporate capitalism itself. Hoover was aware that American labor was not radical, and he wanted to keep it from moving in that direction.

In formulating his ideas concerning such a co-operative, or corporate, capitalistic political economy, Hoover understood that the corporation had asserted its fundamental supremacy over the banker. Between 1900 and 1916, the corporation had been forced to rely temporarily on the financier for capital. But soon after the war the corporation began producing enough surplus capital to finance and thereby control most of its own decisions. The bankers were still important, and struggled bitterly for a time to regain their earlier power, but they were on the defensive.

Some of their last-ditch battles had an important bearing on foreign policy. In Latin America and Asia, for example, the financiers fought hard for policies that would help them gain new economic power which they could use at home. Those efforts delayed or blocked some of the more sophisticated programs advocated by Hoover, such as his desire to limit investments to productive enterprises. The bankers often disregarded such rational, equitable, and long-range considerations. They operated far more as narrow, interest-conscious entrepreneurs. Partly as a result of that nature of their dealings, but also because of the general impact of their expansion, the undertakings of the financiers antagonized many foreigners. That only complicated and increased their difficulties. Along with the Great Depression, those considerations ultimately convinced the bankers of two things: they needed to evolve a new, and more equal, kind of relationship with the corporations; and both economic groups had to increase, regularize, and institutionalize the kind of government assistance that Willard Straight had helped initiate before World War I. Such an approach finally brought the bankers, the corporations, and the government into a very intimate working arrangement concerning domestic and foreign affairs during the years of the New Deal and World War II, but it did not change the underlying primacy of the corporations.

Based on his understanding of the central role of the corporation, Hoover developed his conception of associational capitalism around two themes. First, all economic co-operation would center on the corporation; and second, the government, representing the populace at large, would co-operate with the corporation to insure national prosperity and democratic procedure. Hoover first announced his approach at the national economic conference of 1921, which was originally called by President Wilson to implement his own idea of "some sort of partnership" between capital and labor. The problems were dangerous and difficult, Hoover admitted, but "a large degree of solution could be expected through the mobilization of co-operative action of our manufacturers and employers, of our public bodies and local authorities. . . . While our industry and commerce must be based upon incentive to the individual, yet the national interest requires a certain degree of co-operation . . . in order that we may reduce and eliminate industrial waste, lay the foundation for constant decrease in production and distribution costs, and thereby obtain the fundamental increases in wages and standards of living" that would guarantee "increased social stability" and world peace.

Hoover understood that labor had to participate in this cooperation, and upon many occasions voiced public support for unionization and for collective bargaining. It is of course true that Hoover feared and opposed socialism; and in the years after the Bolshevik Revolution and the end-of-the-war labor unrest in the United States he was concerned that the unions might through their practice if not their intent push the emerging corporate capitalism ever further to the left. But most of the usual criticism of Hoover on the labor issue is very misleading because it is based upon such a narrow conception of the general question.

The point is not to imply that Hoover was prolabor in the sense of giving it first priority in his policies or in taking its side in any situation. He was not. Yet several elementary truths are always overlooked in judging Hoover by that rather simple standard. The American labor movement of the 1920's was not very large, for example, and it accepted the basic features of the existing capitalist system. Furthermore, those few of its leaders who concerned themselves with the underlying problems of the relationship with management, and of markets, revealed broad areas of agreement with Hoover.

This was particularly significant in connection with foreign affairs. The labor movement did have two primary reservations about the policy of overseas economic expansion. It worried that jobs lost to foreign workers when an American corporation established a branch factory in another country were not balanced out by new investment at home or by the increased trade. And a few labor leaders fretted about the possibility that such expansion would lead to wars involving the United States. In general, however, the labor movement in the 1920's supported America's overseas economic expansion because it did provide more sales and because labor itself was interested in expanding its own influence over the labor movements in foreign countries. The latter consideration was nothing new, for labor had backed the Spanish-American War and President Wilson's intervention in Mexico for the same reason.

In his approach to the problem of stabilizing agriculture at the level of prosperity created by the war, Hoover again stressed his central idea in terms of co-operation between individual farmers. They should work together to control production and marketing, which would in turn maintain and even enlarge their foreign markets as well as helping them at home. Though it may seem unrelated to foreign affairs, the issue of agricultural surpluses actually offers in many respects the neatest overview of how overseas economic expansion was the central theme of American foreign policy in the 1920's. It is also worth exploring because it provides a clear picture of the more general problems facing Hoover and other American leaders.*

While one would expect the farmers to be concerned about their markets, it may be surprising to realize the extent to which bankers and industrialists shared that concern. Hoover described the problem very clearly. Farmers were in "great difficulties," he explained in 1921, because of their "position of inequality in purchasing power as compared with other industries." That imbalance was "already digging a grave of unemployment" for those nonagricultural sectors of the economy. Part of Hoover's understanding very probably came from his experience in handling war relief, and from his close friendship with Julius Barnes, who was a major grain exporter. But the most important point concerns the way he analyzed the farm problem as an integral aspect of the whole political economy. "We must have," he concluded, "the co-operation of our bankers and our industry." They "must be brought together" with the farmers by the government—and specifically by Hoover's Department of Commerce—to work out a solution for the problem. It is not unusual, of course, that George N. Peek, a manufacturer of agricultural implements, shared that view. He thought it was a question of solving the farm problem by exporting the surpluses or else "we are going to have state socialism." But Baruch and other eastern urban leaders like Otto Kahn had the same idea. So did Charles G. Dawes, a

---

* Mrs. Brady Hughes and James McHale have written illuminating master's theses on the post-World War II aspects of this relationship of agriculture to foreign policy.

midwestern financier who had economic and political connections with eastern bankers.

The trouble arose over how the exporting was to be done. Farmers generally wanted the government to sell their surpluses abroad, paying them the difference between the world price and the American price out of government funds, or out of money collected from the processor and the consumer at home. Senator Peter Norbeck provided a blunt summary of the basic approach at the end of 1922. "Slowly but surely, the idea is getting home that it [the issue] is the surplus, and that the way to stimulate the market is to find some way to dispose of the surplus. Sell it at a good price, if we can; sell it at a poor price if we must; give it away if we cannot do better. . . . In other words, let agricultural products have the same benefit of a similar control that big business gives its products."

Acting through their representatives in the Congress, the farmers pushed their program into law in 1927 and again in 1928, only to have it vetoed both times. The key to understanding those vetoes lies in the negative and positive sides of Hoover's broad outlook as applied to the agricultural crisis. On the negative side, he militantly opposed the plan advocated by the farm bloc. First: it put the government into business. That not only threatened to speed up a movement toward syndicalism, socialism, or bureaucratic tyranny, *but it also increased the risk of serious international conflict by formally tying the government to economic activities. Conflicts in the market place automatically became political conflicts.* Second: the two-price system proposed by the farmers was unfair to the consumer because it forced him, either through increased taxes or higher retail prices, to pay twice for a loaf of bread.

On the positive side, Hoover and others like Baruch, Kahn, and Dawes had their own solution which tied agricultural prosperity to industrial and financial well-being. Their approach was to loan money abroad, particularly to European industrial countries. That would not only provide funds for buying American farm surpluses (directly, and as a result of general prosperity), but it would also facilitate the building of that broader community of interest which Hoover and Hughes were so eager to establish. They also anticipated at least four other benefits: (1) such loans would give the United States influence on foreign countries creating lines of direct and formal responsibility to Washington (and hence limitations on its action); (2) the loans would help solve the broader problem of post-war recovery throughout the world; (3) by giving strong if unofficial approval to the loans, the government would help the bankers obtain the kind of assistance they needed in accumulating capital from the average citizen; and (4) the plan would satisfy the agricultural bloc and thereby strengthen the Republican Party at a time when it was in danger of losing the farm vote.

For that matter, the easiest way to fix all such considerations in one's mind is to remember that Dawes won the Republican nomination for vice president in 1924. He got the call because of his role in negotiating the huge, inclusive international economic arrangement known as the Dawes Plan, and more directly because he was a midwesterner who could plausibly argue that the program would solve the farm problem. The plan itself was much more than a device to sell agricultural surpluses. It was based on American loans to Germany, which would enable that nation to start reconstruction while also paying reparations to England and France. That triple play would abet economic development among the defeated as well as the victors and thus increase the demand for all kinds of American exports.

Clearly, then, Hoover, Hughes, and other American policymakers of the 1920's viewed overseas economic expansion as the crucial element in establishing a secure foundation for peace, and in guaranteeing the successful functioning of the American political economy. Secretary of State Hughes explained the point in a particularly direct manner: "All political questions . . . broadly, have some economic aspect or some economic force lying back of them." It was only natural, therefore, that the "businessman has the most direct interest in the conduct of foreign relations." And to the Secretary, at any rate, it was obvious that one of his main responsibilities concerned "the enlarging of the opportunities for industry and commerce by the recognition and extension of the policy of the 'Open Door'." A good example of the way this strategy guided all foreign policy actions is provided by the tariff legislation of 1922. For the central importance of that law lies not so much in the rates that it established on various goods, but rather in Section 317, which specified that the principle of the open door was to be written into all enabling agreements negotiated with foreign countries.

Hoover's view of the relationship between domestic welfare and overseas economic expansion was even more explicit. The "export market becomes of peculiar importance to us," he noted in 1924, "in maintaining a stable and even operation of our domestic industries. It has an importance in that regard far beyond the percentage of our exports to our total production." It was a crucial "part of our domestic progress, both socially and economically." Hence it was essential for the government to provide "protection and support to Americans interested in the development of American enterprise abroad."

One of Hoover's most significant acts of assistance involved a thorough reorganization and beefing-up of the Department of Commerce in order to push such economic expansion. The importance of that work is suggested by the way that later Secretaries of Commerce, including Democrats Harry Hopkins, Henry A. Wallace, and Luther Hodges, identified their own programs with both the ideas and the policies stressed by Hoover. Since Hoover picked his assistants with extreme care, it is illuminating to review their basic ideas. Some of the most revealing statements of their outlook were provided by Julius Klein, who served as Hoover's top aide during the time he was Secretary of Commerce. Klein described the general objective as "the internationalization of business" under the leadership (and the predominant influence) of the American corporation. As one who accepted the frontier-expansionist explanation of American history, he offered in 1927 a brilliant two-paragraph statement of the thesis advanced by Brooks Adams, Frederick Jackson Turner, and other philosophers of the frontier. Presented as a major policy statement under the title, "The Tendency of the Frontier is to Move Westward," Klein's essay opened with the unequivocal assertion that "the economic history of the world has been a history of frontiers." "This movement started from China," he explained, and then "swept through central Asia," Greece, and Rome on its way to establishing Europe "as the center of world commerce." Then America "became the great frontier [and in turn]. . . .

The history of the United States itself has been a history of frontiers." The result was in Klein's view the final example of the way that the last frontier became in turn the newest center of expansion. "Now the circle is complete, the last great frontier has been conquered, and we come to a new era of world history. America, with an economic and industrial organization which is the fruit of centuries of world progress, is facing across the Pacific what is at the same time the oldest and the newest trade area." The Chinese Empire had become America's economic frontier.

Another document of similar interest was an analysis of the branch factory movement prepared by Louis Domeratzky, Chief of the Commerce Department's Division of Regional Information. He interpreted what he called "the aggressive expansion policy" of American corporations as the final proof of America's economic predominance. It had developed as a balance wheel to offset domestic fluctuations and as a way of evading tariff restrictions thrown up by foreign countries against American exports. He also emphasized the newer significance of the overseas investment program in "the exploitation of foreign natural resources" to provide raw materials for American production. Given the ability to provide their own capital, Domeratzky saw the process as one which the corporations would continue indefinitely. Hoover not only agreed with that analysis, but sought after the crash in 1929 to generate the recovery of the entire economy by stressing such overseas expansion of American corporations.

The Great Depression is always offered as proof of the limitations and the failure of Hoover's ideas and policies. That judgment is neither very accurate nor particularly helpful. Hoover did not cause the depression. It was brought on by the general malfunctioning of American and world capitalism. His after-the-fact critics offered no significant preventatives before the crisis, and in large measure derived their own programs from the general ideas already put forward by Hoover.

For the most part, such critics merely compare Hoover's efforts to end the depression with the state of the economy after the start of World War II, credit the New Deal with the improvement, and offer harsh and unfavorable conclusions about Hoover. That verdict conveniently ignores the failure of the New Deal to generate sustained recovery until armament orders began to roll in during the latter part of 1940; it slides over the social and psychological, as well as many of the political and economic, costs of the prosperity achieved; and in general neglects to mention that President Franklin Delano Roosevelt and Secretary of State Cordell Hull relied ever more extensively on overseas economic expansion to cope with the economy's propensity to stagnate.

Some partisans of the New Deal assert that a double standard of judgment is involved in pointing out such aspects of the Roosevelt record. The reverse is more nearly true, for the weaknesses of the New Deal are certainly as relevant as the failures of Hoover in reaching any general conclusions about recent American history. Beyond the question of explaining Hoover's approach to the depression, the real issues involve the objectives sought by Hoover and the New Deal, the consequences of their actions, and the extent to which they were aware of—and concerned about—those consequences.

Both Hoover and Roosevelt wanted freedom, prosperity, and peace for the United States. Neither of them approached the problems facing twentieth-century America with the attitude and outlook of a narrow nineteenth-century entrepreneur. Hence there is little relevance in shooting down Hoover as a Simon Legree of industrialism. That target is a straw man. The difficulty is to explain why Hoover was unwilling to plunge into the crisis of the depression with the attitude of "do something, anything" manifested by Roosevelt during his first term.

Hoover was not cautious because he was callous or ignorant. He hesitated because of what seemed to him the serious dangers inherent in all the easy or obvious remedies. In contrast, Roosevelt charged forward with little regard for the rather obvious, as well as the more subtle or latent, consequences of his actions. What is so revealing in this connection is the way the critics of Hoover admit—at least when pressed —to many reservations about the effects of the New Deal. They are often very perceptive in their evaluation of those results, but they seem never to realize that their criticisms were offered in advance—as premonitions—by Hoover.

A good example of this irony is provided by President Dwight David Eisenhower's famous warning in 1962 about the dangers to democracy posed by the growth of a military-industrial complex with great influence inside the government. That blunt admonition found favor with most of those who criticize Hoover. Yet Hoover was intensely concerned in 1930–1932 that fascism would begin to develop if big business was allowed to gain great influence in combating the depression. Thus he flatly rejected several versions of the program ultimately adopted as the N.R.A. by the Roosevelt Administration, an approach that did delegate extensive power to business. Hoover also feared the consequences of giving the government primary and formal responsibility for saving capitalism through overseas economic expansion. He argued with great force and insight that such a policy would turn every economic clash into an international political incident and thereby continually increase world tensions.

In a different way, Hoover feared that socialism would result from giving labor a predominant role in the fight against the depression. That was probably Hoover's main mistake. American labor was not inclined toward socialism. It sought no more than a position of parity with the farmer and the corporation. Even so, Hoover's analysis was not demolished by that error. For his most general fear about precipitate action in the depression was based on an astute analysis of the kind of syndicalist capitalism that would emerge from trying to balance the major elements of the political economy through ad hoc government intervention. He thought that approach would produce a nameless but nevertheless insidious kind of bureaucratic and presidential tyranny that would deaden public interest and participation in government, and that would in the end fail to produce either peace or prosperity.

It may be that Hoover is one of the very few truly tragic figures in American history. Each of his analyses of the main alternatives in 1930–1932 contained a significant amount of truth. And it seems quite likely that his failure to commit himself and the nation to any of those possibilities was the result of a temporary psychological bloc in the face of such unhappy choices that prevented him from taking any vigorous action. Be that as it may, the irony of all the liberal and New Deal criticism of Hoover lies in the way that the New Deal and subsequent administrations carried certain essential aspects of Hoover's basic foreign policies to their logical and extreme conclusions.

While it is certainly true that many of those later developments were inherent in Hoover's program, just as his were implicit in the Open Door Notes, it is also very important to realize that his successors went far beyond Hoover's actions. Perhaps the most effective way to dramatize this point is by comparing Hoover's assumption in 1920 that the Soviet Union would collapse if confronted by a hostile world with the thesis advanced by George Frost Kennan in 1947 that the policy of containment would "force" such a result. The similarity is obvious and significant. But Hoover's program was characterized by a moderation and ambivalence that had been lost by the time Kennan made his proposal.

Hoover did not like socialism or communism, and he opposed the Soviet Union. But he also understood the great danger inherent in externalizing evil in the form of one country, in resting American security and welfare exclusively on the outcome of a trial of strength with one other nation. Hence he did not define American foreign policy so narrowly in terms of putting direct pressure on the Russians. He thought that the inherent difficulties of making socialism or communism work in a backward country would, when combined with the successful example of the United States, ultimately turn the Russians away from doctrinaire communism toward the American model. And that, in turn, would create the conditions for steady American improvement.

Hoover did not enjoy Borah's empathy with revolutions in general, or the Senator's specific insight into the Soviet upheaval. But neither did he make the reductionist error of simplifying the problem to the point of thinking that the challenge of the Bolshevik Revolution could be met through policy toward Russia. He understood very clearly that the only effective answer would be in avoiding war between the advanced industrial nations, and in making capitalism produce results in the poor countries as well as in the rich nations. Given his assumptions, that analysis brought Hoover right back to the importance of a program of overseas economic expansion that would actually develop the poor societies. An understanding of this broad outlook makes it possible to resolve the contradictions of his specific approach to Russia.

Hoover was candid and insistent about the proper way to handle the Russian problem. His remarks at the end of 1921 in a letter to Secretary Hughes about American food shipments to the Soviet Union were not only revealing of the specific subject, but were similar to Secretary of State Root's explanation in 1906 of the role of reform in furthering American influence in Morocco. "The relief measures already initiated are greatly increasing the status and kindness of relations and their continuation will build a situation which, combined with other factors, will enable the Americans to undertake the leadership in the reconstruction of Russia when the proper moment arrives." By the proper moment was of course meant the end of Soviet rule. Hoover continued his analysis with a blunt explanation of why the United States could not allow other nations—and in particular Germany—to function as middlemen in shipping American exports to Russia. "The hope of our commerce lies in the establishment of American firms abroad, distributing American goods under American direction; in the building of direct American financing and, above all, in the installation of American technology in Russian industries. We must, of necessity, in the future finance our own raw materials* into Russia and if our manufactured goods are distributed through German hands it simply means that when Germany has established trade of sufficient distribution to warrant her own manufacture we shall lose the market."

Because they wanted the immediate economic market and the longer-range political influence, Hoover and Hughes unofficially encouraged Americans to embark upon the economic penetration of Russia even though they refused to recognize the Soviet Government or to allow it to negotiate loans in the United States. Perhaps the history of American-Russian relations reveals no greater irony than the fact that this covert

---

* By "raw materials," Hoover of course meant food stuffs.

approval of certain specified economic relations, designed to
speed the collapse of the Soviets and strengthen American influence in the following government, led Americans to contribute significantly to the recovery and development of the
Soviet economic system. At the end of the 1920's, indeed, it
was the depression-racked American economy which looked
to Russian markets as a crutch for its own recovery. And by
that time more Americans, including some among the Hoover,
Hughes, and Stimson group, were thinking of Russia as a
potential ally against Japan and Germany.

Such thoughts were far from the minds of Hoover and
Hughes as they undertook to integrate Germany and Japan
into their American-led community of industrial powers. Concerned with making Germany safe against internal revolution
and strong as a bulwark against world communism, Hoover
and Hughes gave high priority to its recovery. Their main
lever to overcome the opposition of France and England was
the astute and forceful use of American economic power.
Hughes finally backed France and England into the entente by
controlling the relationship between, on the one hand, the
debts they owed to the United States and, on the other, the
reparations they demanded from Germany.

Hughes accomplished this by tying the reduction of Allied
debts to the United States to a similar cut in German reparations to Britain and France. This move, formalized in the
Dawes and Young plans of 1924 and 1929, respectively, enabled the United States to speed the end of military occupation of Germany and to open the way for Germany's re-entry
into the Western community. In line with this objective, they
supported the Locarno Pact of 1925, by which Germany,
France and Britain underwrote the boundaries of western
Europe but left the frontiers facing Russia unguaranteed.
More than one American leader viewed the Locarno Pact as
the first political result of the nation's economic policy. It was
in the context of this general settlement in Europe that the
American Government encouraged private loans to Germany
as a further move to speed that nation's recovery.

All of this was done quietly, much of it "unofficially," and
without American entry into the League of Nations. None of
these considerations alters the fact that the effort was part of

a broad program of conscious involvement in world affairs for well-defined objectives. As Senator Borah remarked at the time, "It does not rise even to the level of sophistry" to assert that such actions are described accurately by the term "isolationism." But neither is it true, as others have maintained, that American policy was designed to make Germany dominant in Europe. American leaders wanted peace, and to that end they sought the reintegration of Germany into a Western community led by the United States. They were willing to go— and did go—a long way to facilitate German recovery and to accept or acquiesce in the assertion of German strength. But it was the failure of American policy, not its success, which contributed to the coming of World War II. The motives were unimpeachable; it was the ancient prejudices, the backward outlook, and the outmoded practices which caused the failure.

American policy in Asia after World War I was characterized by similar features, though the problem itself was more complex. China was not only considered important per se as an area which would absorb large quantities of American surpluses, but it had been a region of American interest, activity, and influence for more than a century. It was impossible to ignore developments there, even had the policy-makers wished to do so. But neither was it possible to step in and run the show. On the one hand, Americans did not want a formal empire, and on the other, Japan blocked that kind of action. Japan's position was further strengthened by its color and ethnic affinities with the rest of Asia. Its occupations of parts of Manchuria and Siberia and its old alliance of 1902 with Great Britain also increased its bargaining power.

Working from the basic premise that wars and revolutions had to be prevented in the Far East, and concluding that the best way to accomplish that was to bring Japan into the American-led "community of ideals, interests, and purposes," Hughes offered Tokyo two commitments: a generous and unquestioned share in the development of China and an understanding that the United States would help check China's revolutionary nationalism. In return, he asked Japan's agreement to the Open Door Policy and to a program of balanced naval power in the western Pacific. Given that *quid pro quo*, Hughes was confident that the United States—as represented by the banking consortium and other businessmen—could control the situation over the long haul. Concerned with future markets for the American economic system, not formal empire, he was willing to sacrifice immediate and marginal goals. Here, as elsewhere, Hughes was following the lead laid down by Wilson, who had revitalized the consortium in 1917, acknowledged Japan's special position in Manchuria the same year, and specified in 1919 that it was "essential" to assert and maintain the open door in Siberia and elsewhere throughout Asia.

Hughes overcame Japan's reluctance to commit itself to such a program by a combination of three kinds of diplomacy. First, he made astute use of pressures and attitudes which reinforced his hand. These included the general postwar desire for disarmament, America's traditional support for the Open Door Policy, the agitation in Canada and Australia (as well as in England itself) against Britain's alliance with Japan, economic and social unrest in Japan, the growing strength of the Bolsheviks in Siberia (which worked to push Japan out but also to encourage other nations to compromise their differences), and the general opposition to China's attempt to assert its economic and political sovereignty. Second, his tactic of opening the discussions at the Washington Conference with a concrete plan for disarmament, under which America would take the lead, kept Japan and other opponents off balance. Most important of all, however, was his willingness to give Japan "an extraordinarily favorable position" in northeastern Asia in order to establish "co-operation in the Far East."

Japan accepted the offer (though with some skepticism and private reservations), and the agreement was formalized in the Four- and Nine-Power Treaties signed in Washington in 1922. These documents defined the community of industrial powers in the Pacific, just as the Dawes and Young plans and the Locarno Pact did in the Atlantic. The United States, Japan, France, and Great Britain agreed to respect each other's rights in various island possessions, to uphold the status quo in Asia, and to proceed with the development of China and other areas within the framework of the Open Door Policy. Answering some of his critics at home, who feared that the treaties weakened America's position, Hughes justifiably asserted that the negotiations and settlement "were conducted within limitations defined by the American Government."

American leaders honored their understanding of these commitments throughout the ensuing decade. China's protest against the limitations imposed upon it by the Washington treaties was brushed aside with the cryptic reply that "various American expressions of sympathy with an academic position may have misled the Chinese," and that the "matter had been decided at Washington adverse to the Chinese view." Entertaining this attitude toward Chinese conservative nationalists, it was natural for Hughes to ignore the appeals for sympathy and help made to the United States by Sun Yat-sen, leader of the revolutionary nationalist movement in China. He did not even open Sun's letter.*

Russia was more responsive to Chinese requests. It offered Lenin's theory of imperialism, which gave Chinese nationalists an explanation of their country's weakness; Marxian economic theory, which outlined a way to gain strength rapidly; the example of a successful revolution; and advisors in the art of such revolution. Thus armed with ideas and encouragement, and goaded by Western policy and actions, the revolutionary nationalist movement in China gathered momentum and took on a strong sense of direction and purpose.

Leaders in the United States replied with the assertion that America had "a responsibility for effort directed toward saving the Chinese from their own folly." This remark, a somewhat astringent and blunt synthesis of all the themes implicit in open-door imperialism, characterized an attitude which limited America to a very few alternatives. Since they ignored, or disapproved of, the possibility of working either with Russia to check Japan or with liberal Chinese nationalists, American leaders had one basic choice. They could join four-power action against the left-wing revolutionary movement in China, but simultaneously effect a broad understand-

---

* While some of the quotations in this section come from unpublished documents, American policy toward China between 1917 and 1923 can be followed in its basic outlines in the appropriate volumes of *Papers Relating to the Foreign Relations of the United States.* Also see: D. Borg, *American Policy and the Chinese Revolution, 1925–1928* (New York: Macmillan, 1947); and A. W. Griswold, *The Far Eastern Policy of the United States* (New York: Harcourt, Brace & Co., 1938).

ing with conservative nationalists in China. Within that context, they could then undertake a vigorous program of economic development in China. Or, on the other hand, they could work with and through Japan, considering that nation as an agent of American policy and a channel through which American economic power would develop China.

The difficulty in resolving the issue stemmed from several considerations. Either proposal could be defended as a continuation of the Open Door Policy designed to establish American predominance in Asia without recourse to war. The idea of working with and through Chinese conservative nationalists who were dependent upon American aid was the traditional concept of putting the policy into operation. The central drawback of the approach was the probability that it would, if undertaken with vigor and determination, lead to war with Japan. That was undesirable per se, and doubly so because after 1917 American leaders feared war as the hothouse of revolution.

The other proposal involved working with and through Japan until American economic power asserted itself in that country as well as in China. This argument took into account the dangers of war and revolution, considerations which tended to compensate for the fact that it again postponed the day of American pre-eminence in Asia. Despite its short-run disadvantages and frustrations, however, it was a persuasive answer to the question of how best to implement the open door in Asia. Though continually challenged by different groups for conflicting reasons, this developed as the basic outlook of American policy-makers from the Bolshevik Revolution of November, 1917, to the very strong American note delivered to the Japanese Government in November 1941. Neither Wilson, Hughes, nor Hoover considered going to war against Japan; and later leaders argued that American economic power could confine Japanese action within limits defined by the United States.

Beyond the broad considerations of preventing wars and revolutions, the policy in Asia was strongly influenced by the last phase of the struggle between the bankers (supported for the time by certain traders and exporters) and the corporations to control the basic character and tone of American foreign policy. The domestic conflict between the corporations and the bankers had a complex relationship to foreign policy. Beginning in the 1840's, and moving rapidly after the Civil War, the corporation established itself by the 1890's as the central insitution of the American economic system. By 1899, for example, two-thirds of all manufactured goods were produced by corporations, and by 1929 the figure was more than nine-tenths. In 1904 the corporations employed seven-tenths of all wage earners in manufacturing, and by 1929 they employed nine-tenths.

Though centered in the factory, the corporation soon addressed itself to the business of integrating and rationalizing the entire economic process of industrialization—from capital formation, through raw materials and labor supplies, to marketing the finished merchandise. Its early emphasis on a foreign policy designed to facilitate and underwrite all phases of that process was continued unabated into the 1920's. Concerning the fundamentals of a policy of expansion, especially over the long-run, the bankers agreed with the corporations.

But on the issue of which institution should control basic decisions, as well as on particular aspects of expansion, the two groups often disagreed vigorously. Between 1900 and 1920, moreover, the corporations suffered from a fundamental disadvantage in their struggle with the bankers. They lacked all of the capital that was necessary to consolidate, expand, and rationalize the process of production and marketing at home. Such capital was available from the bankers. Hence the corporations gave up some key decisions, and part of their influence, as a portion of their payment for loans from the bankers.

During this period, which usually is referred to as "the era of finance capitalism," the bankers also exerted more influence on foreign policy. But the phrase "finance capitalism" is misleading because it creates the impression that the bankers took over the economic process itself. They did exercise extensive control in some industries, as in steel, but even at the height of finance capitalism the bankers functioned more as troubleshooters for the corporate system than as outsiders who moved in and took over—or changed—the economic system. It remained a corporate system throughout these years.

Since the corporations were the true entrepreneurs in the

system, they held the trump cards in any battle with the
bankers. They were asserting this power by 1913, and the
flood of government contracts during World War I pushed
them on to victory over the bankers. Between 1922 and 1929,
for example, the undistributed earnings of the corporations
averaged more than $2,500,000,000 a year. Bankers had no
claim on this capital and but little influence over what was
done with it. The steady decline of commercial loans during
this period also indicated the returning independence of the
corporations.

Though they reasserted their power during and immediately
after World War I, the corporations did not have enough
surplus capital to embark immediately on further expansion
every place in the world. For one thing, the severe depression
of 1920-1921 caused some temporary loss of influence to the
bankers. Then, after recovery began in 1922, the corporate
leaders emphasized domestic investments as well as direct
overseas investments in factories, service installations, and the
development of raw material supplies. Such companies as
Ford, General Motors, International Business Machines, and
American Telephone and Telegraph concentrated their activities in European and other industrialized countries. Others,
including oil and mining corporations and such raw material
processing firms as the Aluminum Corporation of America,
centered their attention on the Middle East, Latin America,
and parts of Asia. This activity led to a great expansion of
direct overseas investments during the 1920's. In 1919 they
totalled 94 million. By 1925, they had jumped to 268 million.
Up again to 351 in 1926, they ballooned to 602 million in
1929.

For their part, the bankers were caught in a more difficult
situation and their actions were more complex and contradictory. On the one hand, they agreed with corporation executives and government leaders that expanded exports were
"essential to industrial prosperity." They accepted the analysis prepared by William B. Fleming, the State Department's
adviser on commercial treaties: "A number of our big manufacturers . . . in normal times can produce enough to supply
the home market in seven months." As the editors of the
Acceptance Bulletin, one of the key journals of the financial

community, pointed out in January 1922, "it is useless to attempt to further develop our own country until a satisfactory
market is created for our surplus products." Thus the bankers
supported Secretary of State Hughes in his drive for "effective
recognition of the Open Door Policy."

On the other hand, the bankers admitted that they lacked
the capital for an all-out loan campaign. Fred I. Kent of the
Bankers Trust Co., George H. Kretz of the National Park
Bank, and George Woodruff of the First National Bank of
Joliet, Illinois, offered typical testimony on that crucial point.
Perhaps the most dramatic and impressive evidence was provided by the failure of the National City Bank to establish
and sustain a *world-wide* chain of branch banks to finance such
expansion. This fundamental weakness forced the financiers
to follow less perfect alternatives. Some, like the House of
Morgan, continued to pursue their broad strategy of working
with and through the British and French while expanding
their connections in Germany. Others decided that Europe
should be given priority for the capital that was available.
Some of that group argued that there would be no possibility
of expanding into the underdeveloped countries if Europe
collapsed. The rest of them thought that they would be able
to move into the poor nations through the European door.
In general, therefore, the capital that was directly available
for the underdeveloped countries was relatively small in
amount and was further limited to short-term loans. The
result, as in Latin America, was a scramble for investments
that were neither very sound nor very productive.

This drive for accounts did, however, intensify two existing
features of banking policy. Financiers continued their maneuvers to obtain government assistance in accumulating
capital. They first tried to enlarge and sustain the operations
of the War Finance Corporation; such a move would not only
have given them the kind of direct aid they wanted, but would
also have reassured smaller investors in the general security
market that the government supported the undertakings.
While that effort failed, the bankers (along with some of the
weaker corporations) did not give up trying to get what the
Journal of Commerce called "federal credit" as a means of
accumulating "the capital necessary" for major overseas op-

erations. But it was not until after the start of the Great Depression that such funds were forthcoming.

The financiers were more successful in preventing government control of their operations. Hoover wanted to set limits on the bankers, restricting them to loans that were in line with the tactics of the Open Door Policy, and which actually promoted viable economic development in the poor, underdeveloped nations. He certainly tried hard to obtain such authority during the first years of the Harding Administration, even though he was aware that it might set a dangerous precedent for government intervention. The bankers blocked him by appealing to the fears (and to the narrower philosophy) of Harding and others in the administration. Their argument was stated with considerable power by John Foster Dulles, who in those years was a leading lawyer for the financial community. "Control of foreign loans," he explained with obvious concern, "involves a vast power over our national economy." It "would obviously be unfortunate if [an] established precedent warranted the use of control over foreign loans as a medium for carrying into effect any economic or financial policies which might happen at the moment to be those of the heads of our executive departments." It proved difficult for Dulles, as for others in the financial community, to attain the more inclusive, long-range view of Hoover. In the 1920's, at any rate, the interests of the bankers obscured their vision. "No foreign policy could be intelligently conceived and carried out," Dulles judged, "by a Department of State which was ignorant of or indifferent to the past and current acquisitions by American interests in foreign lands."

These conflicts incident to the maturation of America's corporate economic system manifested themselves in Asia in a complex fashion. At one level they appeared as a battle between the banker Thomas Lamont, who was aligned with Japan, and several corporations which proposed to do business in China. But Lamont was supported by those corporations which had developed significant trade connections with Japan. Other corporations pushed trade with China, however, and those firms lined up with the companies interested in direct investment in that country.

Such economic crosscurrents caused Hughes and Hoover

considerable trouble throughout the 1920's. Official strategy was to push American penetration in China while holding a checkrein on Japan. But Hoover and Hughes also wanted all the foreign markets they could get, including those in Japan. Hence they acquiesced in Lamont's tie with Japan, and in exports to Japan, hoping meanwhile to encourage and extend America's position in China. Ultimately, of course, American leaders thought to resolve the dilemma by influencing Japan through its economic ties to the United States. But this posed serious difficulties of its own, and the United States finally went to war to preserve the open door in Asia.

In other areas of the world, meanwhile, such as in Latin America, eastern Europe, and the Middle East and Africa, the policies of the United States were formulated to facilitate the "internationalization of business" through the expansion of the American corporation. Aware of the voracious appetite of American industry, and of its commensurate waste, Hoover, Hughes, and corporation leaders united in a concerted program to discover, develop, and control various key raw materials throughout the world. This drive was integrated with the traditional campaign for markets, and both were heightened by the determination to protect direct, on-the-spot operations from foreign competition and revolutionary opposition.

Latin America posed in classic form two basic difficulties connected with such corporate expansion. It was necessary to control and mitigate the region's opposition to the predominance of the United States and, at the same time, extend and rationalize the system of American authority. The effort to expand American exports, develop and control raw materials, and initiate corporate enterprises—while at the same time developing a regional political system based on local rulers loyal to the basic interests of the United States—made of Latin America the laboratory of American foreign policy for all underdeveloped areas.

That comparison offers considerable insight if the foreign policy experiment of the 1920's is thought of as an effort to change the methods and style of American intervention developed by Roosevelt and Wilson while at the same time sustaining and even extending the long-range influence of the United States.* In many respects, moreover, the effort of the 1920's represented the same kind of convergence between reform ideas and hard-headed economics that characterized American policy toward Morocco at the time of the Algeciras Conference in 1905–1906. The developments of the 1920's in the Latin American policy of the United States were simply an adaptation of American policy to altered circumstances that was continued in the Good Neighbor Policy of the New Deal and culminated in the Alliance For Progress proposed by President John F. Kennedy.

In the 1920's, as well as in the 1960's, this modification of policy was brought about by two main considerations. First, new ideas about the nature of American predominance in the Western Hemisphere led different groups in the United States to propose and initiate policy changes. Second, and interacting with the first, the failure of traditional and existing policies to achieve the desired results prompted alterations. Specifically, American policy-makers became convinced by the end of the 1920's that the 21 military interventions undertaken between 1898 and 1924 had not served either to stabilize the region or to institutionalize American power and influence.

The beginning of the shift in approach might usefully be dated from the recognition of the Mexican Government of Alvaro Obregon by the Harding Administration on August 31, 1923. While it is true that Mexico agreed as a condition of recognition to respect subsoil rights acquired by Americans prior to 1917, the move did terminate the direct and even violent intervention carried on by President Wilson. Almost immediately, however, incoming President Coolidge indicated that his outlook was closer to the turn-of-the-century expansionism of Roosevelt than to the approach that Hoover and Stimson were to reveal after 1928. Since he is usually thought of as a pinched-in personality, such a comparison of Coolidge with Roosevelt may appear rather strange. But Coolidge actu-

---

* The laboratory metaphor itself is borrowed from Fred Harvey Harrington, now President of the University of Wisconsin. The two most recent books bearing on Latin American policy are: D. M. Dozer, *Are We Good Neighbors?* (Gainesville: University of Florida Press, 1959); and B. Wood, *The Making of the Good Neighbor Policy* (New York: Columbia University Press, 1961).

ally entertained an expansive conception of American foreign policy. He described the process of American businessmen going abroad and "opening up underdeveloped countries" as—and note the similarity with the language of Roosevelt— "the natural play of the forces of civilization." The United States, he asserted, was "a patron of tranquility abroad." People who questioned that judgment were "treading the way that leads back to the jungle." Holding that American "investments and trade relations" made it "almost impossible to conceive of any conflict anywhere on earth which would not affect us injuriously," Coolidge concluded that "the one great duty that stands out requires us to use our enormous powers to trim the balance of the world."

In keeping with that sense of responsibility, Coolidge sent Marines into Honduras in 1924 because, in the phrase of the State Department, "a condition of anarchy seems likely to develop." In the same year, the administration also formally advised Plutarco Calles, the newly elected Mexican President, that recognition was contingent upon continuing protection and respect for American lives and property. That blunt warning served only to strengthen the groups in Mexico that wanted to push ahead with measures limiting foreign economic penetration and influence. Three such laws were passed by the Mexican legislature to take effect on January 1, 1927. One limited foreign concessions to 50 years; another specified that foreign corporations (such as American oil firms) must forego any appeal for protection to their own governments; and the third, a more general land law to break up large holdings, impinged directly upon American agricultural and mining operators. Even before the laws went into effect, the tension and fear arising from the conflict between Washington and Mexico City had prompted Coolidge in 1926 to send Marines into Nicaragua. The President and others in the State Department were afraid that the Mexican Revolution would spread—directly as well as in spirit—throughout Central America; they were determined to prevent the challenge to the United States from growing any stronger. The intervention in Nicaragua was undertaken to put conservatives friendly to the United States in power. It can be simply described as a military and diplomatic maneuver undertaken to achieve a political objective that, it was expected, would in turn prevent long-range economic difficulties and losses.

The actual results were quite different. For one thing, the Marines stayed six years. More important, the intervention in Nicaragua created fears of a war with Mexico. The reaction against that possibility (as well as against the move into Nicaragua) accelerated and strengthened a movement among diverse groups that opposed military intervention and sought instead to restore and strengthen American influence through more peaceful and sophisticated means. One of those elements, a coalition of pacifist and reform organizations, mobilized considerable public opinion against Coolidge and his policy. They were probably aided, at least to some extent, by the way that England and other countries referred to the President's actions as "frankly imperialistic."

Such general expressions of disapproval were reinforced by criticism from two other sources whose influence was considerable though their size was smaller. Reform politicians of both parties attacked Coolidge vigorously. Senator Borah's opposition was especially militant and had added significance because of his influential position on the Senate Foreign Relations Committee. "The great problem in international affairs at present," he observed bluntly in February 1927, "[grows] out of the relationship between strong and weak nations. . . . It is not war between the great powers but spoliation of the weak nations which seems most vital and imminent in international affairs at this time." Borah was supported in the Congress, moreover, by men like Senators George W. Norris, Hiram Johnson, and Joseph Robinson, and Democratic Representative Fiorello H. La Guardia. They provided the leadership that produced on January 25, 1927, a unanimous vote (79–0) in support of Robinson's resolution calling on Coolidge to settle the dispute with Mexico through arbitration.

Since most Senators were more conservative on matters of foreign policy than Borah or Norris, it is helpful in explaining that vote to realize that many large corporations and other business interests also opposed the nature and implications of Coolidge's policy. Perhaps the most convincing evidence of the central importance of such corporation opinion takes the form of a State Department memorandum prepared during the period when Hoover and Stimson were trying to evolve a less militant approach to relations with Latin America.*

"The participation of American corporations in the development of Latin America involves an incalculable corrective to existing trade figures and implies a distinct and direct American influence in Latin American policies. Irrespective of the policy at Washington and the personality of the statesmen, the operations of such enterprises as the United Fruit Company or the several American oil companies create independent political interests in the territories subject to their economic operation which supplement and often determine official policy both at Washington and in the various Latin American capitals."

In the Mexican-Nicaraguan affair, such firms as Standard Oil and the Boston Bank opposed continued militance on the grounds that it would "injure American interests" far more than it helped them. Another indication of such opinion in the business community was provided indirectly in the editorials of the *New York Times*. At the outset of the crisis they were brazenly nationalistic, even imperialistic. By the end of January 1927, however, the editors were advising a change in policy because a continuation of the existing one "might easily tip the balance in favor of European exporters." Such economic considerations apparently contributed to their advocacy of a "prudent and conciliatory spirit." And finally, such evidence of business influence appeared very clearly when Coolidge picked his trouble-shooters to resolve the crisis. He sent Henry L. Stimson, a lawyer for corporate interests, to Nicaragua in April 1927. And four months later he dispatched Dwight W. Morrow of the House of Morgan as a special emissary to Mexico.

The best general explanation of this attitude on the part of large corporation spokesmen (and their associates in law and politics) was probably offered by Leo S. Rowe, Director General of the Pan American Union. "We have advanced," he pointed out, "from the period of adventure to the period

---

* This document, dated January 12, 1930, can be found in the National Archives (Record Group 59; Decimal File 710.11/1518).

of permanent investment." As a man who probably understood the meaning of that change for foreign policy as well
as anyone of his generation, Hoover moved very quickly after
his election as President in 1928 to sustain the momentum
away from the older tradition of open, forceful, military
intervention. Indeed, even before he took office he made a
long good-will trip throughout Latin America. "We have a
desire," he assured his various hosts, "to maintain not only
the cordial relations of governments with each other but the
relations of good neighbors."

Hoover's desire to improve relations with Latin America
in a manner that would also strengthen the economic expansion of the United States was wholly sincere. Moreover, it was
based upon a perceptive and sophisticated estimate of the
phenomenon that was in later years called "the revolution of
rising expectations." He recognized that World War I had
broken open the long-festering wounds of economic inequity
between the advanced and the poor countries, and between
classes within the underprivileged societies. "The great in-
equalities and injustices of centuries," he explained in 1921,
"[have been] flogged beyond endurance by the conflict and
freed from restraint by the destruction of war." He also saw
the corollary of that new determination and self-consciousness
on the part of the suffering millions: that the United States,
emerging from the war as the richest and most powerful
country in the world, could easily become the focus of that
bitterness, frustration, and antagonism. "A large part of the
world," he warned the country at large (as well as businessmen), "has come to believe that they were in the presence of
the birth of a new imperial power intent upon dominating
the destinies and freedoms of other people."

Hoover's problem was to meet that danger while at the
same time sustaining the overseas economic expansion that he
and other American leaders considered essential to prosperity
and representative government at home. He attempted to
resolve that dilemma by modifying the methods of expansion
so that they were more in line with the ideals he held. "The
basis of an advancing civilization," he observed in 1923, "must
be a high and growing standard of living for all the people,
not for a single class." From that it followed, as he empha-

sized in 1928, that an "essential part of the sound expansion
of our foreign trade [is] that we . . . interest ourselves in the
development of backward or crippled countries by means of
loans from our surplus capital." "In stimulating our exports,
we should be mainly interested in development work abroad
such as roads and utilities which increase the standards of
living of people and thus increase the demand for goods from
every nation, for we gain in prosperity by a prosperous world,
not by displacing others."

A decade later, after the harsh recession of 1937–38 revealed that the depression had by no means been overcome,
New Deal policy-makers finally began to use government powers and public monies in line with the analysis that Hoover
offered in 1928–29. Quite rightly, they won credit for the
developmental loans they granted to some Latin American
countries. But to conclude that they were also the men who
first thought of, or acted on, the approach is both historically
inaccurate and personally unfair to Hoover.

In many ways, moreover, Hoover had a much more difficult
task. He had, in the short space of four years, to close out and
reverse a tradition of military intervention and to initiate a
new program. Nor is there any doubt that that was his aim.
"It ought not to be the policy of the United States to intervene by force to secure or maintain contracts between our
citizens and foreign states or their citizens. Confidence in that
attitude is the only basis upon which the economic cooperation of our citizens can be welcomed abroad." Hoover infused
that rhetoric with substance in many ways, but one of his
earliest acts involved releasing for publication in 1928 the
anti-interventionist *Memorandum on the Monroe Doctrine*.
Prepared in the State Department by J. Reuben Clark, and
held up by the Coolidge Administration, the document openly
and officially disavowed the approach of Theodore Roosevelt.

In moving toward his objective, Hoover was confronted by
more than the obvious handicaps of tradition and an inherited
intervention in Nicaragua. Secretary of State Stimson, for
example, had a good bit of the crusading upper-class reformer
in his temperament that had to be restrained if not overcome.
But Stimson had the relatively rare kind of courage that enabled him to modify or change his opinions on some vital

issues when they were battered beyond a certain point by reality. Nicaragua's factional politics, and its resistance to the Marines, gave some of his assumptions that kind of a beating. He concluded by 1931 that it was time to withdraw. Any effort to keep Nicaragua pacified, and to establish American-style political life, would involve the United States in "difficulties and commitments which this Government does not propose to undertake." They would impose "a very serious burden." In a similar way, Stimson wholly agreed with Hoover that the United States should not intervene in the Cuban Revolution which erupted in 1929–30. And in a way that offered a striking contrast with the later interference by New Deal policy-makers, they did not intervene *or* intermeddle.

As the *London Times* remarked on April 21, 1931, the approach to relations with Latin America revealed by Hoover and Stimson amounted to a "reversal of the methods" of the past. Stimson offered his own neat summary of the difference in connection with the Cuban uprising. "The situation in Cuba ought to so develop that less and less pressure would be necessary on the part of the United States to keep matters straight." Whether or not Hoover and Stimson are given formal credit for founding what later became known as the Good Neighbor Policy is probably not a vital issue. Given the consequences in Cuba and to the United States of Roosevelt's support of Batista as he made his initial bid for power in 1933–34, perhaps they themselves would not press the claim too vigorously. The important things are that they broke with past methods, that their analysis and reasoning also served to guide later policy-makers, and that their objective was to sustain the overseas economic expansion and political influence of the United States under the strategy of the Open Door Policy.

Elsewhere throughout the world during the years after World War I, American policy developed within that framework. In every instance, the key move was the assertion of the policy of the open door. And in each case, the objectives were markets for American industrial exports, raw materials for American factories, and the right to enter directly into the economic life of a country by establishing factories and other enterprises. That economic expansion made it possible to exercise a growing influence on local political and economic decisions, served to provide a base for further penetration, and ultimately took on military significance. But its initial character and importance was only extended—it was neither changed nor abandoned.

The basic approach toward eastern Europe was characterized by Hoover's insistence that the American economic penetration of Russia be handled directly rather than through Germany. Germany was needed to block Russia, and to strengthen the community of industrial powers, but it remained a competitor. Within this framework, American activity in eastern Europe included industrial and communications development and the search for raw materials such as phosphate and oil. Having penetrated the economies of the area, as in Poland, Bulgaria, Romania, Yugoslavia, and Albania, the businessmen turned to Washington for help against restrictive legislation enacted by these nations and against competition from Germany, Britain, and France. The first official move usually was a note to the country in question, reminding it of the principle and practice of the Open Door Policy. If that hint proved insufficient, American leaders resorted to economic pressure: directly, by withholding approval of projected loans or similar projects; or indirectly, by threatening, subtly or blatantly, to break diplomatic relations. Reinforcing their own vigorous political and economic activities on the scene, such diplomatic support enabled American businessmen to establish and develop significant interests in eastern Europe throughout the 1920's.*

Better known, and certainly more dramatic, was the postwar pattern of open-door expansion in the Middle East. Oil was the major objective of American policy, but American leaders did not overlook the long-range importance of a "new and as yet unorganized market of prodigious size." For these reasons, as well as in behalf of its own logistic and other interests, the Navy supported such expansion. Its program, along with President Wilson's assumption that Russia would be kept "bottled up" in the Black Sea, was based on the proposition that the

---

* This involvement should not be forgotten when considering American differences with Russia at the end of World War II.

strongest navy would control the straits of the Dardanelles. With this general support, Secretaries Hughes and Hoover in Harding's Cabinet first acted to force Britain and France to accept and honor the policy of the open door in their colonies and in the areas assigned to them under the League of Nations system of mandates. After several false starts, American interests finally began their penetration of the area by infiltrating European companies rather than by independent operations.

Several factors account for the initial preference for indirect action. For one thing, it was cheaper and easier; it gave American companies a share of current production while enabling them to conduct private and secret explorations designed to outflank their European "partners." Also, American companies were occupied for the moment in the Western Hemisphere, fighting Mexico, on the one hand, and, on the other, exploring and getting title to newly discovered reserves throughout the rest of the region. And finally, Hughes and Hoover continued and extended the practice of favoring, however subtly and covertly, one American corporation as the "chosen instrument" of the Open Door Policy in any given area.

In the case of the Middle East, the partiality benefited the complex of Standard Oil companies. Outfits such as Barnsdall, which wanted to work with the Russians in the Baku region, or Sinclair, which tried to do the same thing in the Far East, were blocked by the Department of State. Barnsdall discovered that it was permissible to do some trading with the Bolsheviks but not to help them develop important natural resources. And Secretary Hughes bluntly told Sinclair that he would not support the company in its battles with the Japanese, who claimed the sole right to exploit the oil reserves in the Russian half of the island of Sakhalin.

There is some evidence which suggests that the official bias in favor of Standard Oil helps explain Sinclair's efforts to secure access to American domestic reserves held by the government itself—a campaign which ended in the Teapot Dome scandal of 1924. One thing is certain: favored by the government, Standard Oil could afford the luxury of delaying active production in the Middle East until it had penetrated and canvassed such areas as Saudi Arabia. This result might be described as a most successful example of co-operative corporate capitalism in action. The nature and consequences of these activities became diplomatic issues for the Roosevelt Administration and for its successors.

Though neither as dramatic nor as extensive as the undertakings in Latin America, eastern Europe, and the Middle East, American penetration of Africa and Southeast Asia also increased during the 1920's. After considerable maneuvering by Liberian leaders (as well as by Hoover and Hughes), designed to prepare the natives for foreign economic intervention, the Firestone Tire and Rubber Company began its development of rubber plantations in that nation. It was more difficult to penetrate European colonies in Africa and southeastern Asia in such direct fashion, but the patterns of investment, purchasing, and marketing which originated in the 1920's ultimately made those raw-material producing areas vitally important to the existing methods and processes of the American corporate economy.

There were other ways of planning and providing for the continuing development of the American economy, but they were never seriously considered, let alone adopted. Thus the ties with the colonies of western European powers and other underdeveloped regions gradually came to be viewed as the *only* source of raw materials, services, and markets, whether or not current operations were based on such connections. And the threatened loss of supplies earmarked for future development was considered as dangerous as the possible loss of current ones, both by the corporations and the American Government. Perhaps more so, for the method and that rate of current exploitation were based in part on the assumption that the future was under control—that the frontier was unlimited.

When such assumptions, as well as current operations, were threatened by Germany and Japan (and later by revolutionary agitation), American leaders came to define the issue as one involving the principle of the open door and the strategic position of the nation itself. Men who began by defining the United States and the world in economic terms, and explaining its operation by the principles of capitalism and a frontier thesis of historical development, came finally to define the

United States in military terms as an embattled outpost in a hostile world. When a majority of the leaders of America's corporate society reached that conclusion, the nation went to war—at first covertly, then overtly.

Far from being unimportant, therefore, the Open Door Policy became increasingly more significant and crucial in the years after it was first enunciated by Secretary of State John Hay. The pattern of American expansion under the principles and procedures of the Open Door Notes came to maturity during the 1920's. And it was the threat posed to that program by the combined impact of the Great Depression and the competing expansion of Germany and Japan, both of which gained strength by falsely identifying themselves with one or more of the broad revolutions against classical liberalism, which ultimately accounted for American entry into World War II.

CHAPTER FIVE

The only thing we have to fear is fear itself.
FRANKLIN DELANO ROOSEVELT, 1933

When everyone began to realize finally that the country was really filled up, that there were no more good homesteads and no frontier to fill up in times of depression, there was great uneasiness.
HENRY AGARD WALLACE, 1934

Foreign markets must be regained if America's producers are to rebuild a full and enduring domestic prosperity for our people. There is no other way if we would avoid painful economic dislocations, social readjustments, and unemployment.
FRANKLIN DELANO ROOSEVELT, 1935

The rest of the world—Ah! there is the rub.
FRANKLIN DELANO ROOSEVELT, 1936

The reason for all this battleship and war frenzy is coming out. We Democrats have to admit we are floundering. The Democratic administration is getting down to the condition that

THE WAR FOR
THE AMERICAN FRONTIER

*Mr. Hoover found himself [in]. We have pulled all the rabbits
out of the hat and there are no more rabbits.*

REPRESENTATIVE MAUREY MAVERICK, 1938

*There can be no military disarmament without economic
appeasement.*

SECRETARY OF STATE CORDELL HULL, 1938

*Unless substantial economic offsets are provided to prevent
this nation from being wholly dependent upon the war expenditures we will sooner or later come to the dilemma which
requires either war or depression.*

JOHN L. LEWIS, C.I.O., 1940

*What interests us primarily is the longer-range question of
whether the American capitalist system could continue to
function if most of Europe and Asia should abolish free enterprise.*

FROM THE FIFTH FORTUNE ROUND TABLE DISCUSSION
ON THE U.S. AND WAR, 1940

Yes, war did come, despite the trade agreements. But it is a fact that war did not break out between the United States and any country with which we had been able to negotiate a trade agreement. It is also a fact that, with very few exceptions, the countries with which we signed trade agreements joined together in resisting the Axis. The political line-up followed the economic line-up.

CORDELL HULL, 1948

Initiated in the 1880's, and formalized in the Open Door Notes of 1899 and 1900, America's imperial expansion seemed on the threshold of legendary triumphs as Herbert Hoover was inaugurated as President in 1929. The domestic economic system was producing more wealth than any competitor. America's power, authority, and prestige throughout the world were enormous and seemed to be expanding as the nation continued to develop, extend, and rationalize its informal empire around the globe. It appeared, indeed, that the foundation and the superstructure of the *Pax Americana,* so candidly avowed by Secretary of State Hughes in 1924, were firmly established.

And so they were, though the events of the years between 1929 and 1945 are still so near and charged with emotion that they often obscure the configuration of American foreign relations during that period. President Hoover had barely established a routine of administrative procedure before the basic assumptions underlying the open-door conception of America and its role in the world were undercut in a fundamental way by the Great Depression. The entire policy was predicated on the proposition that the overweening economic power generated by the American economic system would enable it to overcome competitors and wrong-headed revolutionaries and bestow prosperity and democracy upon the entire world. Yet within two years the American economic system was not providing for its own citizens.

A second event dramatized and extended the domestic crisis of the corporate order. For by the end of Hoover's term in office, it was apparent that the broad revolutionary challenges to America's program for the world, which first appeared to plague President Wilson, were being taken up, in part or in toto, by other major powers. However they distorted or misused the upsurge of dissatisfaction with the status quo, the leaders of Germany, Japan, and Italy were working with the most powerful weapon available—the determination, born equally of desperation and hope, of large numbers of people to improve, radically and immediately, the substance and tone of their daily lives. And though at great hardship and suffering, these revolutions seemed to have survived and converged in a Russia beginning to assert its right and ability to lead the world out of economic and spiritual depression into a better future. Confronted by this domestic and international crisis, American leaders were forced to re-examine their basic outlook, modify it as necessary, and then devise means that would restore and sustain the nation's position in the world.

The key decision made by American leaders, and accepted by the rest of the nation, was a bipartisan agreement to preserve the existing system of corporate capitalism governed according to the existing practices of constitutional democracy. Far from being a revolution, the New Deal was a consensus and a movement to prevent a revolution. Thus it is most aptly defined and described as a movement to provide for the emergency relief, the short-run rehabilitation, and the long-term rationalization of the existing corporate society. Its objective was to define and institutionalize the roles, functions, and responsibilities of three important segments of any industrial society—capital, labor, and the government—and to do so according to the principles of capitalism. In such fundamental ways, therefore, the New Deal continued and developed the central approach and outlook formulated by advocates of a corporate society such as Theodore Roosevelt, Herbert Croly, Herbert Hoover, Bernard Baruch, Gerald Swope, and Samuel Gompers.

While the initial necessity to grapple with the domestic crisis temporarily de-emphasized the foreign policy that was an integral part of that outlook, the New Deal did not signify any fundamental change in the traditional policies of economic and ideological empire. Even in the depths of the depression, and increasingly so in subsequent years, the overseas expansion of the American corporate system was considered a basic means of recovery and further development. Franklin Roosevelt quickly reasserted, moreover, the kind of aristocratic *noblesse oblige* that his cousin Theodore had infused into American diplomacy. He also revealed a good bit of the crusading fervor for the extension of American ideas and ideals that had characterized the outlook and actions of Woodrow Wilson.

Roosevelt's sense of *noblesse oblige* and mission gave his foreign policy a more assertive and expansive tone than was produced by Hoover's emphasis on efficient economic expansion. This difference did not become readily apparent until the mid-1930's, but its early manifestations can be observed in the events of 1929 to 1933. President Hoover's response to Japanese military expansion in Manchuria was conditioned by his long-term objective of establishing a community of interest with Japan in Asia, and by his fear of war as the pump-primer for revolution. He neither liked nor approved of Japan's actions, but he concluded that Japanese expansion was much the lesser evil when judged against Chinese revolutionary nationalism or the Soviet Union. War by itself was dangerous enough, but undertaken in the context of depression it would produce general disaster.

Roosevelt and Stimson shared Hoover's outlook in general. Both men favored working with Japan throughout the 1920's and agreed with Hoover's emphasis on the importance of peace—both generally and in the circumstances of the depression. But they differed with Hoover over the best means of insuring peace. The divergence was the product of two factors: Roosevelt and Stimson came to question Japan's willingness and ability to accept America's conception of the world without coercion of some sort; and they entertained an active sense of America's mission in China. These considerations led them to disagree with Hoover over what should and could be done to sustain peace, even though they were willing to accept his policy under the existing circumstances. Nevertheless, they inclined toward economic pressure and a show of force to warn Japan back toward an acceptance of American leadership in the world community. In 1932 and 1933 this divergence of opinion among American leaders was not severe and dramatic, and it was not acted upon either by Stimson or by Roosevelt, but it did reveal a difference of opinion that became extremely significant within five years.

That willingness to employ economic coercion against Japan at the end of the 1930's seems to be the main explanation for what is a rather general impression that Roosevelt recognized the Soviet Union in 1933 for the purpose of exerting similar pressure on Tokyo. It is true that some Americans like Senator Borah suggested the maneuver very openly. And the Russians did their best to foster that interpretation at the time to improve their own position in dealing with Japan. But it was not the reason Roosevelt acted.

The recognition of Russia was very largely the result of a persistent campaign by large and small business interests who felt that it would lead to a vast increase in their export of goods, capital, and services. Their efforts began in 1926, when the first signs of economic trouble appeared in many industries. For that matter, Hoover began financing such exports through the Reconstruction Finance Corporation before he left office (though neither the President nor Secretary Stimson responded favorably to Borah's proposals). Roosevelt did not recognize the Soviets simply, or only, as an economic move (the first Export-Import Bank, however, was organized explicitly to handle the anticipated export boom). His upper-class urbanity, for example, led him to consider the game of make-believe about the nonexistence of such a major country as something more than slightly ridiculous on the part of the world's most powerful country. And he did want to establish some kind of communication and discussion about peace between the United States and all major nations. But he never considered the kind of an entente sought by the Russians, as was indicated by his persistent refusal to respond to their overtures for a nonaggression pact with China and the Soviet Union.

Short-term as well as traditional long-run economic considerations also played an important role in Roosevelt's dramatic moves to improve and regularize relations with Latin America. The Good Neighbor Policy was infused with the tone and substance of *noblesse oblige* and announced in the rhetoric of

America's mission to defend and extend democracy, but its context was defined by the immediate and specific needs of American businessmen and by the long-range objective of a broad integration of the economy of the United States with that of Latin America. It was Roosevelt's Latin American policy, not his recognition of Russia in 1933, which offered the strongest hint that he entertained from an early date the idea of a major intervention in world politics at some later time. For from the very beginning, the leadership of the United States was asserted, defended, and extended in terms of meeting the European challenge to America's open-door empire in the Western Hemisphere. And the continued development of that interpretation and argument culminated in the treaty organization of the American system. Even so, the European challenge of the early 1930's was economic, not military.

Roosevelt's conception of America's general role in the world, and of its economic expansion, became clearer and more forceful in 1934, when it appeared that the early policies of the New Deal were generating recovery from the depression. This illusion of success enabled the Roosevelt Administration to give more attention to world affairs than it had during its first year in office. The most striking feature of this development was the degree to which Roosevelt and his advisors reasserted the traditional foreign policy of the United States. As with Theodore Roosevelt and John Hay, they assumed the necessity, desirability, and ability of the American economic system to expand throughout the world. And with Woodrow Wilson, they asserted America's leadership in the establishment and maintenance of an orderly peace. At home and abroad, peace and order were the main objectives of the New Deal.

In general, therefore, the United States at first gave ground before the assertiveness of Germany, Japan, and Italy. Neither private corporate nor official political leaders approved all the actions of those powers, but the bipartisan consensus among American leaders during these years was based on acquiescence in Axis actions and appeasement of Axis demands. The underlying attitude was that world problems would be taken care of by American recovery. Various critics did agitate for unilateral action in Europe or Asia, for an entente with the Soviet Union, or for more vigorous alignment with Great Britain and France, but they effected no significant modification, let alone a fundamental change in American policy.

Quite in keeping with traditional policies, American leaders undertook a vigorous campaign during these same years to renew and extend America's economic expansion. The corporations, for example, steadily renewed and extended their overseas operations after 1934. As early as 1928, moreover, Roosevelt had talked of solving domestic economic problems in terms of "exportable surpluses." And from the fall of 1932, Roosevelt and Hull stressed the importance of foreign trade and investment for domestic revival and for controlling conditions abroad which caused wars and revolutions. Based on the proposition that "the political line-up followed the economic line-up," this program for the expansion of the American economic system was presented as the answer to specific and general problems. Inherent in the approach was a definition of trade that went far beyond the idea of an exchange of commodities and services. The denotation of the definition emphasized trade as the expansion and control of markets for America's corporate *system,* while the connotations stressed the control and development of raw-material supplies.

Secretary Hull's reciprocal trade program was designed to meet both needs. The strategy was simple: in return for lowering American tariffs on selected items exported by a foreign country, that nation would decrease its tariffs on certain American exports. And by insisting upon the unrestricted most-favored-nation clause, the United States sought to extend its own potential or actual market even further. In practice, America traded tariff reductions on items which it needed (such as selected raw materials) or on goods which did not seriously challenge producers at home, in return for foreign reductions on American surpluses.

The reciprocity program offers basic insights into New Deal foreign policy and also serves to document its continuity with the decade of the 1890's. First proposed as a key element in foreign policy during the late 1880's, and then tentatively written into law in a limited way in the McKinley Tariff Act of 1890, the concept of reciprocity treaties was taken up by the National Association of Manufacturers in 1895 as an integral part of its drive for foreign markets. From the very beginning, moreover, the principle of the unconditional most-favored-nation clause (by which America gained any benefits extended to other nations) was closely associated with the idea of reciprocity. .

Neither Secretary of State Hull nor any other New Deal policy-maker ever improved very much upon McKinley's clear and candid explanation of the policy. "It is to afford new markets for our surplus agricultural and manufactured products," he had remarked in 1896, "without loss to the American laborer of a single day's work that he might otherwise procure." The statement of purpose written into the first and basic New Deal trade act of 1934 was no more than a rather clumsy reiteration of the outlook and logic evolved by intellectuals, businessmen, and politicians during the Crisis and Depression of the 1890's. The law announced that it was "for the purpose of expanding foreign markets for the products of the United States (as a means of assisting in the present emergency in restoring the American standard of living, in overcoming domestic unemployment and the present economic depression, in increasing the purchasing power of the American public, and in establishing and maintaining a better relationship among various branches of American agriculture, industry, mining, and commerce)."

Secretary Hull had long advocated greatly expanded penetration of Latin American markets, with a complementary influence over that region's sources of raw materials. His move upward from Tennessee politics to the House of Representatives was in considerable measure a result of the reputation and backing he had won by pushing that issue. Actually, of course, his emphasis on exports to Latin America was merely one facet of his almost religious faith in the nineteenth-century doctrine of free trade as a solution to the political and social, as well as economic, ills of the United States and the world. That commitment led him, not unnaturally, to make unfavorable moral judgments of any and all countries which opposed his plan, which tried other techniques of handling foreign trade (such as balancing accounts with each country separately), or which had economic systems that limited the activities of American businessmen (such as Russia and Mexico).

Hull's outlook further provided him with a circular argument involving cause, effect, and prescription that seemed to him, at any rate, unanswerable either by example or logic. Long before the Great Depression actually began, for instance, he predicted and explained such a crisis in terms of his theory. Speaking on January 3, 1929, he first documented the great gap between America's productive capacity and its actual output. Then he noted that there were great surpluses in spite of the idle facilities. "These glaring facts and conditions," he concluded, "soon will compel America to recognize that these ever increasing surpluses are her key economic problems, and that our neglect to develop foreign markets for surpluses is the one outstanding cause of unemployment." Because they were confusing and seemingly indecisive, President Roosevelt's early actions in the foreign trade area apparently upset Hull considerably. In one of his most famous campaign speeches delivered before the Commonwealth Club in San Francisco, for example, Roosevelt referred explicitly and with considerable emphasis to the end of the frontier and implied that this called for a more self-contained and planned economy. It developed later, however, that he had neither written nor studied and evaluated the speech before he stood up and delivered it. Even so, a careful reading of the document reveals that the argument pointed not so much toward national planning as toward finding a new frontier in such areas as foreign trade.

And despite his concern and preoccupation with immediate domestic relief measures, Roosevelt quickly indicated that he was thinking along those lines. Hull understood this. The true source of the Secretary's anxiety (and resentment) resided in the signs that Roosevelt was attracted to the idea of expanding foreign trade through bilateral balancing and bartering with a steadily increasing number of countries. *The issue was never whether or not to continue America's overseas economic expansion, but rather the question of how it should be furthered.* The showdown came over such a bilateral deal negotiated with Germany by George N. Peek, who was challenging Hull for control of foreign trade matters. Hull won. The victory not only opened the way for the reciprocal trade program, but offered one of the earliest indications that Hull was not in fact the kind of secondary figure in New Deal diplomacy that many commentators and historians later assumed. Roosevelt swung over to Hull's policy with an enthusiasm based upon his own commitment to the basic objective. "The full measure of America's high productive capacity is only gained," he warned in 1935, "when our businessmen and our farmers can sell their surpluses abroad." The President went on to reveal (and dramatize) his acceptance of the same either-or attitude that had characterized American thinking on the subject ever since the 1890's. Prosperity and democracy were contingent upon the program. "Foreign markets must be regained if America's producers are to rebuild a full and enduring domestic prosperity for our people. There is no other way if we would avoid painful economic dislocation, social readjustments, and unemployment."

Administration leaders connected with the trade program left no doubt as to its underlying philosophy. Diplomat George S. Messersmith held, for example, that any other approach "would call for a complete rearrangement of the entire economic setup of the United States." But the most significant spokesman was Assistant Secretary of State Francis B. Sayre, a law professor and the son-in-law of Woodrow Wilson, who became chairman of the President's Executive Committee on Commercial Policy. Sayre's departmental and public documents offer an illuminating example of how American policymakers had consciously accepted, and were acting upon, the same analysis developed in the 1890's. "By that time [the 1890's]," Sayre explained, "our national surpluses which could not be sold profitably in this country had come to assume formidable proportions, and it was becoming clear that the loss or curtailment of foreign markets would mean severe economic dislocation." He even quoted McKinley to cinch the point: "The expansion of our trade and commerce is the pressing problem." Sayre laid great and persistent stress on the idea that trade offered the only way to avoid changing the existing political economy. "Unless we can export and sell abroad our surplus production, we must face a violent dislocation of our whole domestic economy."

It is not surprising, therefore, that trade was defined in a most particular and narrow manner. On the one hand, it meant finding and expanding markets—*and making them "secure for the products of the United States."* [Italics mine.] On the other hand, it involved careful studies to pinpoint the countries supplying raw materials to American industry, followed by negotiations to tie those economies to the United States through reciprocal trade treaties.

This New Deal conception of trade as an integral part of the overseas expansion of the economy had three consequences of major importance. All of them operated and influenced events over the long-run as well as during the decade of the 1930's, and all of them contributed significantly to the maturation of the broader tragedy of American diplomacy.

The first was the role of the New Deal in reinvigorating, extending, and sustaining, in the mind of the general public as well as the policy-makers, the traditional view of overseas economic expansion. Lord Keynes and other economists who stressed the role of public spending and other measures to counteract underconsumption and underinvestment did influence New Deal thinking and policies. But they did so within the old system of thought. Their ideas did not displace the existing outlook. Thus the pattern of either-or thinking about representative government and economic welfare was reasserted and even intensified. Different solutions were dismissed because they would undercut the existing order of business and politics.

Secondly, the emphasis on trade expansion, and upon the Open Door Policy, served to define the nature and the causes of danger and conflict in international affairs. As Sayre explained, the trade expansion program was "an instrumentality for throwing the weight of American power and influence against the current disastrous movement toward economic nationalism." It was "only" as the American program was adopted that the United States could "recover her foreign markets." For the New Deal administration as for its predecessors, therefore, American recovery and prosperity were made dependent upon the acceptance of American policies by the rest of the world. By externalizing good, so also was evil externalized: domestic problems and difficulties became issues of foreign policy. In the immediate context of the mid-1930's, and as Roosevelt, Hull, Sayre, and others explicitly noted as

early as 1935, that meant that Germany, Italy, and Japan were
defined as dangers to the well-being of the United States. This
happened before those countries launched military attacks into
or against areas that the United States considered important
to its economic system. It occurred instead as those nations
began to compete vigorously with American entrepreneurs in
Latin America and Asia. In the broader sense, the American
outlook defined as a danger any nation (or group) that challenged or limited such expansion. The successful drive by the
United States in 1962 to define any "Marxist-Leninist" government as an alien and dangerous outlaw in the Western Hemisphere was a projection of the same basic idea.

The third major consequence of New Deal trade philosophy
was the way it sustained, and even deepened, the pattern of
free trade imperialism or informal empire that had evolved
out of British economic policy in the nineteenth century.
America's relationship with the chief suppliers of raw materials became economically and politically ever more imbal-
anced in its own favor. And, at the same time, the policy
reinforced the existing *internal* political economy of those
poorer, weaker nations. For the changes introduced by American penetration served primarily to create islands of modern-
ism that intensified the skewed and inequitable character of
those societies.

In response, many people in these nations began to wonder
if the United States was not merely a more subtle—and hence
more dangerous—imperial power. Americans were shocked or
angered by this reaction, arguing that their policies increased
the national wealth and prestige of the raw-material areas. On
the surface, this seemed to be true in most cases, but the American operators took much of the wealth back to the United
States. Their actions, and those of American political leaders,
also strengthened groups and classes in the underdeveloped
regions that prevented the wealth that remained from being
distributed equitably—or even wisely from a conservative
point of view—or used in a way to initiate and sustain the
balanced development of a poor country. For the most part,
moreover, the pro-American groups were not very democratic
in political and social matters. This further weakened American leadership.

Not only did this aspect of New Deal foreign policy serve to stockpile explosives for future social upheavals, but it can almost be said to have lit the fuses. The tragedy is that none of it was done with evil intent. Good intentions granted, however, that was nevertheless the basic dynamic inherent in the program. For having defined overseas economic activity as essential to the welfare of the United States, American policymakers were exceedingly prone to view social revolution in those countries as a threat to the vital national interests of their own nation. The irony is that while the New Deal did gradually become less militant in defending *individual* American business interests against the actions of underdeveloped countries, it continued at the same time to consolidate the traditional definition of such economic activities as essential to domestic prosperity and political welfare of the United States.

However more openly humanitarian (and more adept with the polished phrase), New Deal leaders did not in action go very far beyond the foreign policy of Hoover until the economic needs of American overseas business enterprise, and the competition from Axis rivals, forced it to do so. Since this may seem too severe a judgment, particularly for the generations which either led or came to maturity under the New Deal, it may be useful to make two points very explicit. The first concerns the sincerity and the liberal sentiments of New Deal policy-makers. No question, direct or indirect, is raised about either characteristic. The second involves something that is generally overlooked; namely, the basic denotation about conduct that is inherent in the famous phrase, "The Good Neighbor Policy." Here the issue is very important even though it is implicit. By American definition, and practice, good neighbors do not rock the boat.

But rocking the boat is precisely what Latin Americans were doing, at least by the standards current in the United States, throughout the 1930's. It was only after many years of intervention and intermeddling that New Deal leaders began to act as well as talk like good neighbors in a more mature and sophisticated manner. The early attitude was revealed by Hull's remark after he had signed a hemispheric pledge in 1933 holding that "no state has the right to intervene in the internal or external affairs of another." Speaking privately, the Secretary commented that the proposition was "more or less wild and unreasonable."

Hull, Roosevelt, and Ambassador Sumner Welles proceeded to act in keeping with the Secretary's judgment in connection with the Cuban Revolution that was under way when they came into office. Pressure exerted through and by Welles first contributed to the final collapse of the old regime headed by Gerardo Machado y Morales. But it was in dealing with the new government headed by Grau San Martín that New Deal interference became persistent and determined. Though it ran Cuba from September 1933, through January 1934, the Grau Government was never recognized by the United States. Secretary Hull and Ambassador Welles made it clear that the ability of Grau to maintain order was *not* the issue. "No government," Welles remarked to Hull during a phone conversation in mid-September, "will be able to maintain absolute order here for some time to come." Both men accepted that as natural under the circumstances. Welles was extremely upset, however, by any and all indications that "a social revolution" was in progress. "Our own commercial and export interests in Cuba," Welles warned in October, "cannot be revived under this government." Viewing the Grau Government as composed of "the most irresponsible elements," the Ambassador was determined to replace it by an instrument of "all the better classes of the country."

Three Cuban groups opposed Grau: the officer corps, the communists, and the business community and its associated politicians. Grau crushed two attempted coups by the officers, a demonstration of power and general support that impressed the British representative but served only to intensify American antagonism. And though certainly spearheaded by Welles, the opposition to Grau was supported by Hull and Roosevelt. Indeed! By the end of 1933, for example, the United States had some 30 Navy ships on station around Cuba. Even more important, at least in some respects, was the way that nonrecognition disrupted the Cuban economy. For that weakened the Grau Government as effectively, if more subtly, as detachments of American Marines doing guard duty throughout the country.

By all accounts, it would seem that President Roosevelt enjoyed his games of verbal hide-and-seek with American reporters who asked him whether or not his policy amounted to intervention. He once told them adamantly that the United States was not intervening at almost the precise hour that Welles was busily engaged in trying to organize a coalition against Grau. Even Welles once admitted to Hull that he was rather embarrassed by "the measure of control" he was exercising in Cuba. Finally, after many false starts, the support and encouragement that Welles and the United States gave to Batista led to the overthrow of the Grau Government.

By the end of the decade, Roosevelt had modified his method of handling Latin American affairs. The change was nevertheless very slow in developing. Bolivia found that out in March 1937, when it annulled the oil concession held by Standard Oil and confiscated the company's property. The United States supported the firm in two ways. It brought pressure on other Latin American countries to prevent Bolivia from obtaining help in developing or selling its oil, and it refused to give Bolivia any economic aid (loans or technical assistance). The latter position was stated very directly in a memorandum of December 26, 1939. "In order to secure the necessary support and cooperation of American private interests [for such aid]," the State Department explained, "it is believed to be essential before American financial assistance is given that a settlement will have been reached." That statement revealed not only the kind of economic intervention that was used against Bolivia, but also the relationship between official policy and the views of large corporate spokesmen. This connection between big business leadership and the government is often misconceived as a simple, direct kind of push-or-pull relationship in which outsiders lean on insiders—or vice versa. Many businessmen as well as many reformers are prone to make that kind of an interpretation. But it is misleading, particularly by the time of the mid-1930's, even though there were (and still are) many examples of such interaction.

But thinking of the New Deal so narrowly (or wholly) as a reform movement tends to blind both its critics and its defenders to the way that it steadily drew more and more of its

leadership from the community of large, established corporation executives, their counsels, and their economic advisors.
This does not necessarily mean that the New Deal became less
reformist. It does mean, however, that the reforms were of a
certain kind; namely, they rationalized the system as it existed,
and did not lead to significant modifications of its character.

This aspect of New Deal leadership offers an important insight into the developments in American policy specifically
toward Latin America, but also more generally, between 1937
and 1941.* It helps explain, for example, the gradual willingness (after mid-1939) to grant a loan to Bolivia on the basis
of a gentleman's agreement that Standard Oil would then be
given prompt satisfaction on its claims. This slow and halting
process of change was brought about by four principal factors.
On the basis of the available evidence, they can be ranked in
the following order of importance.

There was first a general reassertion during and after the
sharp and serious recession of 1937–38 of both central themes
of American diplomacy as it evolved during and after the
Crisis of the 1890's: that vigorous overseas economic expansion
was essential to the functioning of the system; and that, as
stated so explicitly by Secretary of State Root in 1906, policy
had to be formulated so "that the door, being open, shall
lead to something." This feeling, and the new urgency behind
it, was manifested by government spokesmen and also by
leaders of the corporate system who did not hold public office.
Official policy-makers like Lawrence Duggan, Eric Johnston,
and Nelson Rockefeller, for example, advanced this view with
great vigor. But corporation leaders outside the government
shared the same outlook. A group of them meeting in 1939
under the auspices of *Fortune* magazine agreed that it was
important to "provide adequate economic opportunities to the
so-called 'have-not' countries."

Secondly, American private and official leaders were by

---

* My general knowledge and understanding of New Deal diplomacy
has been vastly increased as a result of many long discussions with Professor Lloyd Gardner. We have exchanged research notes and ideas on
an extensive and wholly reciprocal basis. He has contributed greatly to
my comprehension of the development of American policy in Latin
America during the years 1937–1941.

1939 very disturbed by German and Japanese economic competition in Latin America (as well as in Asia). It may be, indeed, that this factor was most important of all. On the other hand, there were many important Americans who felt as late as 1940 that it would be possible to work out some kind of economic compromise with the Axis powers. Two things, however, are certain: Axis competition worried a significant number of men in policy-making positions after 1938, and that concern served to convince some of them that it was necessary to modify some of the existing practices of America's overseas economic expansion in order to protect the expansion itself. Sumner Welles offers a good example of the way that kind of interaction altered earlier attitudes and actions.

The third consideration was the determination on the part of some of the larger Latin American countries, such as Mexico, to stand firm in their efforts to reform, control, and restrict American business activities in their countries. This resistance unquestionably speeded up the modification of American policy.

Fourth, the humanitarian idealism of American policy-makers affected their decisions. Never absent in the making of American policy, it enjoyed a renaissance in the late 1930's. This is no doubt partly explained as a reaction against Axis domestic and foreign policies whose nature was growing more obvious and more disturbing after 1936. But it was also the result of a few strong and even assertive reformers having positions of some authority, probably the best example being Josephus Daniels as Ambassador to Mexico. He not only softened some of Hull's outbursts to the Mexicans, but also enjoyed a direct correspondence with Roosevelt. More significant, however, the existence of a growing crisis by nature involved Roosevelt more directly in all relations with Latin America. And that brought his sense and spirit of *noblesse oblige* more actively into the policy-making process.

The developing and on-going interaction of these four factors can be seen and followed in the renewed crisis with Mexico over American oil properties. The election in 1934 of President Lázaro Cárdenas led to a resurgence of revolutionary enthusiasm and a program of vigorous reform legislation. After concentrating on domestic property issues for two years,

Cárdenas pushed through in November 1936, a law providing the government with authority to move against foreign companies that controlled oil resources. The American response was prompt and negative. Hull minced no words. "It would be extremely unfortunate," he commented in August 1937, "if any action should be taken by the Mexican authorities which would jeopardize the [American oil] industry in any manner."

Hull was concerned about the Mexican situation in several broad and fundamental respects. The threat in Mexico was only the specific issue. For one thing, he was worried about the impact of such action in countries like Venezuela, where Standard Oil had developed huge operations, or in Bolivia, which would be encouraged in its own expropriation battle. It might also slow down or disrupt entirely the efforts that were under way to win a favorable settlement of outstanding economic issues with Brazil. Thus the United States made it clear, even before any expropriation had actually taken place, that loans to Mexico would be held up indefinitely.

Other considerations made it difficult, however, to settle upon a policy of unmitigated opposition to Mexico. Ambassador Daniels in Mexico City and Secretary of the Treasury Henry Morgenthau were both beginning to fear Axis economic competition. Daniels argued that it was imperative to expand trade with Mexico, both for its own sake and to keep the door closed against Germany and Japan. Morgenthau was even more emphatic, probably because of his deep horror at Nazi persecution of Jews. "We're just going to wake up and find inside of a year," he fretted in December 1937, "that Italy, Germany, and Japan have taken over Mexico." In a similar way, State Department policy-makers like Adolph A. Berle, Jr., and corporation leaders like Juan Trippe of Pan American Airways, were upset by German airline activity in the region. "We initiated a campaign," Berle remarked tartly, "to clear these lines out."

Some policy-makers were emphasizing the need for developmental loans that would lead to expanded trade and investment throughout Latin America. This need had been intensified by the recession of 1937. Along with businessmen who experienced the difficulties in their daily operations, men like

Duggan understood one of the fundamental problems of dealing with the Latin American economies. They were in many respects so backward and rudimentary that it was almost impossible to link them up with the economic system of the United States in any effective, efficient, and profitable manner. It did little good, for example, to have the Export-Import Bank grant a loan to an American manufacturer to finance a shipment if he could not even transport the goods inland to potential consumers. Similar difficulties faced Americans who wanted to expand and rationalize the collection and shipment of raw materials. Beginning in 1938 with a loan to Haiti for building roads and drainage projects (and followed by a similar arrangement that Welles negotiated with Brazil in March 1939), the New Deal began to finance the very kind of operations that Hoover had called for a decade earlier. There was, of course, one rather significant difference. Hoover wanted American entrepreneurs to make the loans. The New Deal used public funds supplied by taxpayers.

The complications and complexities of these efforts to cope with the problems of economic expansion in Latin America were certainly sufficient to account for the intensity of the American reaction to Mexico's move against the oil companies. Granted Hull's assumptions, it does not require much imagination to understand his anger, worry, and concern. Those feelings were intensified, at the very time it became clear that Mexico was going to use the expropriation law, by Japan's renewed military operations in China in July 1937. Hull's commitment to the Open Door Policy in Asia was complete and unequivocal, and Japan's attack unquestionably influenced the New Deal's handling of the crisis with Mexico. Indeed, President Cárdenas expropriated American oil properties on March 18, 1938, at the very moment the Congress was considering President Roosevelt's request for a dramatic increase in the Navy. In response, Hull forgot the rhetoric of the Good Neighbor Policy and fired off an ultimatum. It was fortunately deflected by Ambassador Daniels and finally ricocheted into the Mexican Foreign Office as an unofficial document. Daniels was deeply concerned with better relations and "increased trade" with Mexico, and he realized that Hull's initial fear and anger might create a situation which could be resolved only through force. And Daniels had learned about the diminishing returns of military action while serving in the Navy Department when President Wilson had tried that method of dealing with Mexico.

Hull acquiesced in Daniels' maneuver (a fact often slurred over by those who praise the Ambassador); but he and other policy-makers in Washington retreated only far enough to pick up the weapon of economic coercion. They planned to force Mexico to accept arbitration of the issue. The ban on loans was continued. An effort was made to cut into Mexican dollar reserves by manipulating the price it received for its silver exports. And, finally, the government gave unofficial approval to the efforts by the oil companies to keep Mexico's newly nationalized industry from developing the country's resources and entering the world market with its petroleum.

There the crisis rested until July 1940, when the United States agreed, in view of "circumstances presently impending," to go along with the Mexican counterproposal to settle the conflict by appointing a joint commission to work out a compromise.* That diplomatic phrase about circumstances obviously referred to the accelerating pace of German and Japanese expansion, and to the increasing opposition manifested by the United States. Those were the most important considerations in determining the *timing* of the American decision to sit down with the Mexicans at the negotiating table. Even so, the community of American policy-makers was still split as late as the fall of 1941 over whether to hold out in the joint commission talks until Mexico's need for American investment capital modified its offer on compensation to the oil companies.

Considered alone, the combined economic and strategic challenge from the Axis could, and might well, have prompted the United States to maintain its intransigence (and even to increase its economic pressures). That was, after all, the course followed in dealing with Argentina. Such a might-have-been proposition is useful primarily to help clarify the reason that it did not occur. And that seems clearly to have been because Roosevelt was reached and persuaded by those policy-makers who insisted upon the need for a sophisticated reform in the

---

* Mexico's offer to embargo the shipment of certain strategic minerals to the Axis powers contributed to the change in American policy.

methods of America's overseas economic expansion. The Duggan-Rockefeller-Johnston group had worked out a broad tactical conception which, as Professor Lloyd Gardner has described it, amounted to modifying the *laissez faire* system of Adam Smith so that separate national economies rather than individuals were defined as the entrepreneurs.

Now it is true, at least in one sense, that this was not so much an adaptation of Adam Smith as simply a decision to honor in practice the precepts of the theory as originally stated. Smith did lay great emphasis on the international division of labor, and that one point could be (and was) interpreted to mean that raw-material producing countries remained raw-material producing countries even though they became more efficient. But Smith also stressed freedom of enterprise where the resources existed, and many nations which in 1939 were still raw material producers enjoyed human and material resources that were capable of building and sustaining far more diversified economies. *To a certain extent, and one still to be controlled and structured by the economy and the policies of the United States, this latter interpretation of Smith is the one advanced by the sophisticated American reformers.* The idea was to create somewhat more diversified political economies under the direction of the United States. The economic objectives were more markets and more efficiently produced raw materials. The political objective was middle-class government stabilized in a pro-American posture.

Roosevelt himself put it as neatly—and as revealingly—as anyone ever did in his casual remark of 1940. "[There is] a new approach that I am talking about to these South American things. Give them a share." It was to be a more generous share. It was to be a more intelligently defined share. And it was to be a share that might ultimately produce more psychological and social welfare along with a larger gross national income in the South American countries. But it was still a share to be granted by the United States.

Since Mexico is often pointed to as the glowing example of the success of this New Deal version of the Open Door strategy, it seems useful to digress briefly and examine the claim. Mexico unquestionably benefited from its ever more intimate economic integration with the United States after 1940. The economy became more diversified, the national income increased significantly, and the daily lives of some Mexicans became easier and more affluent. Let this be granted as the achievement.

The caveats and questions which remain are nevertheless very crucial. First: it should be recalled that the policies of the open door and the good neighbor were supposed to create prosperity and welfare in the underdeveloped countries as well as in the United States, and to do so short of war. They should be judged by their own claims. And by that standard they have not succeeded. The difference between the Mexico of 1935 and the Mexico of 1962 is not the result of the Open Door Policy and the Good Neighbor Policy functioning in a period of peace. *The improvement that has been made since 1935 is very largely the product of World War II and the Cold War.*

Second: the claim as stated neglects entirely the psychological, social, and even economic results of American expansion into Mexico. Here again the evidence is strongly negative. Mexicans discovered by 1961 that they were steadily losing effective control of some areas of their economy. Indeed, it was a conservative government that began in that year to consider and act upon measures designed to regain some measure of that authority. As for the oil industry itself, American companies won their secondary objective: because of being excluded from the private international government of oil and because of Mexico's shortage of investment capital over which it exercised full control, the nationalized industry has never contributed its potential share of the nation's development.

Third, and in a more general sense (that is often neglected), it is hardly too much to say that the Mexican political economy maintains a precarious stability only because it sloughs off into the United States, in the form of legal and illegal migratory and transient labor, a sizable portion of its own population. That group of *braceros* is increasing by a million people a year. Americans think of those men, women, and children as employed workers. But they actually form a huge unemployment problem in Mexico. Neither the existence of that mass of ill-used human beings, nor the way they are dealt with, can be adduced as proof of a sound and healthy system.

Finally, millions of Mexicans still live in poverty. They are not just middle-class people in debt beyond their means. They

are not simply poor. They live in poverty. Hence it is both
practically and morally necessary, before praising American
policy as the benefactor of the Mexican Revolution, to consider the sober and yet deeply moving estimate presented by
anthropologist Oscar Lewis in his classic study of *The Children of Sánchez.* His judgment on the migratory workers, for
example, is this: "Were the United States suddenly to close its
borders to the *braceros,* a major crisis would probably occur
in Mexico." But his most telling comments come in the context of his stark review of American penetration. American
investment totalled almost $1,000,000,000 as of 1960. And the
major television programs are sponsored and controlled by
American firms. But the chronic inflation since 1940, when
American influence began to rise so dramatically and continually, has raised the cost of living for workers in Mexico
City some 400 per cent. And the "uneven distribution of the
growing national wealth has made the disparity between the
incomes of the rich and the poor more striking than ever before." "At least the lower third of the rural and urban population" know only what Lewis calls "the culture of poverty."
He characterizes it as a "constant struggle for survival, unemployment and underemployment, low wages . . . child labor,
the absence of savings, a chronic shortage of cash . . . crowded
quarters, a lack of privacy, . . . a high incidence of alcoholism,
[and] frequent resort to violence." As for the improvement and
development that has occurred, Lewis offers a judgment that is
far closer to the truth than any explanation which stresses the
role of American influence. "It is the poor who emerge as the
true heroes of contemporary Mexico, for they are paying the
cost of the industrial progress of the nation." Unfortunately,
the New Deal adaptation of Adam Smith did not prove sufficient unto the task of transforming the promises of the Open
Door Policy into reality.

American policy-makers also discovered, again in a way
contrary to its axioms and expectations, that the strategy of
the open door did lead to war. None of them wanted war.
They did not plot to involve the United States in armed conflict with the Axis. Indeed, and as symbolized by Roosevelt's
support of the Munich Agreement of 1938 between Nazi Germany and Great Britain, they tried very seriously and persistently to accomplish their objectives without war. But given

their *Weltanschauung,* their explanation of how the prosperity and welfare of the United States was to be achieved and
maintained, they had no recourse but war. And as it happened,
the United States was engaged in a shooting conflict with
Germany before Japan struck Hawaii. The question of how
and when that combat would have formally been joined if the
Japanese had not attacked Pearl Harbor is fascinating but
nevertheless irrelevant to an understanding of how American
leaders came to accept the necessity of violence. It is also possible, perhaps even probable, that they would have reached
that decision even if they had not entertained a frontier-
expansionist conception of history. But again, and however
pertinent it may be for later consideration, that hypothetical
question is not germane to an explanation of how the United
States did actually become involved in World War II.

Perhaps the most helpful way to approach that problem is
by reviewing the attitudes toward foreign policy that existed
after Roosevelt had been in office two full years. Encouraged
by the economic revival that seemed in 1935 to herald a general recovery from the depression, the community of public
and private decision-makers looked ahead to a continuing
extension of overseas economic activities. Those men also reasserted their conviction that such expansion would prevent
foreign revolutions (and future depressions in the United
States itself) and that peace was essential to recovery at home
and profitable operations abroad.

Beyond those areas of agreement, however, the policy-makers
split into differing—and often bitterly antagonistic—groups.
Two main features of their dialogue and argument must be
kept in mind if the evolution of policy is to be understood.

First: these divisions over policy not only cut across political
lines, but also across what was by then an increasingly artificial
boundary between private economic (including labor) leadership and formal office holders. The decision-making community at all times included men of great power and influence
outside the government as well as those inside the nation's
official establishment. Thus the support for a given policy
always came from men in both groups. The natural corollary
was that both the private leadership and the government
bureaucracy disagreed among themselves as well as with mem-

bers of the other bloc. One striking result of this hammering out of a consensus on policy between 1935 and 1941 was that a consolidated corporate group emerged under the banner of bipartisanship for security and prosperity. That coalition came to enjoy a very extensive measure of control over foreign policy. Often, for example, their internal debates were not even known to—let alone participated in by—their critics or the general public. And their broad authority over both private and official information and news media further closed down the discussion of alternatives.

It is vital to understand this pattern of power if the role and the authority of the military itself is not to be exaggerated. Beginning in 1938 and 1939, the evolving corporate coalition of private and official leaders called in the military to execute a policy that they—*the civilians*—were formulating and adopting. *It was the civilians who defined the world in military terms, not the military who usurped civilian powers.* Once the military had been called in, they quite naturally gained more influence because the situation had been defined in a way that put a premium on their particular knowledge and experience. But a change in the definition of reality would decrease the power of the military. Even granting a generous measure of new authority, the military had not even by 1962 established themselves in an independent and superior position. Along with recognizing that fact, it is essential to remember that it was the civilians who called in the military, and that they did so between 1935 and 1941.

Second: the argument within the policy-making community developed around four issues. At the outset, by 1935, the debate concerned whether or not it was possible to work out some compromise with the Axis powers. That discussion shaded into an argument about whether the effort to remain neutral in another war would lead to an economic depression through the loss of overseas markets. Then, in 1937, the majority, who still held feasible some kind of accommodation without war, began to divide over whether or not to coerce the Axis into an acceptable settlement by using economic sanctions and the threat of military force (if not its actual use in combat short of a formal declaration of war). Finally, and beginning in 1939 after the Nazi victory over Poland, there opened a final argument over whether or not it would be necessary for the United States to become a total and formal belligerent. Though that angry debate was settled by the Japanese, it seems apparent that the policy-makers and the public were reaching, however reluctantly, the conclusion that war was necessary.

The detailed reconstruction of that evolution into trial by arms has yet to be made by any historian or group of historians.* But it is possible to characterize the changing attitudes of various groups and personalities within the corporate leadership of the country, and to outline the main phases of the debate. One of these was the argument over neutrality policy that began early in the 1930's with a discussion of blocking the sale of munitions to belligerents in another war. American leaders (and the public at large) generally agreed on the wisdom of that restriction, but they rapidly drew back from any commitment to full neutrality when it became apparent that such a policy would undercut existing and prospective overseas economic expansion.

Along with the strikingly frightened reaction of American leaders to the threat posed to exports and foreign investments by the outbreak of World War I, this marked fear in the 1930's about the economic consequences of real neutrality offers impressive proof of the degree to which Americans *thought* their domestic welfare depended upon overseas economic activity.† Theoretical and statistical arguments concerning the actual extent of that dependence are of course relevant, particularly in connection with any consideration of alternate foreign policies, but this idea about its great importance is the crucial factor in understanding and interpret-

---

* The two volumes by W. L. Langer and S. E. Gleason, *The Challenge to Isolation,* and *The Undeclared War* (New York: Harper and Bros., 1952, 1953), have a general but undeserved reputation as being the last word. Another approach, fairly represented in a collective volume edited by H. E. Barnes, *Perpetual War for Perpetual Peace* (Caxton, Idaho: Caxton Printers, Ltd., 1953), is challenging but by no means definitive. The best single volume is P. W. Schroeder, *The Axis Alliance and Japanese-American Relations* (Ithaca: Cornell University Press, 1958).

† Some of the most revealing evidence concerning this response to the World War I situation is to be found in the *Hearings before the Special Senate Committee Investigating the Munitions Industry* (39 parts: Washington: Government Printing Office, 1934–1936).

ing American foreign policy in the 1930's— and in subsequent decades. Americans thought and believed that such expansion was essential, and their actions followed from that supposition.

This became apparent early in the discussion which developed around the ideas of Charles Warren, an international lawyer who had served President Wilson as an Assistant Attorney General prior to 1917. Warren argued that the only way to avoid involvement in a future war was to abandon all claims to neutral rights and rest content with whatever trade the belligerents would permit. In the face of prompt opposition, he shortly modified his original proposal by suggesting that trade with belligerents be limited to the average amount carried on during a five year period prior to the outbreak of hostilities.

Secretary Hull and other key advisors in the State Department, and such quasi-official figures in the corporation community as Allen Dulles, continued to criticize even Warren's revised plan as a surrender of traditional rights and as a body blow to American commerce. As might have been expected, many businessmen joined the attack on Warren. No doubt influenced by Senator Gerald P. Nye's investigation of the traffic in munitions at the time of World War I, and even in the period of peace thereafter, the pro-trade group accepted the need for an arms embargo. But everyone actually involved in the debate, if not all those who followed it in the popular press, knew that the commerce in arms was not the central issue.

The crucial point involved trade in other manufactured goods, and in raw or semi-processed materials. Not only were those the products sought by belligerents, but they were the items that Americans wanted to sell abroad. Senator Nye understood and defined the dilemma as early as 1935. "My own belief," he concluded, "is that a complete embargo on trade is the only absolute insurance against the United States being drawn into another prolonged major war between great powers. I am convinced that drastic legislation to accomplish this could not be passed even in time of peace."*

---

* This analysis and interpretation was originally prepared from materials in the National Archives, manuscript collections of such figures as

Nye had strong reasons for reaching such a conclusion. Secretary Hull and Herbert Feis of the State Department argued quite openly that restrictions of that kind on American overseas economic activity would be extremely harmful if not disastrous to the nation's economy. In a typical bit of calculated understatement, for example, the Secretary observed that a general embargo would be "undesirable." The bipartisan nature of this resistance to real economic neutrality was indicated by the agreement of Henry Cabot Lodge, Jr. And Roosevelt was warned in 1935 by the President of the New York Chamber of Commerce that "exporters and merchants on our eastern seaboard are now more interested in the freedom of the seas for American ships than at any time since the World War." The same view was advanced by General Motors, the giant cotton firm of Anderson, Clayton, and even by the Business Advisory Council of the Department of Commerce.

One of the bluntest analyses of these economic considerations was offered by Edwin Borchard, an outstanding professor of international law at Yale who was deeply concerned to strengthen American neutrality. Commenting in 1936 on proposed legislation that followed some of Warren's early ideas, Borchard warned that "we are likely to begin to lose our markets the minute this bill is passed." "Nobody," he feared, "has apparently thought through the full effects of this legislation." Those consequences would be "revolutionary" because they involved the issue of "self-sufficiency." Neutrality of that kind was dangerous because it would "incite disorders and distress at home."

Senator Key Pittman's judgment of the situation in 1936 made it clear that Borchard underestimated the extent to

---

President Roosevelt and Senator Borah, the *Congressional Record,* and the various investigations into neutrality undertaken by the Congress during the late 1920's and the 1930's. Just as this manuscript was going to press, however, I had the good fortune to receive an advance copy of R. A. Divine, *The Illusion of Neutrality* (Chicago: University of Chicago Press, 1962), which deals with the fight over neutrality within a similar framework. I have borrowed this quotation from Nye, and a later one from Pittman, from Professor Divine, who found them during his research in the manuscript files of the congressional committees.

which government and business leaders had in fact very carefully "thought through the full effects of this legislation."
"The necessity for foreign commerce is so great and political
pressure at this particular time is so strong," Pittman explained, that it was unrealistic to expect real neutrality legislation. The compromise was Cash-and-Carry Neutrality, a concept and an idea apparently conceived by Bernard Baruch.
The long-term result of that approach was clear even at the
time of its adoption by the Congress—it created an economic
alliance between the United States and Great Britain.

Even before that implicit connection led to formal political
and military discussions and agreements, however, American
leaders were defining the Axis powers as dangerous economic
rivals in Latin America. That conflict played an early and significant role in the thinking of decision-makers about the possibilities and probabilities of war with Germany and Italy,
and even with Japan. Much of the shift toward a policy of
vigorous opposition short of formal belligerence took place
in connection with Axis activities in Latin America. In the
intellectual and emotional sense, that is to say, an important
number of American leaders began to go to war against the
Axis in the Western Hemisphere.

This attitude was intensified in those who already held it,
and adopted by others, as a result of two events during 1937–
1938. One was the Spanish Civil War, and the other was the
Japanese attack in China. Although the Spanish conflict generated more emotional involvement and more vociferous agitation, particularly in the populous Eastern part of the country,
the Japanese action made a more significant impact within
the policy-making community. This was in part due to the
triumph in Spain of General Francisco Franco, who was openly
supported by Germany and Italy. His total victory liquidated
the issue. If the Republican Government had held out for a
longer period, as did the Chinese, it is possible that the Spanish Civil War would have brought the United States into a
general European coalition against Germany before Japan attacked Pearl Harbor. That is possible but not very probable.
Spain served to arouse and involve two rival groups in the
United States, but they were quite unevenly matched in power
and influence. The reformers who opposed fascism and thought

it was time to slow or halt its ideological, political, and military momentum did mount a dynamic public campaign in behalf of their policy. But it is highly doubtful that a majority of those reformers favored direct American intervention. The opposition in the debate, especially the hierarchy of the Catholic Church and a broad segment of private and public Protestant leaders, enjoyed much more influence. As a result, the Roosevelt Administration followed a policy of strict and formal neutrality which weakened the Republican Government. American policy in its deeper nature is rather well characterized by a bit of chronology: Franco captured Madrid on March 28, 1939, and the United States recognized his government on April 1, 1939.

Japan's attack in China on July 7, 1937, which followed upon its withdrawal from the London Naval Conference in 1936, had a far greater effect on the entire community of American policy-makers. Several considerations explain this difference. The most important of these was the emphasis on Asia as the Eldorado of America's overseas economic expansion ever since the time of the Sino-Japanese War in 1894, which had led to the strategy of the Open Door Policy. This had always been focused on China, even though tactical and other considerations had prompted economic and political dealings with Japan that sometimes seemed to create a different impression. It is at most a slight exaggeration to say that China was by 1937 firmly established in the minds of most American policy-makers, *and even below the level of conscious thought,* as the symbol of the new frontier of America's ideological and economic expansion. This was as true for those who advocated working through and with Japan as it was for others who persistently agitated for a stronger direct effort in China. The commitment to China was much greater than the identification with any European power except England—and possibly France. This cast of mind and emotion, this utopian image, was strengthened and infused with new substance between 1935 and 1937 by very practical economic developments. A significant number of private and official decision-makers became convinced during those years that the long-awaited blossoming of China as a market was finally under way. There was, as one of them phrased it, a "new spirit" of confidence that the open door was about to lead to something big and profitable.

This enthusiasm was the offspring of two economic facts. One involved the way that China had actually begun to modernize its own system; that meant it was buying more and more industrial goods and services from the United States. The other concerned American trade with China. After a slump during the 1920's, it began to increase very rapidly. In 1932, for the first time in over a decade, American-Chinese trade totalled more than Chinese-Japanese trade. That exciting trend continued, moreover, through the next two years. This led, in 1935, to a little remembered but very significant liaison between the National Foreign Trade Council and various people and groups (including a bloc in the State Department) who held official positions in the Roosevelt Administration. The result was two-fold. Men inside the government who favored implementing the Open Door Policy by dealing directly with China and taking a firmer stand against Japan became more active in policy discussions. And the N.F.T.C. organized a quasi-official American Economic Mission to the Far East. Headed by W. Cameron Forbes, it visited Japan and China for the purpose of gathering data upon which to base future policy.

Upon his return, Forbes announced that there was little enthusiasm for the mission in Japan. "In China, on the other hand," he reported, "American participation and American investment along all lines was sought." He then spelled out the implications by reminding American businessmen that in 1935 they had outscored Japan in trade with China to the amount of some $22,000,000. Finally, he made it clear that it was time to use firm pressure to keep the door open. "This policy of the open door does not seem to have been observed in the conduct of affairs in Manchuria." Should that Japanese conduct be extended to more of China, he warned, "there will inevitably be built up a greater and greater resistance." Japan's attack was particularly disturbing to Forbes and men who shared his outlook because it came at a time when American economic activity in China "was considered especially bright." "Probably never in its history," Forbes remarked in his judgment on the assault, "has China offered greater promise for its future trade, industry, and general economic progress than . . . just prior to the outbreak of the present hostilities." Nor were the implications limited to China, or to Forbes and his followers. In 1937, for example, Asia furnished 51.5 per cent of all raw and crude materials imported into the United States. British Malaya and the Dutch East Indies supplied 86 per cent of its crude rubber and 87 per cent of its tin. Asia provided, in addition, 85 per cent of its tungsten, a third of its mica, 99 per cent of its jute, and 98 per cent of its shellac.

This confrontation between, on the one hand, America's specific and general economic interests and expectations and, on the other hand, Japan's move south into China, affected the posture and the policy of the United States very directly. Through September and October 1937, the issue was debated very vigorously within the State Department in preparation for the Brussels Conference on the Far East. The argument took the traditional form: some wanted to make a strong stand with China, a smaller group suggested working with the Russians, and others reiterated that it was necessary to follow the tactic of trying to control Japan.

At this juncture, the Soviet Union renewed the traditional Russian bid for an entente with the United States. Its spokesmen warned American officials at Brussels that, while the offer was wholly sincere, it might well represent the last stand of those in the Kremlin who advocated collaboration with the Western Powers against the Axis. Russia felt it "had taken some terrible beatings" while striving to work out such an alliance, and it might very soon change its policy and emphasize unilateral moves to insure its own security. (The general assumption that the Soviets can never be trusted in such situations is not borne out by the Brussels experience. The failure of the conference did verify the warnings given to American policy-makers. The decline in influence of Maxim Litvinov, and of the pro-Western views he advocated, can be dated from that time. American policy-makers continued to make this kind of error in dealing with the Soviet Union, however, right down to 1962.)

Roosevelt seems to have considered, however briefly, a more positive response to this overture. But his final instructions followed the pro-Japanese line. He defended his choice by arguing that, short of war, Japan could be stopped only by arranging a truce in China. Even so, the American policy at Brussels was based on extracting extensive concessions from China. It may be that the President had even then concluded that war was all but inevitable, and was only buying time with a down payment provided by the Chinese. It seems more probable, however, that Roosevelt and Hull felt that unilateral American economic and military pressure would force the Japanese to retreat. They were no doubt encouraged in this traditional assumption behind the strategy of the Open Door Policy by the speed with which Japan accepted American demands for an apology, reparations, and promises for the future in connection with the sinking of the Navy river gunboat *Panay* in December 1937.

There is no doubt, in any event, that the United States proceeded very quickly after the Brussels Conference to reassert and act upon both its frontier-expansionist outlook and its traditional strategy of the Open Door Policy. Hull clarified that with one blunt remark on February 19, 1938, shortly after the administration had asked for a huge increase in naval construction. "There can be no military disarmament," he explained, "without economic appeasement. . . . Only healthy international trade will make possible a full and stable domestic economy." And by "healthy international trade," Hull obviously and exclusively meant trade defined in American terms.

Assistant Secretary Sayre reviewed the events of 1937 and 1938 a bit more laconically: "The economic world became a battlefield in which the issues were sometimes political as well as economic." And military as well as political, he might have added. But the most classic explanation of the crisis was offered by William S. Culbertson, who had begun his service as an economic advisor and policy-maker on trade matters under President Wilson, had continued to exercise such influence in the 1920's, and was still active in the New Deal period. "Our economic frontiers," he remarked, "are no longer coextensive with our territorial frontiers." No one ever offered a more succinct description and interpretation of the single most important aspect of twentieth-century American diplomacy—

either in general, or pertaining explicitly to the nation's involvement in World Wars I and II.

Administration leaders in Congress made the same point in less striking style during the consideration in the late winter of 1938 of Roosevelt's bill for the expansion of the Navy. In a long debate that was far more revealing of the nature of American foreign policy than were the arguments over the Neutrality Acts of 1935, 1936, and 1937, New Deal Senators David I. Walsh and Tom Connally stressed two factors. They began by pointing to German and Japanese activity in Latin America and cautioned that it was necessary to be "very careful" about such competition. Their conclusion was a warning that the danger might rapidly become greater.

Then they compared the American economic system to the British Empire. "We, too, have trade routes," Walsh explained. "It is estimated by our experts that unless we are able to keep open certain trade routes the United States could not maintain itself more than two years without being defeated by a powerful enemy." Any delay in building a big Navy would court final surrender. "We cannot build battleships in time of war unless we keep the trade routes open to bring in manganese. We cannot make munitions in time of war unless we keep the trade routes open to bring in certain essential raw materials." Backed by such leadership and logic, the bill passed the House of Representatives 294 to 100, and the Senate 56 to 28.

Armed with this steel in his diplomatic glove, Secretary Hull called for a moral embargo on shipments to Japan in June 1938. Six months later the United States loaned China $25,000,000. And in July 1939, it denounced its commercial treaty with Japan. One segment of the policy-making community which had access to governmental authority was clearly moving to stop the Japanese by economic pressure and the threat of force. A spokesman of that group who was also an active member of the Council on Foreign Relations put it very bluntly. "Seen in its Far Eastern setting," William Diebold, Jr., explained, "our concept of commercial policy expands. . . . It becomes our most potent instrument of foreign policy, a long-range weapon with which to settle the fate of nations."

That intensity and tempo of opposition was not apparent,

however, in dealings with Germany in 1938 and 1939. And it slacked off for more than a year in affairs with Japan. The reason for this lies in the ambivalence and the split within the community of American policy-makers. Fears of war and hopes of compromise with the Axis were still very strong. John L. Lewis and other leaders in the C.I.O., for example, manifested that combination of attitudes very clearly. Aware and concerned by 1939 that the United States was "gradually being driven out of trade relationships with the various markets of the world," Lewis did not turn to war or preparations for war as a solution. He first accepted the reality that "the open door is no more" in Asia. Then he advocated an increased effort in Latin America to take up the slack. Government loans should be granted to provide the peons with buying power. Lewis shared the feeling of the steel workers that foreign policy should not "be formulated or made dependent upon the protection of the vested or property interests in foreign countries of the large corporations in this country." Of course, labor leaders feared such preparations for war as the draft, because the government—and its industrial contractors—could then control the conditions and the market for labor. Lewis saw the squeeze and disliked it. "Unless substantial economic offsets are provided to prevent this nation from being wholly dependent upon the war expenditures," he cried out in anguish in 1940, "we will sooner or later come to the dilemma which requires either war or depression."

Corporation leaders and their associates were caught in the same corner, as were other policy-makers who held positions in the government. The great majority of American leaders emerged from World War I fearing war as the midwife of international revolution and domestic unrest. A good many of them remained unconvinced even by 1939 that it was the greater part of wisdom to make war in order to make peace. Worried about "world-wide ruin," and frightened of the political and social consequences of "another generation of misery," such leaders opposed war as a "great destroyer and unsettler of their affairs." Bernard Baruch, for example, thought that "the institutions of government, as we have known them, [would] fall down . . . and that the whole moral attitude of the world would change." Many corporation leaders and a significant though probably smaller number of national politicians extended that line of reasoning on through the 1930's. They argued that serious preparation for war would subvert the kind of political economy they equated with freedom and democracy. "As certain as night follows day," asserted the editors of *Iron Age* in 1939, "while we were fighting to crush dictatorships abroad, we would be extending one at home."

"It is fairly certain," agreed a corporation executive who was prominent in the financial and policy affairs of the America First Committee, "that capitalism cannot survive American participation in this war." Others broadened the analysis, seeing American intervention as leading "to the end of capitalism all over the world" with a resulting "spread of communism, socialism, or fascism in Europe and even in the United States." Winthrop W. Aldrich spoke from a similar estimate in his remarks to the National Foreign Trade Council shortly after the Munich Agreement of 1938 had been signed. "We ought to take full advantage of the opportunity for the continuance of peace which has resulted from the events of the last few weeks," he advised in very strong terms. "It is of paramount importance that the efforts of the diplomats and of the heads of governments should speedily be reinforced by measures of economic appeasement." The depth and power of the crosscurrents within the community of policy-makers is clearly revealed by Aldrich's remarks. He was head of the Chase National Bank, which not only was a very powerful element in the Federal Reserve System, but also handled most of the Soviet Union's transactions in the United States. He was advising conciliation with the Axis while Secretary of State Hull was militantly fighting the pressures for such economic appeasement.

Tormented by their estimates of the consequences of intervention, leaders of the Aldrich bent argued, when pressed to the wall, that America could and should avoid war by building and integrating an impregnable empire in the Western Hemisphere or that it could and should assert America's ultimate supremacy by waiting for the belligerents to exhaust themselves. Senator Harry S. Truman was one of the politicians who inclined toward the latter proposal. "The role of this great Republic," he explained in October 1939, "is to save civilization; we must keep out of war." Later, after the Nazis attacked Russia, he went so far as to suggest aiding both of them in such a way as to promote their mutual exhaustion.

The way those attitudes began to change was nicely revealed in the course of a discussion among leading businessmen held late in 1939 under the auspices of *Fortune* magazine. The participants formally and vigorously rejected entry into the war. But almost everything else they said indicated either that they expected American involvement or that they were still trying with considerable success to avoid facing the fact that the things they did want could not be obtained short of war. No war, they agreed, and then voted "unanimously" to oppose giving way to Japan's New Order in Asia. No war, they reiterated, and then flatly refused even to discuss the possibility of a more self-contained economy. Overseas economic expansion was mandatory. No war, they repeated, and then agreed that the Philippines had to be defended in order to protect "the rich resources" of Southeast Asia. No war, they concluded, and proceeded to reject "abandonment of the U.S. world position through surrendering neutral rights, adopting economic self-containment, or acquiescing in Japanese demands in the Orient."

The contradictions became somewhat blatant when they went on to discuss "the important tasks confronting the next peace." "What interests us primarily," the businessmen explained in perfect candor, "is the longer-range question of whether the American capitalist system could continue to function if most of Europe and Asia should abolish free enterprise." Their conclusion was not too surprising: the next peace settlement would have "to organize the economic resources of the world so as to make possible a return to the system of free enterprise in every country."

It required very little more Axis expansion to push men who were that ambivalent over to the side of intervention. They were further exhorted and encouraged by industrial leaders like James A. Farrell of the steel industry, who had been agitating for more expansion, and more militant opposition to the Axis, for at least two years. "Our internal economy," Farrell explained in 1938, "is geared to export trade on an increasingly higher level. . . . We must be prepared," therefore, "to increase our outlets abroad for manufactured products or make adjustments of far-reaching consequences." Hence to Farrell it was "imperative that business interests and government agencies act together to assure American business a proportionate and equitable share in the [world's] trade. . . . The door of equal opportunity to all trading areas should be kept open." Farrell strongly implied that war would come: "It suffices to say that no compromise seems possible between [economic] doctrines so wide apart in principle."

The Business Advisory Council of the Roosevelt Administration gave Farrell the assurances he wanted. "An enlargement of our opportunities for trade and investment in foreign countries is *now essential* to maximum national prosperity." In addition, many of those who had in 1938 and 1939 feared the totalitarian consequences of going to war had by 1940 turned the argument upside down. They began to assert that staying out of the war would bring the end of free enterprise and democracy. Lewis W. Douglas, who had served as Budget Director in the early days of the New Deal, typified such thinking. "To retreat to the cyclone cellar here means, ultimately, to establish a totalitarian state at home."

Such a convergence of thinking within the corporate community of policy-makers encouraged the administration to act more openly. It continued to lie about, and in other ways conceal, some of its key policy decisions. But Roosevelt and Hull felt strong enough by September 1940, to embargo aviation gasoline and end iron shipments to Japan. Germany's rapid conquest of France brought even more support for their policies. Hitler might be said to have provided the deciding vote that passed the first peacetime draft in the same month of September. Thereafter events and decisions moved in an ever-accelerating spiral downward into war. Within a year, on September 4, 1941, the United States was engaged in undeclared naval warfare with Germany. Japan attacked three months later.

The final explanation of the tragedy at Pearl Harbor has yet to be made. It most certainly lies in some combination of American arrogance and negligence and of Japanese brilliance. But there is no doubt about the final convergence of thought between the Roosevelt Administration and the leaders of

America's corporate economic system. For by mid-1943, when the issue of postwar foreign policy came to the fore and was thrashed out in Congressional hearings and departmental discussions, it was apparent that the Roosevelt Administration was dominated by men whose personal experience and intellectual outlook were conditioned by their careers as leaders or agents or students of the large corporation. Dean Acheson, Averell Harriman, Donald M. Nelson, Edward Stettinius, Adolf A. Berle, Jr., John Foster Dulles, Eric Johnson, Paul Hoffman, William C. Foster, and James Forrestal are but the most obvious names from the top layer of American leadership in foreign affairs.

These men symbolized a consensus that had been foreshadowed in the winter of 1939–1940, when American economic leaders began to support Roosevelt's policy toward the Axis. By January 1940, key leaders of America's large corporations were defining crucial problems in terms of economic stagnation at home and postwar peace terms. Having had the central issue spelled out for them in that fashion, the editors of *Fortune* devoted their attention to the questions of "The Dispossessed" at home and a redefinition of "The U.S. Frontier."

From the candid admission that the American system was in serious trouble ("For nearly one-fourth of the population there is no economic system—and from the rest there is no answer"), the editors of *Fortune* drew three major conclusions. First, they acknowledged that "the U.S. economy has never proved that it can operate without the periodic injection of new and real wealth. The whole frontier saga, indeed, centered around this economic imperative." Second, and in consequence of this fact, the editors defined two new frontiers. A new emphasis on enlarged consumer sales at home would have to be paralleled by a tremendous expansion of "foreign trade and foreign investment." Secretary of State Hull's trade agreements program was "a step in the right direction," but to "open up real frontiers, under a general policy of raising the standard of living of other countries, we shall have to go much further."

In outlining its conception of such a program, *Fortune* argued that "the analogy between the domestic frontier in 1787, when the Constitution was formed, and the present international frontier is perhaps not an idle one. The early expansion of the U.S. was based upon firm political principles; and it may be that further expansion must be based upon equally firm—and equally revolutionary—international principles." *Fortune's* third point concerned the importance of having more and more corporation leaders enter the Roosevelt Administration and subsequent governments.

As they devoted more of their attention and energy to the challenge of extending the new American frontier, many economic leaders became enthusiastic converts to the mission to reform the world. The convergence of a sense of economic necessity and a moral calling transformed the traditional concept of open door expansion into a vision of an American Century. In this fashion, the United States entered and fought World War II. Americans were convinced that they were defending an anticolonial democracy charged with a duty to regenerate the world. They also had come firmly to believe that their own prosperity and democracy depended upon the continued expansion of their economic system under the strategy of the open door.

CHAPTER SIX

The President [Roosevelt] . . . said that he himself would not be in favor of the creation of a new Assembly of the League of Nations, at least until after a period of time had transpired and during which an international police force composed of the United States and Great Britain had had an opportunity of functioning.

REMARKS TO WINSTON CHURCHILL, AUGUST 1941,
AS REPORTED BY SUMNER WELLES

For unless there is security here at home there cannot be lasting peace in the world.

FRANKLIN DELANO ROOSEVELT, JANUARY 1944

It is important that I retain complete freedom of action after this conference [in Moscow] is over.

FRANKLIN DELANO ROOSEVELT, OCTOBER 1944

We cannot go through another ten years like the ten years at the end of the twenties and the beginning of the thirties, without having the most far-reaching consequences upon our economic and social systems. . . . We have got to see that what the country produces is used and sold under financial arrangements which make its production possible. . . . My contention

THE NIGHTMARE OF DEPRESSION
AND THE VISION OF OMNIPOTENCE

is that we cannot have full employment and prosperity in the United States without the foreign markets.

DEAN ACHESON, NOVEMBER 1944

. . . if the Russians did not wish to join us they could go to hell.

HARRY S. TRUMAN, REMARK OF APRIL 23, 1945,
AS REPORTED BY CHARLES E. BOHLEN

In Rumania and Bulgaria—and rather less decisively in Hungary—the Russian Government has sponsored and supported Governments which are democratic in the Russian rather than in the English-speaking connotation of the term and whose friendship for Russia is one of their main qualifications. This policy would fit in well enough with a "zones of influence" conception of the [peace] settlement; and it would be idle to deny that other great nations, both in the remoter and in the recent past, have pursued the same policy in regions of the world which they deemed vital to their security. During the past few weeks, however, the English-speaking Powers have adopted an attitude towards Balkan affairs which seemed to imply the contrary view that any of the three Powers may claim a right of intervention even in regions especially affecting the security of one of the others; and the clash of these opposing views, each of which can be formidably sustained by argument, underlay all the difficulties of the Foreign Ministers in their discussion of Balkan affairs.

LONDON TIMES EDITORIAL, OCTOBER 3, 1945

. . . the United States has it in its power to increase enormously the strains under which Soviet policy must operate, to force upon the Kremlin a far greater degree of moderation and circumspection than it has had to observe in recent years, and in this way to promote tendencies which must eventually find their outlet in either the break-up or the gradual mellowing of Soviet power.

GEORGE FROST KENNAN, FEBRUARY 1946—JULY 1947

The situation in the world today is not primarily the result of the natural difficulties which follow a great war. It is chiefly due to the fact that one nation has not only refused to cooperate in the establishment of a just and honorable peace, but—even worse—has actually sought to prevent it.

HARRY S. TRUMAN, MARCH 1948

I. ROOSEVELT AND STALIN CONFRONT THE DILEMMAS OF VICTORY

Politicians become statesmen, not by honoring pious shibboleths, nor even by moving men to action with inspiring rhetoric, but by recognizing and then resolving the central dilemmas of their age.

When measured against this demanding standard, Franklin Delano Roosevelt's performance after 1940 poses a difficult problem in judgment for the historian. On the one hand, he seems clearly enough to have sensed the contradiction between his intellectual, emotional, and policy commitment to America's traditional strategy of the open door, and the new circumstances arising out of World War II which called for the acceptance of limits upon American expectations and actions, and for the working out of a concert of power with other major nations. Though it was not in any sense unique, Roosevelt's recognition of that new reality does entitle him to a place of honor within the community of American policy-makers. It also explains and justifies the praise of his partisans.

On the other hand, Roosevelt did not resolve the dilemma posed by that contradiction between tradition and reality. He occasionally spoke candidly of the problem. He offered a few very general ideas about the kind of things that could be done to adapt American thinking and policy to the new conditions. And he even suggested a few concrete proposals for dealing with specific aspects of the developing crisis. But he never worked out, initiated, or carried through a fresh approach which combined necessary domestic changes with a fundamental re-evaluation of American foreign policy. He did not resolve the dilemma. At the time of his death, he was turning back toward the inadequate domestic programs of the New Deal era, and was in foreign affairs reasserting the traditional strategy of the Open Door Policy.

Explorations into the forest of conditional history are sometimes fruitful, for they occasionally suggest new insights into what did occur. This is perhaps the case with the debate over what would have happened if Roosevelt had lived. The most sympathetic interpretation explains Roosevelt's ambivalence as a result of his declining health. But while his fatigue was a relevant consideration, there is little evidence that Roosevelt seriously entertained even the idea of initiating a re-evaluation of America's conception of itself and the world. For the further such an inquiry is pushed, the more it becomes apparent that Roosevelt had not abandoned the policy of the open door; and that, even if he personally had been on the verge of trying to do so, few of his advisors and subordinates had either the intention or the power to effect such a change.

The leaders who succeeded Roosevelt understood neither the dilemma nor the need to alter their outlook. A handful of them thought briefly of stabilizing relations with the Soviet Union on the basis of economic and political agreements, but even that tiny minority saw the future in terms of continued expansion guided by the strategy of the Open Door Policy. The great majority rapidly embarked upon a program to force the Soviet Union to accept America's traditional conception of itself and the world. This decision represented the final stage in the transformation of the policy of the open door from a

utopian idea into an ideology, from an intellectual outlook
for changing the world into one concerned with preserving it
in the traditional mold.

American leaders had internalized, and had come to *believe,*
the theory, the necessity, and the morality of open-door expansion. Hence they seldom thought it necessary to explain or
defend the approach. Instead, they *assumed* the premises and
concerned themselves with exercising their freedom and power
to deal with the necessities and the opportunities that were
defined by such an outlook. As far as American leaders were
concerned, the philosophy and practice of open-door expansion
had become, in both its missionary and economic aspects, *the*
view of the world. Those who did not recognize and accept
that fact were considered not only wrong, but incapable of
thinking correctly.

The problem of the Soviet leaders was defined by the confrontation between the expansive prophecy of Marx about
world revolution (which was supported by the traditional
Great Russian and Slavic ideas of world leadership) and a
realistic, Marxian analysis of world conditions (which was
reinforced by sober calculations of nationalistic self-interest).
Russian leaders clearly recognized their dilemma, and realized
that rehabilitation and military security were the points upon
which its resolution had to hinge. But American policy offered
the Russians no real choice on those key issues. Particularly
after the atom bomb was created and used, the attitude of the
United States left the Soviets with but one real option: either
acquiesce in American proposals or be confronted with American power and hostility. It was the decision of the United
States to employ its new and awesome power in keeping with
the traditional Open Door Policy which crystallized the cold
war.

To say that is not to say that the United States started or
caused the cold war. Nor is it an effort to avoid what many
people apparently consider the most important—if also the
most controversial and embarrassing—issue of recent and contemporary history. For, contrary to that general belief, the
problem of which side started the cold war offers neither a very
intelligent nor a very rewarding way of approaching the central
questions about American foreign relations since 1941. If anyone can be said in that sense to have caused the cold war,

then the responsibility rests primarily if not exclusively upon Adolf Hitler and Nazi Germany. What might or might not have happened if those protagonists had not torn central and eastern Europe to pieces in a vain effort to unify them is not (contrary to the one raised about Roosevelt) a very useful kind of hypothetical question. It is not a matter of what Hitler might have done. Hitler and Nazi Germany did make that attempt. And it was in the course of defeating their ignoble ambition that the United States and the Soviet Union came into direct and sustained confrontation from the Baltic to the Black seas.

The real issue, therefore, is not which side started the cold war. It is rather the far more subtle one of which side committed its power to policies which hardened the natural and inherent tensions and propensities into bitter antagonisms and inflexible positions. Two general attitudes can be adopted in facing up to that issue. One is to assume, or take for granted, on the basis of emotion and official information, that the answer is obvious: Russia is to blame. That represents the easy, nationalistic solution to all questions about international affairs. That attitude also defines history as a stockpile of facts to be requisitioned on the basis of what is needed to prove a conclusion decided upon in advance. The technique is rather like redesigning the famous Memory Hole in George Orwell's book, *1984*, so that it works in reverse. Instead of burning up all embarrassing facts, they are merely labeled and stored according to official standards. Disturbing facts cease to be troublesome because they are never put in the proper context. When they do appear, therefore, they do so as anachronisms.

The other approach is to consider history as a way of learning, of mustering the intellectual and moral courage to acknowledge the facts as they exist without tampering with them. If they are unpleasant or disturbing, then new facts—in the form of our ideas and actions—must be created that modify the unsatisfying scene. This is the more difficult and the more demanding method. Recognizing this, John Foster Dulles offered in 1946 a classic bit of encouragement to push on with the effort: "There is no nation which has attitudes so pure that they cannot be bettered by self-examination."*

---

* Dulles apparently mislaid his own advice in subsequent years.

In undertaking such self-examination, the first and essential requirement is to acknowledge two primary facts which can never be blinked. *The first is that the United States had from 1944 to at least 1962 a vast preponderance of actual as well as potential power vis-à-vis the Soviet Union.** Nothing can ever change that fact about the absolute and relative power relationship between the two countries during that chronological period. This relative weakness of the Russians did not turn them into western parliamentary democrats, and it did not transform their every action into a moral and equitable transaction. But it does confront all students of the cold war, be they academicians or politicians or housewives, with very clear and firm limits on how they can make sense out of the cold war if they are at the same time to observe the essential standards of intellectual honesty. For power and responsibility go together in a direct and intimate relationship. Unless it tries all the alternatives that offer reasonable probabilities of success, a nation with the great relative supremacy enjoyed by the United States between 1944 and 1962 cannot with any real warrant or meaning claim that it has been *forced* to follow a certain approach or policy. Yet that is the American claim even though it did not explore several such alternatives.

Instead, and this is the second fact that cannot be dodged, the United States used or deployed its preponderance of power wholly within the assumptions and the tradition of the strategy of the Open Door Policy. The United States never formulated and offered the Soviet Union a settlement based on other, less grandiose, terms. For that matter, it never made a serious and sustained effort even to employ in dealing with the Russians the same kind of tactics that had been used for a generation before World War II in relations with the Japanese.

It is true that the offer to include the Soviet Union in the Marshall Plan can be interpreted as a similar move. For, if the Soviets had accepted the conditions set forth for receiving such assistance, the United States would have been in a position to exercise extensive influence over internal Soviet affairs, as well

* The most recent and most cogent estimate of this relative balance of military power between America and Russia is P. M. S. Blackett, "Steps Toward Disarmament," *Scientific American* (April, 1962).

as over its foreign policy. To cite but one known example, American leaders would have demanded that the Russians allocate large quantities of raw materials to western Europe. That in itself would have delayed and complicated Soviet recovery, let alone its further development.* Even so, American policy-makers greeted the Russian refusal to participate on such terms with an audible sigh of relief. They never made the kind of serious effort to negotiate a satisfactory compromise with the Russians as they had done with the Japanese. If it be objected that the effort would have failed anyway because it had not worked with the Japanese, then those who advance that argument must go on to confront one of three conclusions that are inherent in their logic. It must be admitted either that the strategy itself cannot succeed without war, or that it can succeed without war only if the other country accepts and works within limits set by the United States. Otherwise, the policy must be changed—formally or informally.

Instead of being changed, however, the traditional strategy was merely reasserted and put into operation at the end of the war under the famous and accurate phrase about "negotiation from strength." But negotiation from strength meant in practice that there would be no meaningful negotiations. The very concept defined negotiation as the acceptance of American proposals, and American leaders acted upon that definition. The broad and fundamental failure of the policy demonstrated the basic misconception of man and the world inherent in the policy of the open door. For it established beyond cavil that the policy of the open door, like all imperial policies, created and spurred onward a dynamic opposition to which it forfeited the initiative. Not even a monopoly of nuclear weapons enabled America to prove itself an exception to that involuting momentum of empire.

Even before they formally entered World War II, American leaders assumed that the United States would emerge from the conflict in a position to extend, stabilize, and reform the empire of the open door. Roosevelt's assumption that Anglo-American

---

* See, for one of many pieces of evidence concerning this attitude: J. M. Jones, *The Fifteen Weeks* (New York: Viking Press, 1955), 253.

forces would police the world for a "transition period" after the defeat of the Axis was given overt expression in August 1941. That was almost four months before Pearl Harbor but after the decision had been made to help the Russians defeat Hitler in Europe. His casually optimistic outlook foresaw the ultimate creation of an international organization committed to the policy of the open door, a circumstance that would enable the United States to proceed with the work of developing the world.

Supported by a thoroughly bipartisan assortment of liberals and conservatives, this reassertion of the traditional open door strategy guided the community of American policy-makers throughout the war and on into the cold war era. Ultimately it became, in the best tradition of the open door, and in the words of G. L. Arnold, a sympathetic British observer, a view of the world resting "upon the expectation of a prolonged era of peace, Anglo-American hegemony (with the aid of China) in the United Nations and in the world generally, free trade outside the Soviet orbit and gradual liberalization within, a weakened and profoundly pacific Russia far behind the Western powers in the utilization of atomic energy." The assumption of virtuous omnipotence, implicit in the Open Door Notes and formulated explicitly on the eve of American entry into World War I, reached full maturity in that image of an American Century. As with Theodore Roosevelt's concern to save civilization and Wilson's crusade to make the world safe for democracy, however, the urge to give the future a New Deal was powered by a persuasive sense of the necessity to expand economically in order to sustain democracy and prosperity in the United States.

In keeping with this outlook, the United States declined in the winter of 1941–42 even to consider the Soviet Union's bid to settle the postwar boundaries of eastern Europe on the basis of the situation as it existed just prior to Hitler's attack.*

---

* The best printed sources for this crucial episode are: W. S. Churchill, *The Grand Alliance* (Boston: Houghton Mifflin Co., 1950); *The Memoirs of Cordell Hull* (New York: Macmillan Co., Vol. II, 1948); S. Welles, *Seven Decisions That Shaped History* (New York: Harper and Bros., 1951); and especially *Foreign Relations, 1942: Vol. III, Russia* (Washington: Gvt. Printing Office, 1961).

Russia raised the question in conversations with the British during November and December 1941, at which time Soviet spokesmen made clear and pointed references to being left out of the Atlantic Conference discussions of August 1941, between Churchill and Roosevelt.

Stalin suggested five major areas for agreement: (1) the boundaries of the Soviet Union should be guaranteed largely as they existed just prior to Hitler's assault in June 1941 (including the Curzon Line in Poland); (2) Austria should be restored as an independent nation; (3) Germany's industrial and military base should be weakened by splitting off the Ruhr manufacturing complex, by incorporating East Prussia into Poland, and perhaps by breaking off one other large province; (4) Yugoslavia and Albania should be re-established as independent countries, and Czechoslovakia and Greece should have their prewar boundaries reaffirmed; and (5) Russia should receive reparations in kind from Germany.

These proposals pose a fascinating "iffy" question: what if Russia had been committed to those conditions, and they had been honored by both sides? Certainly the postwar era would have developed in a significantly different manner. Another consideration is more relevant to what did happen, because the Soviets continued in large measure to emphasize their proposals of 1941 during the war and on into the subsequent period.

At the time, however, the American response was wholly negative. Hull considered it "unfortunate" even to discuss such "commitments," and simply refused to agree to them. He first put strong pressure on the British to delay and then spurn the Soviet offer. There is no particular mystery about his adamant. In the most general sense, American leaders did not want to negotiate any settlements until they were in the strongest possible position, and they thought that would be at the end of the war. More specifically, their guiding attitude was that of the Open Door Policy, and they had neither the desire nor the intention to negotiate away any equality of opportunity in eastern Europe.

Stalin nevertheless continued to press his proposals during discussions with Anthony Eden in Moscow in December 1941, and on into 1942. Hull never gave way. He secured Roosevelt's support in April 1942, for the view that such commitments were "both dangerous and unwise." A month later the Secre-

tary and his advisors in the State Department prepared a protest "so strong that we were in some fear lest the President
disapprove it." The concern was unfounded. Roosevelt, so
Hull reported, "quickly returned it with his O.K." The Soviets
were blocked. The postwar configuration of eastern Europe
was left moot—to be settled by other means.

This episode was extremely significant in American-Soviet
relations, and English and American leaders realized that at
the time. In many ways, the crisis can be understood most
clearly in terms of the paradoxical attitude of the United
States toward the Baltic States. Before World War I, Estonia,
Latvia, and Lithuania had been provinces of Russia. Then,
at the time of the Bolshevik Revolution, Germany had forcibly
annexed them. During the subsequent years of intervention,
the Allies encouraged and finally established the three countries as part of the *cordon sanitaire* designed to contain the
Soviet Union.

Acquiescing in, but not accepting, that loss of its traditional
"window on the West," the Soviets signed peace treaties with
the new states in 1920. But the United States did not recognize
the independence of those nations for several years, insisting
that they were legitimate parts of the Russian state. Ultimately,
however, America gave way and established diplomatic relations with the three countries. Having re-established its traditional authority over the Baltic states in 1939, the Soviet Union
fully expected and intended to retain that control after the
defeat of Hitler. In the discussions that took place during the
winter of 1941–1942, however, the United States refused to
return to its original position. Stalin's blunt reaction to being
blocked on this issue by Hull and Roosevelt (and thereby the
British) casts an exceedingly bright light on subsequent tension between East and West.

"It is very important to us," Stalin explained at the outset
of the negotiations, "to know whether we shall have to fight
at the peace conference in order to get our western frontiers."*

The record of the discussions reveals that the Russians became convinced that such a battle would be necessary.

---

* This and subsequent quotations from Stalin come from the stenographic report of the discussions printed in *Foreign Relations, 1942:
Russia.*

"Surely this is axiomatic," Stalin shot back when Eden continued, as the advance guard for Hull and Roosevelt, to balk at an agreement. "We are fighting our hardest and losing hundreds of thousands of men in the common cause with Great Britain as our ally, and I should have thought that such a question as the position of the Baltic states ought to be axiomatic. . . . [I] am surprised and amazed at Mr. Churchill's Government taking up this position. It is practically the same as that of the Chamberlain Government. . . . This attitude of the British Government toward our frontiers is indeed a surprise to me so I think it will be better to postpone the proposed agreements."

"It now looks," he added in a remark that implicitly tied Roosevelt and the United States to the British position, "as if the Atlantic Charter was directed against the U.S.S.R." Stalin was of course aware of America's responsibility for preventing an agreement. Any doubts are removed by Eden's very blunt summary of the whole affair. The American attitude, he warned on March 12, 1942, "will surely appear to Stalin so uncollaborative a state of mind as to confirm his suspicions that he can expect no real consideration for Russia's interests from ourselves or the United States."

Roosevelt took an almost identical position three years later, in the fall of 1944, when the issue was reopened by the Russian counteroffensive against Hitler. The British repeated their warning about the dangers inherent in Roosevelt's efforts to avoid a commitment: the Russians were on the scene, and the only possible way of sustaining Western interests was through serious negotiations based on a series of *quid pro quos*. Instead, Roosevelt and Hull again stood by the strategy of the open door. They insisted that any agreement between Stalin and Churchill would have to be limited to a period of three months duration. It seems very probable that Stalin concluded that he would "have to fight at the peace conference in order to get our western frontiers."

In the meantime, the refusal to negotiate a basic settlement with the Soviet Union in the winter of 1941–1942 was almost immediately followed by another serious difference between the two countries. For, later in the spring of 1942, the Russians were given ambivalent and confusing assurances about when a second front would be opened in Europe. By August, when it had become apparent that Allied troops would not land on the continent that year, relations with Moscow had encountered very rough sledding. Even so, several developments reduced the tension and produced an interlude of improved relations between America and Russia. Foremost was the Russian victory at Stalingrad. That triumph convinced everybody, including the Russians, that Hitler would be defeated. As a result, and even before they launched their major counteroffensive, the Soviets embarked upon a fundamental debate over what to do after the war. Their discussions ranged across political, philosophical, and economic lines, but its essential nature was defined by Russia's tremendous physical and human losses in the war.

After Stalingrad, the Russians knew they would survive, but as a terribly weakened nation. Hence they were aware that the way they handled the recovery problem would influence all other decisions. Perhaps the most revealing insight into Russia's basic outlook at that time was offered (unconsciously, in all probability) by Molotov on February 18, 1956—after the Soviets had developed their nuclear weapons, and after the Chinese Communists had triumphed in Asia. "We now have an international situation," he remarked, "of which we could only have dreamed ten or fifteen years ago." Implicit in Molotov's comment was the fact that the Russians had viewed their position in the 1940's as one of weakness, not offensive strength.

Though there were various shades of opinion as to how the central issue of reconstruction should be dealt with, the Russians divided into three broad groups. One of them, occasionally called "our softies" by their Russian opponents, held that it was necessary and desirable to undertake reconstruction at a relatively moderate tempo, obtaining assistance from the United States. The softies stressed the need and desirability of relaxing the pervasive and extensive controls that had been exercised over Soviet life ever since the first Five Year Plan and the wisdom of revising, decentralizing, and rationalizing the industrial system that had been built. They also emphasized the danger of deteriorating relations with the United States. Perhaps most significant of all, they advanced the thesis that Western capitalism could probably avoid another serious depression, and hence the appeal and the safety of the Soviet

Union depended upon its ability to improve the quality of life in Russia and thereby induce other peoples to accept communism by the force and persuasiveness of example.

Others within Russia argued that the softies were wrong in theory or in fact. Some of these men, who may be called the conservatives, agreed with the softies that it was desirable to ease up at home and were half convinced by the more favorable analysis of foreign capitalism, but they doubted that the Western nations, and in particular the United States, would help the Soviet Union solve its reconstruction problems. Hence they concluded that Russia would have to establish a basic security perimeter in Europe, the Middle East, and Asia and once again pull itself up by its own bootstraps.

Opposed to the softies and the conservatives was a group which may be called the doctrinaire revolutionaries. The diehards scoffed at the analysis and proposals advanced by the moderates and asserted that the only practical and realistic program was to secure a base for militant revolutionary activity throughout the world. Such doctrinaires stressed the need to force the pace of reconstruction while doing all that was possible to export revolutions.*

Stalin's temperament and experience inclined him toward resolving the dilemma posed by the problem of reconstruction and the tradition of revolution in a conservative manner. But that approach depended on two things for success: (1) limiting and controlling revolutionary action by foreign communists, which otherwise would antagonize the United States, and (2) reaching an economic and political understanding with America, an agreement that would enable Russia to handle the problem of recovery and at the same time relax certain controls

---

* Perhaps the best introduction to the nature and feel of debate within the Soviet Union is A. Erlich, *The Soviet Industrialization Debate, 1924–1928* (Cambridge: Harvard University Press, 1960); then, in addition to the materials cited below, see on the World War II phase of such disagreements the following items: Z. K. Brzezinski, *The Soviet Bloc. Unity and Conflict* (Cambridge: Harvard University Press, 1960, and paperback, 1961); V. Dedijer, *Tito* (New York: Simon & Schuster, 1953); I. Deutscher, *Stalin* (New York: Oxford University Press, 1949); M. Gordey, *Visa to Moscow* (New York: Alfred A. Knopf, 1952); E. Snow, *Stalin Must Have Peace* (New York: Random House, 1947); and A. Werth, *The Year of Stalingrad* (New York: Alfred A. Knopf, 1947).

and pressures inside the country. To use the language of Wall Street, Stalin was a bull on communism. He was confident that if given a peaceful opportunity to develop its program in Russia, communism would gradually appeal to more and more countries of the world. He felt this was particularly likely in the underdeveloped areas and in poorer industrialized nations. If this could be managed by getting aid from America and by restraining foreign communists from seizing power through revolutions, then the movement toward socialism and communism would move slowly enough to avoid frightening the United States into retaliation against the Soviet Union itself.

There are two important aspects of this ferment and clash of views within the hierarchy of Soviet leadership that have to be kept in mind throughout any discussion of American-Soviet relations after 1941. They are particularly important to an understanding of the interaction between the two countries during the period between April 1945 and the summer of 1948.

The first is that this conflict over policy within the Soviet Union cannot be discounted or dismissed on the grounds that it did not (or will not) produce Western-style representative government in Russia. Both the American public in general and its individual leaders tend very strongly to interpret the absence of Anglo-Saxon institutions in another country to mean that there is also an absence of significant or meaningful disagreement and debate about important issues. This is simply wrong. The ways in which differences of interest and opinion are organized and exert influence are many and varied. Even in the United States, for that matter, many crucial issues are debated and decided wholly outside the institutions of local, state and national elections. Furthermore, as events since 1952 have demonstrated, such debate in Russia did continue and did begin to take on institutional form and substance. It also affected policy.

This development leads directly to the second main point. American policy exerted an early, continuing, and significant influence on the course of such debate in the Soviet Union. Indeed, it had done so since the very first weeks of the Bolshevik Revolution in 1917. American policy therefore influenced Soviet policy and action. These considerations can not be re-emphasized every time they appear in the subsequent pages of this essay, but it is extremely important to understand them and use them as intellectual tools in thinking about later events.

In order to bypass all the misunderstanding that it is possible to avoid, let these points be stated as simply and as directly as possible. As Stalin made clear in the winter of 1941–1942, the Soviet Union fully intended to re-establish what it considered to be its minimum natural and desirable frontiers in eastern Europe. He further concluded that the United States and England would resist that effort. His opposition raised in the minds of Soviet leaders the very natural question as to whether or not they did not need an even firmer security perimeter.

Hence the problem for American leaders was one of developing an attitude and a broad set of proposals involving such security and economic aid for the Soviet Union that would enable them to negotiate some kind of modus vivendi with the Russians. The failure of American leaders to do that is the central theme of American diplomacy after the abortive negotiations of 1941–1942. If studied and written as a critique of Soviet policy, the emphasis involved in treating these matters would be different. In that case, the story might very well focus on the way that the breakdown of the talks of 1941–1942 strengthened those Soviet leaders who laid primary stress on extending communism as the Red Army moved westward. That might very possibly be the real tragedy of Soviet diplomacy. But since this essay is about American diplomacy, and—even more—since it was the United States that refused to offer any clear and unequivocal basis for such fundamental negotiations, the essay has to concentrate on America's actions and the ideas behind them.

Returning, then, to the events of the winter of 1942–1943, there were several developments which encouraged Stalin in his propensity to resolve his dilemma in a conservative (i.e., nationalist) fashion. One was the Western landing in North Africa, which did apparently modify his suspicion and anger over the failure to make an assault on the European continent. More important, however, was an American approach concerning postwar economic relations with Russia which seemed to

suggest that the Soviet Union could obtain help in dealing
with its reconstruction problems. Stalin responded quickly and
decisively. But as he was ultimately forced to conclude, the
American overture did not represent a changed outlook on the
part of the majority of America's corporate leaders.

In its origins the plan was a continuation of the old idea
that America's economic system had to have a constantly expanding foreign market if it was to survive and prosper. At
bottom, therefore, it was the fear of another depression (or the
resumption of the old one) that prompted a few American
leaders such as Donald M. Nelson and Eric Johnston to think
of large-scale exports to Russia. Johnston, for example, was
convinced after careful investigation in 1944 that the primary
concern of Soviet leaders was "to rebuild Russia." They also
worried about America's depletion of certain raw materials
and thought that Russia could continue to supply such items
as manganese after the war. This small minority of American
leaders began to realize that, whatever his many faults, Stalin
was not another Hitler and that the Soviet Union had not developed by the same dynamic as Nazi Germany.

During 1943, therefore, Nelson and a few other Americans
pushed the idea of a large loan to Russia. Stalin told Nelson
that he was very much in favor of the plan and even gave him
a list of priority needs as a first step in working out a specific
program. Their negotiations had much to do with the improvement in political relations between the two countries, exempli-
fied by Stalin's voluntary promise to Secretary of State Hull in
October 1943 that Russia would enter the war against Japan.
A bit later, in November, the conversations at the Teheran
Conference also reflected the improved atmosphere.

For his part, Roosevelt was by that time revealing a more
realistic attitude about including the Soviet Union as a full
partner in any plans for the postwar world. He did not talk
any longer, for example, about the way that England and
America would between themselves police the world at the end
of the war. In a similar way, he apparently grasped the fact
that Stalin was "most deeply interested" in Russian recovery
problems, and indicated at least some recognition of the way
that issue was tied in with Soviet foreign policy. The President
also seemed to be gaining some awareness that more reforms

were needed in the United States. He talked, at least to some extent, about the importance of an "economic bill of rights" to balance, supplement, and reinforce America's traditional political freedoms. In certain respects, he appeared to be echoing the argument of the speech he had read at the Commonwealth Club in San Francisco during the 1932 presidential campaign. "America's own rightful place in the world," he asserted, "depends in large part upon" its handling of domestic issues. "For unless there is security here at home," he explained, "there cannot be lasting peace in the world."

Such remarks can be interpreted to mean that Roosevelt was beginning to understand that America's traditional policy of open-door expansion had contributed significantly to its domestic and international difficulties. Even so, his concrete proposals for development at home were pale copies of old New Deal legislation. And while he said he was "sorry" that he did not have time to discuss Russia's postwar recovery problems with Stalin at Teheran, the fact is that he never took—or made—time to do so during the remaining sixteen months of his life. He did not even see to it that his subordinates committed and prepared themselves to discuss and negotiate the issue with the Soviets. Roosevelt's declining health may account in part for this, but in that event it is clear that such an approach to the Russians was very low on the President's list of priorities.

There is at least one account, moreover, which suggests that Roosevelt's position was very similar to those who wanted to use Russia's needs to win major political and economic concessions. The story is told by James Byrnes in his second volume of memoirs, *All In One Life.* He reports that Leo Crowley, who was to terminate Lend-Lease shipments to the Soviet Union as soon as Germany surrendered, told him of a conversation with Roosevelt that took place about April 1, 1945, shortly before the President died. "Crowley told me that . . . he told the President about a rumor that our government was considering a loan to the Soviets of $10 billion, and that he [Crowley] thought it wise to refrain from making any loan until more was known of their postwar attitude. He said the President agreed." This account should not be taken as full proof of Roosevelt's attitude. But it does, even when evaluated with caution, support the main point at issue. It is simply not possible to account for the continuance of the Open Door Policy by blaming Roosevelt's successors, for the President did not carry through on persistent Russian overtures for major economic assistance to help them rebuild their shattered economy.

Had Roosevelt done this, it would be more meaningful to charge his successors—or the Russians—with sabotaging his plan for the future; for it is quite true that the small group around Nelson favoring some rapprochement with the Russians was opposed by a much larger number of America's corporate leaders. It seems likely that Averell Harriman, one of the many wealthy industrial and banking leaders who supported Roosevelt, and who was one of the President's top advisors, was one of the more influential leaders of the anti-Russian group. Harriman's natural antagonism to the Soviets was reinforced by his vigorous belief in the necessity of open-door expansion, a belief that may have been heightened even more by an unhappy experience with the Russians in the 1920's, when his attempt to control a sizable segment of the world's manganese market by developing Russian supplies ended in mutual dissatisfaction. Harriman was but one of many corporate leaders, however, who had gone into the Roosevelt Administration with anti-Russian views. Others included James B. Forrestal and Bernard Baruch. All of these men were skeptical of Nelson's approach to dealing with the Soviets and were supported in their view by State Department experts such as George F. Kennan (who was in Russia much of the time with Harriman).

These men shared Harriman's extremely reserved reaction, early in 1944, to the news that the Russians "were anxious to come to a prompt understanding" about postwar economic relations. His view became even clearer when, a bit later that year, Stalin made a formal request for a loan of six billion dollars. Harriman advised cutting the initial amount under discussion to one-tenth of that sum and proposed that the project should be defined as a credit, rather than as a loan, so that if it ever actually went through, the United States could exercise extensive controls over Russia's use of the money. Thus, while he agreed with the Nelson group that "the question of long-term credits represents the key point in any negotiations with the Soviet Government," he also shared the State Department's view that the lever provided by Russian weakness and devastation could and should be used to insure a predominant role for America in all decisions about the postwar world.

Harriman and most American leaders knew precisely what kind of choice they made. One of the most unequivocal pieces of evidence on this point comes from Admiral William H. Standley, who served as American Ambassador to Russia during the first part of the war. Speaking publicly on November 14, 1944, he offered a candid review of the situation. Some kind of rivalry with the Russians was unavoidable simply because they would be the only other victorious power on the continent of Europe. But that tension could be kept within bounds, Standley argued, if the United States accepted its primary responsibility in the situation.

"We must assume two important premises," he pointed out. "First, that Russia's security is vital to her and that she cannot turn to industrialization and development of her raw material resources unless she has that security. . . . After victory, security is their next consideration. . . . [And unless we help establish it] they will have to proceed on their own to provide it."

Harriman based his policy on an identical analysis. He candidly acknowledged "that the sooner the Soviet Union can develop a decent life for its people the more tolerant they will become." That interpretation obviously implied a basic policy of helping the Russians recover from the devastation of the war. But quite unlike Standley, Harriman proposed instead to exploit Russian weakness and force them to accept American policies. The Russians "should be given to understand that our willingness to co-operate wholeheartedly with them in their vast reconstruction problems will depend upon their behavior in international matters." "I am opposed to granting her that credit," he stated flatly in May 1945. "I would apportion that credit out piecemeal, demanding in return concessions on the political field."

From the very beginning of the discussions with Stalin in 1943, Roosevelt was aware of the Soviet overtures for economic aid and of the importance Stalin attached to such negotiations.

Yet the President never took the lead himself in handling the
issue. Nor did he direct the State Department or a special
committee to push the matter. In the end, therefore, there was
no concerted American effort to match the Russian approach
of handling related political and economic questions on an
integrated basis.*

Roosevelt's attitude, which so clearly reflected the traditional outlook of the Open Door Policy, was revealed even
more vividly in the spring of 1944, when the Soviet Army
began to advance into eastern Europe. Confronted by Churchill with the need to come to some clear arrangement with the
Russians, Roosevelt at first agreed to the idea of a clear and
precise division of authority. Then, in an abrupt turnabout,
he asserted that he must have "complete freedom of action,"
whatever the agreement arranged by Churchill and Stalin.
After considerable effort, Churchill and Stalin worked out an
understanding—"a good guide," said Churchill, "for the
conduct of our affairs"—whereby Russia would exercise predominant authority in southeastern Europe, Great Britain
would do so in Greece, and the Allies would share responsibility in Yugoslavia. Roosevelt reluctantly accepted this division of power on the basis of a three-month trial.

During subsequent months, the British intervened to crush
a revolution in Greece and prepare the way for the installation
of a government they wanted and could control. Though he
urged the British to take a more liberal line, Roosevelt went
along with Churchill on the need to control affairs in Greece
and acquiesced in the Prime Minister's action. *Both in fact
and in the eyes of the Russians, that committed Roosevelt
on the eve of the Yalta Conference to the agreement worked
out between Churchill and Stalin.* For his part, Stalin refrained from attacking or blocking the British move in Greece.
Churchill reported that Stalin "adhered very strictly to this
understanding." Stalin also initiated his efforts to forestall
trouble with the Western Allies arising from foreign communist agitation and revolution. He advised, and apparently even

---

* On these matters consult the very illuminating, but all too often
neglected volume by E. F. Penrose, *Economic Planning for the Peace*
(Princeton: Princeton University Press, 1953).

warned, Tito and Mao Tse-tung to abstain from revolutionary action in their nations and instead to accept subordinate positions in coalition governments led by pro-Western parties.

Against this background, and in the context of Germany's imminent defeat, Roosevelt met Churchill and Stalin at Yalta in February 1945. In addition to their knowledge of the Churchill-Stalin agreement, and of Stalin's self-containment during the Greek episode, American leaders were aware that the Chinese communists, after a long debate, had concluded in September 1944, that they preferred to work with the United States rather than with Russia in the future development of China. Thus it is absolutely clear that Roosevelt and his advisors knew that the Soviet Union was prepared to negotiate seriously about the character of postwar relations with the United States and that America had an equally fruitful opportunity in Asia. But during the conference American leaders were not concerned to push such negotiations. They were not prepared to abandon, or even seriously to modify, the traditional strategy of American expansion.

Disturbed by America's ambivalence and Churchill's increasingly open opposition, which increased the difficulty Stalin had in controlling the doctrinaire revolutionaries within his own camp, Stalin went to Yalta with two approaches to the postwar world. One was based on receiving a large loan from the United States. His overtures in this direction were answered with vague and unrewarding replies. Stalin's alternative was to obtain, by agreement or by self-exertion, economic reparations from Germany and a strong strategic position in eastern Europe, the Black Sea area, and the Far East. America went to Yalta, on the other hand, guided by little except a sense of mission to reform the world, a growing fear of postwar economic crisis, and an increasing confidence that Russian weakness would enable America to exercise its freedom and solve its problems by further open-door expansion.

Commentators have criticized President Roosevelt very severely on the grounds that he was naive in believing that he could persuade Stalin to co-operate with the West after the war. Such attacks are weak and misdirected in several important respects. In the first place, it is almost absurd to think —or charge— that a man with Roosevelt's mastery of political infighting was naive. He may have overestimated his power or his skill, but he was not naive. Significantly, too, Roosevelt had *not* abandoned, at the time of his death, the intention of reasserting American power and influence in eastern Europe. It was suggested to him that the United States should file a vigorous protest over the Soviet action early in 1945 of reconstituting the Rumanian Government along pro-Soviet lines. Roosevelt did *not* reply that the basic issue should be forgotten. His position was quite different. *He said merely that the Rumanian episode, because it involved supplies for the Red Army that was still fighting Germany, did not offer the best kind of ground upon which to take a stand.*

Roosevelt's idea of reaching an accommodation with Stalin was not based on some utopian dream of perfect and everlasting agreement on any and all issues. However, Roosevelt simply did not understand the nature and workings of a modern, complex industrial economy. The result in domestic affairs was that his political acumen and skill were never focused on the central and vital issues of getting the political economy into some kind of fundamentally dynamic balance. The same weakness plagued him in dealing with the Russians. He never got his priorities straight. Short of war, economic aid was the one effective tool he had in negotiations with the Soviets. But he never used it.

Roosevelt's successors understood and used that lever, but they treated it as a weapon to force the Soviets to accept American policies. The conflict over affairs in eastern Europe which developed out of that attitude is usually stressed in discussing the origins of the cold war. Yet it may be that the issues of German reparations and American expansion in the Middle East were equally important as determining factors. Failing to obtain a loan from America, Stalin had to decide between three possible courses of action.

He could give way and accept the American interpretation of all disputed points, abandoning foreign communists to their fate and attempting to control the extremists in his own nation. He could respond with an orthodox revolutionary program throughout the world. Or, relying on large economic reparations from Germany, he could continue the effort to resolve his dilemma in a conservative manner even though he did not have any formal understanding with the United

States. This approach would also do much to keep Germany from becoming a threat to Russia in the immediate future. It left him, however, with the need to effect some basic settlement concerning eastern Europe, the Far East, and the Black Sea region.

Stalin was able to reach such an understanding with the United States in but one of those areas. This was in Asia, where he traded American predominance in China (and Japan) for strategic and economic rights in Manchuria. Concerning eastern Europe, however, Stalin accepted an ambivalent proposal on the Polish issue which represented America's unwillingness to acknowledge his agreement with Churchill as much as it did Russia's security needs. He was no more successful in the Middle East, where American oil companies had moved back into Iran in 1943. Supported by the State Department and special emissaries, the companies were well along in their efforts to obtain extensive concessions. Roosevelt was "thrilled" by the chance to work along with the oil companies and make Iran an example of what America could do for underdeveloped areas of the world, an attitude which helps explain why the United States was not willing to allow the Russians to obtain oil rights in northern Iran. Stalin gave way on the issue at Yalta and also refrained from pushing his desire to gain more security for Russia in the Black Sea area.

Despite his failure to get any positive response from the United States on the question of a postwar loan, or a clear understanding on other vital issues, Stalin still hoped to effect a conservative resolution of his dilemma. Throughout the first half of 1945, for example, *Izvestia* stressed the vitality of the American economy (in striking contrast to the fears being expressed in Congressional hearings), emphasized the importance of resolving outstanding issues by negotiation, and reiterated the fruitfulness of economic co-operation. The British press attaché in Russia reported that Soviet comment remained restrained and hopeful until America initiated a campaign of vigorous criticism and protest aimed at Soviet predominance in eastern Europe.

But the most significant indicators of the predisposition to work out some modus vivendi with the United States, and then to concentrate on internal recovery and development, came in the debates within the Soviet hierarchy, and in the relatively restrained policies followed in eastern Europe after the Nazis were defeated. One of the earliest indications of Russian emphasis on domestic affairs appeared in 1943 in the form of a discussion (in the journal *Under the Banner of Marxism*) over the proper way to teach economics. This took special note, among other things, of Stalin's praise of the United States. The crucial feature was the heavy stress laid upon the extent of the recovery crisis, and upon the need to concentrate on domestic affairs. Many American observers immediately understood and pointed out the nonrevolutionary implications of the argument, but official policy-makers in the United States took little if any cognizance of the matter.*

An even more revealing debate occurred after the publication in 1946 of a major study of capitalism by the Soviet economist Eugene Varga. The date of 1946 is significant in two respects. It means, in the first place, that the discussion had been going on at least since 1944, a consideration which underscores the ambivalent, undecided, and cautious nature of Soviet thinking at the end of the war. It also indicates that the Russians had not made a firm decision on their basic approach as late as 1946; even though, as will be seen, the United States had been exerting strong pressure on the Soviet Union ever since the London Foreign Ministers' Conference in September 1945.

Varga's central point was that capitalism in general, and in the United States in particular, was capable of stabilizing itself in the postwar era. He went on to argue that the role of the government could be positive and creative under capitalism, and in that fashion suggested that the classic Marxian prophecy about the inevitable collapse of capitalism might

---

* The reader who does not have access to, or cannot read, Soviet sources (upon which this discussion is based), can follow the debate in these items: L. A. Leontiev (et. al.), "Teaching of Economics in the Soviet Union," [*Under the Banner of Marxism*, Nos. 7–8 (1943)], translated and printed in *The American Economic Review* (September, 1944); P. Baran, "New Trends in Russian Economic Thinking?", *American Economic Review* (December, 1944); R. Dunayevskaya, "A New Revision of Marxian Economics," *American Economic Review* (November, 1944); and A. Zauberman, "Economic Thought in the Soviet Union," *The Review of Economic Studies*, Nos. 39–41 (1948–50).

need to be revised and modified. Varga's argument pointed very directly toward the need to stabilize relations with the United States, and to concentrate on domestic Soviet development.*

These examples point up a very important kind of continuity in Soviet affairs that is often missed or forgotten. The revisionist debate that erupted within and between communist countries in the mid-1950's was actually no more than a continuation of the discussion that began in 1943-44 within the Soviet Union, and which was pursued very vigorously as late as 1947 and 1948. The two illustrations mentioned here should not be taken as isolated, atypical events. Early in 1945, for example, a very long and strongly argued revisionist article appeared in the magazine *Foundations of Marxism*. Similar debates took place around short stories and novels. And the philosopher Aleksandrov, who had good things to say about Western capitalist thinkers, was in high favor as late as the first months of 1947.† The popular idea that Soviet leaders emerged from the war ready to do aggressive battle against

---

* The Varga Controversy, as it came to be called, has received considerable attention from American students of the Soviet Union. Varga's book was published as *Changes in the Economy of Capitalism Resulting from the Second World War*. An English translation of the stenographic report of a vigorous debate on the book, in which Varga participated, and which took place on May 7, 14, and 21 of 1947, appeared as *Soviet Views on the Post-War World Economy* (Washington: Public Affairs Press, 1948). The reader who wants real insight into the extent to which Soviet leaders do disagree among themselves, and into the vigorous nature of their discussions, should consult the translation. Of the many comments on the debate, the reader may find it useful to begin with these: F. C. Barghoorn, "The Varga Discussion and Its Significance," *American Slavic and East European Review* (March 1948); H. Marcuse, *Soviet Marxism. A Critical Analysis* (New York: Columbia University Press, 1958); and B. Moore, *Soviet Politics—The Dilemma of Power* (Cambridge: Harvard University Press, 1950). Quite surprisingly, D. F. Fleming does not examine these internal debates in his massive and impressive study, *The Cold War and Its Origins, 1917-1960* (New York: Doubleday and Co., 2 Vols., 1961). He does provide, however, a vast amount of supporting evidence in his discussion of Soviet policy at the end of the war. Further material is in I. Deutscher, *Russia: What Next?* (New York: Oxford University Press, 1953); and B. Moore, *Terror and Progress: USSR* (Cambridge: Harvard University Press, 1954).

† See, as representative: V. Alexandrova, "The Russian People and the 'Lost Peace'—In Literature," *Modern Review* (1949); and P. E. Corbett, "The Aleksandrov Story," *World Politics* (1949).

the United States is simply not borne out by the evidence. Varga himself was not attacked in public in any serious way, for example, until after Winston Churchill's militant Iron Curtain speech in 1946, and the enunciation of the Truman Doctrine in March 1947.

Soviet officials who later chose to live in the West often offered the same kind of evidence bearing on Russian policy at the end of the war. One of the American experts who interviewed many such men offered this general judgment about Soviet policy in Germany. "The paramount consideration was not the extension of the revolution to Germany and the establishment of a Soviet Government there, but the rehabilitation of the Soviet Union's war-ravaged industry and transportation . . . regardless of the effect this policy might have on . . . establishing a Soviet Germany." For that matter, the Red Army's railroad lines across Poland into Germany were ripped up in 1945. And in eastern Europe, the Soviet approach was modeled on the popular front governments of the 1930's rather than upon the existing Soviet system.*

The point of these examples (and there are many more) is not to suggest, let alone try to prove, that Stalin and other Soviet leaders behaved either as Western democrats or as men uninterested in exercising influence in eastern Europe. The point is to indicate and to stress the importance of three quite different things: first, the very significant extent to which Soviet decisions from 1944 through 1947 were based on domestic Russian conditions; second, the degree to which the Soviets were assuming that capitalism would stabilize itself around the great and undamaged power of the United States; and third, the way in which those two factors pointed in the mind of many Russians—including Stalin—to the need to reach some kind of agreement with America. They never defined such an understanding on the basis of abandoning

---

* The quotation is from R. Slusser (ed.), *Soviet Economic Policy in Postwar Germany. A Collection of Papers by Former Soviet Officials* (New York: Research Program on the USSR, 1953). Also see: R. A. Rosa, "The Soviet Theory of 'People's Democracy'," *World Politics* (1949); H. G. Skilling, "People's Democracy, The Proletarian Dictatorship and the Czechoslovak Path to Socialism," *American Slavic and East European Review* (1951); and Brzezinski, *The Soviet Bloc.*

Russian influence in eastern Europe or acquiescing in each and every American proposal just as it first emanated from Washington. But neither did they emerge from World War II with a determination to take over eastern Europe and then embark upon a cold war with the United States.

Beginning in 1946, Stalin grew ever more skeptical about the possibility of negotiating any basic understanding with American leaders. But he never became a fatalist about war with the United States. And the so-called softies in the party were not finally downgraded, and then subjected to vigorous and extensive attacks (including imprisonment) until the late summer and early fall of 1947. It was not until even later that the Soviet Union moved ruthlessly to extend and consolidate its control over eastern Europe.

II. THE OPEN DOOR POLICY AND THE ONSET OF THE COLD WAR

Stalin's effort to solve Russia's problem of security and recovery short of widespread conflict with the United States was not matched by American leaders who acceded to power upon the death of Roosevelt. The President bequeathed them little, if anything, beyond the traditional outlook of open-door expansion. They proceeded rapidly and with a minimum of debate to translate that conception of America and the world into a series of actions and policies which closed the door to any result but the cold war.

The various themes which went into America's conception of the freedom and the necessity of open-door expansion, from the doctrine of the elect to the frontier thesis, had been synthesized into an ideology before Roosevelt's death. Once it was frozen into ideology, it became very difficult—and perhaps artificial, even then—to assign priorities to its various facets. Even a single man, let alone a group, emphasized different themes at various times. Yet the open-door outlook was based on an economic definition of the world, and this explanation of reality was persistently stressed by America's corporate leadership as it developed its policy toward the Soviet Union and other nations. It was not the possession of the atomic bomb which prompted American leaders to get tough with Russia but rather their open-door outlook which interpreted the bomb as the final guarantee that they could go further faster down that path to world predominance.

Long before anyone knew that the bomb would work, most American leaders were operating on the basis of three assumptions or ideas which defined the world in terms of a cold war. The first specified Russia as being evil but weak. This attitude, predominant among American leaders from the first days of the Bolshevik Revolution in 1917, was reinforced and deepened by the nonaggression pact signed by Russia with Nazi Germany in 1939. There is little evidence to support the oft-asserted claim that Americans changed their basic attitude toward the Soviet Union during the war. Most of them welcomed Russian help against Germany, and some of them mitigated their antagonisms and suspicions, but several careful studies make it clear that large and crucial segments of the American public remained "dubious about the prospects of building the peace together with Russia."

Even before the end of the war in Europe, many Americans were again comparing Stalin with Hitler and stressing the importance of avoiding any repetition of the appeasement of Nazi Germany. Others, like John Foster Dulles, who had sought persistently and until a very late date to reach a broad compromise with Hitler and Japan, changed their approach when it came to dealing with Russia. They made no such efforts to reach an understanding with Stalin. And by the time of the San Francisco Conference on the United Nations, such leaders as Averell Harriman were publicly expressing their view that there was an "irreconcilable difference" between Russia and the Western powers.

At the same time, however, very few—if any—American leaders thought that Russia would launch a war. Policy-makers were quite aware of the "pitiful" conditions in western Russia, of the nation's staggering losses and its general exhaustion, of its "simply enormous" need for outside help "to repair the devastation of war," and of Stalin's stress on firm economic and political agreements with the United States to provide the basis for that reconstruction. In their own discussions, American decision-makers drew an astute and crucial distinction between Soviet actions to establish a security perimeter in eastern Europe and an all-out aggressive move against the entire capitalist world. They were right in their estimate that Russia was concerned with the first objective. They were also correct in concluding that the Soviet Union—unlike Nazi Germany—"is not essentially constructed as a dynamic expansionist state."*

Far from emphasizing the imminence of a Russian attack, American leaders stressed the importance of denying any and all Soviet requests or overtures of a revised strategic agreement in the Middle East, and at the same time concentrated on reasserting American influence in eastern Europe while pushing the Russians back to their traditional borders. The first such American action came in the spring and summer of 1945 in the form of protests over Soviet influence that developed as the Red Army moved westward in pursuit of the Nazis. These protests were not prompted by the fear that Russia was about to overwhelm Europe or the world in general, but rather by the traditional outlook of the open door and the specific desire to keep the Soviets from establishing any long-range influence in eastern Europe.

Another basic attitude held by American leaders defined the United States as the symbol and the agent of positive good as opposed to Soviet evil and assumed that the combination of American strength and Russian weakness made it possible to determine the future of the world in accordance with that judgment. One important congressional leader, for example, remarked in 1943 that lend-lease provided the United States with a "wonderful opportunity" to bring the United States to "a greater degree of determining authority" in the world. He was quite aware that his view was "shared by some of the members of the President's Cabinet" and that important State Department officials were "fully in accord" with the same outlook. Another key congressman was thinking in terms of the

* See, as a typical report of such discussions within the American policy-making community, the story in the *New York Times*, September 27, 1945 (p. 4), from which the quotation is taken.

"United States seeking world power as a trustee for civilization."* Following the even earlier lead of publisher Henry R. Luce, who had announced in 1941 that it was high noon of the American Century, various business spokesmen began stressing the need to become "missionaries of capitalism and democracy." Shortly thereafter, a leading oil-industry leader asserted that America "must set the pace and assume the responsibility of the majority stockholder in this corporation known as the world." Such remarks were not unique; they merely represented the increasing verbalization of one aspect of America's traditional policy.

The third essential aspect of the open-door outlook, which also made its appearance before the end of the war, was the fear that America's economic system would suffer a serious depression if it did not continue to expand overseas. Stressing the fact that there remained roughly nine million unemployed in 1940, one leading New Deal senator warned in 1943 that the danger of another depression could not be overemphasized. A government economic expert promptly supported this view with his own report that "it unfortunately is a fact that for the majority of the people in the United States the thing we have liked to refer to as the American standard of living is only possible in situations where two people in the family are working."

The reason for this concern, and the extent to which government participation in the financing of such expansion was crucial, is nicely revealed by two sets of statistics. The first figures concern direct exports. In 1928, when the United States enjoyed a net export surplus with every region of the world except some areas in the tropics, the nation sold 17.1 per cent of the world's exports. Ten years later, during the depression, that share had dropped, despite government loans and subsidies to exporters, to 14.9 per cent. The proportion in 1953, 21.3 per cent, seems at first glance to indicate a dramatic recovery and further gain. But 5.6 per cent of that total was

---

* See, as typical of such remarks, the comments of Karl E. Mundt, A. A. Berle, Jr., John M. Vorys, and Charles A. Eaton, in *Extension of Lend-Lease Act. Hearings Before the Committee on Foreign Affairs. House of Representatives* 78th Cong., 1st Ses. (1943).

paid for by government loans and grants financed by the American taxpayer. Hence the net share of world exports was only 15.6 per cent. Not until 1956, when it reached 17.9 per cent, did the net figure surpass the American export position of 1928.

The second kind of data concerns the extent to which various American corporations depend upon overseas operations. Total foreign sales, including those of directly owned overseas branches and subsidiaries as well as exports from parent American companies, amounted in 1956 to $58 billion. When classified according to the percentage of total sales accounted for by all foreign operations, the pattern is indicated by the following examples: 75 per cent—Standard Oil of New Jersey; more than 70 per cent—H. J. Heinz and Colgate-Palmolive; over 40 per cent—American Radiator, International Harvester, F. W. Woolworth, Gillette Razor, and National Cash Register; better than 30 per cent—Parke Davis Drugs, Sterling Drugs, and Otis Elevators; and between 15 and 30 per cent—Johnson and Johnson, Corn Products Refining, Firestone, Goodyear, International Business Machines, Coca Cola, and Eastman Kodak.*

The drive to achieve those postwar results began in earnest while the war was still being fought. For his part, Secretary Hull never eased off on the pace he had established in 1933. "The primary object," he reiterated in 1940, "is both to reopen the old and seek new outlets for our surplus production." One of his principal concerns was to break into the British trading system, a campaign in which he was vigorously encouraged and supported by American exporters. Hull's weapons included lend-lease, and Britain's growing need for a major recovery loan. The United States made its aid conditional upon the acceptance by England of the open-door principle.†

One of the most vigorous proponents of this assault upon the British imperial market was William L. Clayton, a self-

---

* A convenient, though merely surface, survey is: C. E. Silberman and L. A. Mayer, "The Migration of U.S. Capital," *Fortune* (1958). On investments, see the authoritative *U.S. Business Investments in Foreign Countries* (Washington: Department of Commerce, 1960).

† Here see R. N. Gardner, *Sterling-Dollar Diplomacy* (Oxford: Oxford University Press, 1956).

made man who became head of the world's largest cotton
export business and then moved into the Roosevelt Administration as a policy-maker. His underlying attitude was very
similar to Hull's: "The international economic policies of
nations," Clayton remarked in 1943, "have more to do with
creating conditions which lead to war than any other single
factor." He was committed, as one might expect, to the Open
Door Policy as the way to expand exports. Clayton was unusual, however, in that he was considerably more candid than
most American leaders when speaking about the nature of
that overseas economic expansion. He admitted, for example,
that the United States often tried to close the door to competition once it had gone through and established its own
position. "As a matter of fact, if we want to be honest with
ourselves, we will find that many of the sins that we freely
criticize other countries for practicing have their counterpart
in the United States."

Clayton's comment is particularly relevant to America's insistence that former Axis colonies, and other trustee territories, should be handled in such a way that the United States
would be assured of unrestricted economic access. As Assistant
Secretary Sayre explained the policy, it was centered on establishing "sound economic foundations." "Here again," he noted,
"another distinctively American ideal, expressed at various
times as the Open Door Policy, is made a binding obligation in
all trust territories." The remarks of Sayre and Clayton serve
to clarify and dramatize one of the issues that plagued
American-Soviet relations after 1943. The United States interpreted Russian resistance to the Open Door Policy in eastern
Europe as an unfriendly act, even though Stalin acquiesced in
the principle throughout the Pacific and elsewhere in the
world.

Another policy-maker dramatized this ever-increasing concern with overseas economic expansion by comparing the
American system with the old British empire. America, he
explained, was "a great island" dependent upon a "greater
volume of exports" than even the British had needed in the
nineteenth and early twentieth centuries. But what was very
probably the clearest and most direct statement and explanation of the American approach to the postwar world was pro-

vided in November 1944—five full months before the death of
Roosevelt—by Assistant Secretary of State Dean Acheson.
Testifying before a special Congressional committee on Postwar Economic Policy and Planning, Acheson analyzed the
situation in a remarkable and almost unique outburst of blunt
candor. His remarks cast such a dazzling light on American
foreign policy ever since that date that they warrant extensive
quotation.*

Along with almost every other American leader, Acheson
was gravely concerned lest the economy slide back into the
depression of the 1930's or collapse in a new debacle at the
end of the war. That was the danger, and Acheson repeatedly
emphasized it during his entire career in the Department of
State.† If that happened, he began his testimony in 1944,
"it seems clear that we are in for a very bad time, so far as the
economic and social position of the country is concerned. We
cannot go through another ten years like the ten years at the
end of the twenties and the beginning of the thirties, without
having the most far-reaching consequences upon our economic
and social system."

"When we look at that problem," he continued, "we may
say it is a problem of markets. You don't have a problem of
production. The United States has unlimited creative energy.
The important thing is markets. We have got to see that what
the country produces is used and is sold under financial arrangements which make its production possible." The solution, Acheson explained to the Congressmen, was not in doubt.
"You must look to foreign markets."

Acheson then interrupted the main line of his analysis in
a curious way. He voluntarily threw in a comment that seems
remarkably similar to the admission made by Brooks Adams
in 1900, when he was proposing exactly the same kind of

* All of the testimony during these hearings, however, is very pertinent.
*Post-War Economic Policy and Planning. Hearings Before the Special
Subcommittee on Post-War Economic Policy and Planning. House of
Representatives,* 78th Cong., 2nd Sess. (1944).

† When compared with their subsequent political and historical rhetoric
about the success of the New Deal itself, the candid and sworn testimony
of New Deal leaders after 1943 offers a valuable corrective. More historians should examine it.

expansion. Indeed, the full flavor and import of the episode can only be captured in the give-and-take between Acheson and the chairman of the committee.*

> ACHESON.   We could argue for quite a while that under a different system in this country you could use the entire production of the country in the United States.
>
> WORLEY.   What do you mean by that?
>
> ACHESON.   I take it the Soviet Union could use its entire production internally. If you wish to control the entire trade and income of the United States, which means the life of the people, you could probably fix it so that everything produced here would be consumed here, but that would completely change our Constitution, our relations to property, human liberty, our very conceptions of law. And nobody contemplates that. Therefore, you find you must look to other markets and those markets are abroad. . . . The first thing that I want to bring out is that we need these markets for the output of the United States. If I am wrong about that, then all the argument falls by the wayside, but my contention is that we cannot have full employment and prosperity in the United States without the foreign markets. That is point one, and if anyone wants to challenge me on that we will go over it again.
>
> WORLEY.   I think we are agreed on that.
>
> ACHESON.   How do we go about getting it? What you have to do at the outset is to make credit available. . . . I don't believe private capital can possibly do it.
>
> WORLEY.   Why not?
>
> ACHESON.   I don't think there is enough private

---

* This parallel between Acheson and Adams becomes even more fascinating in the light of two other similar episodes. Adams in 1900 used the words *contain* and *containing* to describe how the United States should deal with Russia. George F. Kennan used precisely the same terminology in 1946 and 1947 in writing his famous "X" article which enunciated the policy that took the word *containment* as its name. In the same year, 1947, the New Deal newspaper columnist Marquis Childs republished Adams's essay, *America's Economic Supremacy*, as a guide to the proper policy for the United States in the cold war. My efforts to find out whether these episodes involved more than coincidence have not been successful. In either case, the continuity of American foreign policy is established beyond question.

capital willing to engage in that activity, which is quite risky. There will be a lot of losses. . . .

As for the significance of the Open Door Policy in this drive for markets, Acheson made that very clear:

> WORLEY.   You don't think there would be a peace agreement without collateral agreements of an economic nature?
>
> ACHESON.   I don't see how it would work, Mr. Chairman. If we tried to do that it would really mean that we would be relying exclusively on the use of force. I don't believe that would work.

As the policy developed, however, American leaders did come to rely rather extensively on the threat of force implied by their short-lived monopoly of the atom bomb. That attitude, and the tension it produced in relations with Russia, ultimately provoked strong protests from Secretary of War Stimson and Secretary of Commerce Henry A. Wallace. Prior to their changes, however, both men supported the orthodox line of policy. Deeply concerned about the problem of preventing a depression, Wallace persistently talked between 1943 and 1947 about overseas economic expansion as the new frontier. "Private enterprise in the United States can survive only if it expands and grows," he argued, and pointed out that he was only trying to help the businessmen do what they themselves advocated. "The old frontiers must be rebuilt," as he put it, and pointed to American economic expansion into the poor, underdeveloped countries as "this unlimited new frontier of opportunities." Wallace of course wanted to reform and improve conditions abroad as part of that extension of American enterprise, and was in many respects the epitome of the New Deal version of Woodrow Wilson's reforming expansionism.

But it is very revealing that Wallace himself spoke favorably of Hoover's similar desire to improve the lot of the overseas poor as an integral part of extending American business operations. "I have considerable sympathy," Wallace remarked as he took over the same cabinet post in 1945, "with Herbert Hoover's problem as Secretary of Commerce." The one obvious

difference in their outlooks was Wallace's willingness to provide the private entrepreneurs with public capital. "It is vital,"
he asserted, "that Government co-operate with the export
trade . . . to put on an aggressive sales campaign abroad."

Wallace's version of the expansionist outlook won him sharp
criticism from Senator Robert A. Taft. Along with his repeated warnings that American policy might well provoke the
Soviets into ever more militant retaliation, and perhaps even
war, Taft's attack on Wallace serves to illustrate the misleading nature of the popular stereotype of the Senator. Taft
immediately spotted the contradiction between the rhetoric of
the New Deal and the reality of its policies. "Dollar diplomacy
is derided," he commented very pointedly in 1945, "although
it is exactly the policy of Government aid to our exporters
which Mr. Wallace himself advocates to develop foreign trade,
except that it did not [in its earlier forms] involve our lending
abroad the money to pay for all our exports."

Despite the perception of his analysis, Taft stood virtually
alone. Congressman Clarence Murdock of Arizona offered what
was perhaps the most striking summary of the majority view:
"The proper foreign outlet is our safety valve." Milo Perkins,
a New Deal businessman who for a time headed the Board of
Economic Warfare, offered a pungent statement of the familiar
either-or thesis that had originated in the 1890's. "We must
sell great quantities of machinery and transport equipment
and machine tools abroad if we are to avoid large-scale factory
shutdowns here at home." Labor and farm leaders joined corporation executives and government officials in supporting that
analysis. "We cannot possibly maintain full production and
full employment," the United Auto Workers announced in
1945, "unless we have a world pool of free and prosperous
consumers." "Foreign trade," the union explained, "can be the
margin between a drop into economic chaos and a steadily
expanding economy." Edward O'Neal, President of the American Farm Bureau Federation, was equally vehement. Agricultural surpluses "will wreck our economy unless we can find
sufficient outlets in foreign markets to help sustain the volume
of production." In his view, the "finest" policy proposal involved Wilson's old idea of extending the Monroe Doctrine
to the world at large. "Let us spread it all over," O'Neal sug-

gested to the congressional committee on postwar planning; "let us run it into China, if necessary, and run it around into Russia."

As it moved quickly to take over government affairs after the death of Roosevelt, the Truman Administration made it clear that it would sustain all these aspects of the traditional approach to foreign policy. "The United States cannot reach and maintain the high level of employment we have set as our goal," Secretary of State James F. Byrnes reiterated, "unless the outlets for our production are larger than they've ever been before in peacetime." Byrnes had neither time nor interest for the idea of working out some agreement with the Russians that involved the recovery loan they had requested. He even sidetracked the basic memorandum dealing with the issue. "I had it placed in the 'Forgotten File'," he later revealed, "as I felt sure that Fred Vinson, the new Secretary of the Treasury, would not press it."

President Harry S. Truman was for his part an enthusiastic and militant advocate of America's supremacy in the world. He seemed, indeed, to react, think, and act as an almost classic personification of the entire Open Door Policy. From a very early date, moreover, he led the rapid revival of the analogy between Nazi Germany and the Soviet Union (and Hitler and Stalin) which became one of the fundamental clichés of America's analysis of the postwar world. Given that analogy, which was very rapidly and very generally accepted, American policy can without much exaggeration be described as an effort to establish the Open Door Policy once and for all by avoiding what were judged—on the basis of the analogy—to have been the errors of appeasement made during the 1930's.

There were two central fallacies involved in that estimate of the world. Soviet Russia and Nazi Germany were significantly different in crucial aspects of domestic and foreign policy; and, unlike the situation in the 1930's, the United States was neither weak nor disarmed. Indeed, it enjoyed a great absolute as well as relative advantage in both economic and military power. As the United States Government candidly admitted even as late as 1962, the United States had been the strongest power in the world ever since 1944. For that matter, it was the existence and the knowledge of that strength that encouraged Truman and other leaders after 1945 to think that they could force the Soviets to accept American proposals without recourse to war.

It is no doubt wrong and inaccurate to conclude that the effort to establish the false analogy between Soviet Russia and Nazi Germany was the product of conscious distortion by America's private and official leaders. Many of them adopted and used that argument in complete sincerity. They simply accepted it without serious thought or critical evaluation. However mistaken in fact and logic, such men were not hypocrites. But it also is true that there were a good many men who shared the attitude of Senator Arthur K. Vandenberg. He thought it was necessary "to scare hell out of the American people" in order to win their active approval and support for the kind of vigorous anti-Soviet policy he wanted. Those men did consciously employ exaggeration and oversimplification to accomplish their objectives. Senator Taft would seem to have offered a sound judgment on that conduct. He remarked during congressional consideration of the European Recovery Program that he was more than a bit tired of having the Russian menace invoked as a reason for doing any- and everything that might or might not be desirable or necessary on its own merits.

Truman not only thought about Russia in terms of Nazi Germany, but he made it clear very soon after he took the oath as President that he intended to reform the world on American terms. He casually told one early visitor "that the Russians would soon be put in their places; and that the United States would then take the lead in running the world in the way that the world ought to be run." Then, on April 23, 1945, he told the Cabinet "that he felt our agreements with the Soviet Union so far had been a one-way street and that he could not continue; it was now or never. He intended to go on with the plans for [the] San Francisco [Conference] and if the Russians did not wish to join us they could go to hell." Senator Vandenberg, soon to become (along with John Foster Dulles) the Republican leader of that bipartisan approach to the Soviet Union, caught the spirit—and reflected the absurd exaggeration—of the outlook of his diary entry of the following day: "FDR's appeasement of Russia is over."

As one insider remarked, "the strong view prevailed" from the very beginning, though it did not take on the form and tone of a great crusade against the Soviet Union and international communism until the end of 1946. Thus, for example, additional lend-lease allocations and shipments to Russia were canceled in May 1945. The full story of the cancellation has never been revealed. In the narrow sense, the action can be interpreted as a blunder. Truman later referred to it as "my greatest mistake," and claimed that, given a second chance, he would have handled it differently. Nevertheless, all lend-lease to the Soviets was closed off promptly once the Japanese surrendered. It is also clear that, on a comparative basis, Russia was treated far less considerately than England and France during the process of termination. In those respects, therefore, the action was repeated.*

But in the first instance, and as Truman later explained, the authority to act had been sought by Leo Crowley, the Foreign Economic Administrator, who proceeded to interpret it very broadly and to use it very vigorously. Truman's oblique comment that the whole affair was "clearly a case of policy-making on the part of Crowley and Grew" implies an explanation that can be substantiated by other evidence. Crowley's push for the power was supported by Admiral William D. Leahy, Assistant Secretary of State Joseph Grew, and Harriman. All those men wanted to use American economic power to coerce the Soviets on policy issues. This is established be-

---

* This reconstruction of the affair is based in the main upon the following sources: *Memoirs by Harry S. Truman. Volume One. The Year of Decisions* (New York: Doubleday and Co., 1955); William D. Leahy, Manuscript Diaries, 1941–1945, State Historical Society of the State of Wisconsin, Madison; *Foreign Relations. The Conference at Malta and Yalta* (Washington: Government Printing Office, 1958); *Extension of the Lend Lease Act. Hearings Before the Committee on Foreign Affairs. House of Representatives.* 79th Cong., 1st Sess.; *Export-Import Bank of 1945. Hearings Before the Committee on Banking and Currency. House of Representatives.* 79th Cong., 1st Sess.; *Export-Import Bank. Hearings Before the Senate Committee on Banking and Currency.* 79th Cong., 1st Sess.; and materials from the Manuscript Papers of Henry L. Stimson and Joseph Grew, Harvard University Library.

yond any question in a Grew memorandum of his phone conversation with Crowley on May 12, 1945, as they were working to obtain a grant of authority from Truman. The document makes it absolutely clear that Crowley and Grew had Russia in the very forefront of their minds as they pressured the President. For his own part, Crowley refused to consider the Russian request for a loan as coming under the lend-lease law, even though he did negotiate such an arrangement involving $9 million with France. Crowley's general outlook was revealed when congressmen questioned him about loans in general. "If you did not like the government," he was asked, "you would not have to make them a loan at all?" "That is right," Crowley replied. "If you create good governments in foreign countries, automatically you will have better markets for ourselves."

Whatever further details may ultimately be added to the story of the termination, there is no doubt that the action seriously antagonized the Russians. Stalin interpreted it as a move to put pressure on him to accept American policies, and bluntly called it "disturbing." Then, in a very revealing series of comments, Stalin told Harry Hopkins in May 1945 that such an approach would not produce Soviet acquiescence.*

Stalin first provided an insight into the differences within the Soviet hierarchy. The Russian leader said that "he would not attempt to use Soviet public opinion as a screen but would speak of the feeling that had been created in Soviet governmental circles as a result of recent moves on the part of the United States Government." "These circles felt a certain alarm," he explained, "in regard to the attitude of the United States Government. It was their impression that the American attitude towards the Soviet Union had perceptibly cooled once it became obvious that Germany was defeated, and that it was as though the Americans were saying that the Russians were no longer needed."

To be specific, Stalin continued, the way lend-lease had been cancelled "had been unfortunate and even brutal . . . [and]

---

* The following quotations come from a stenographic record of the conversations reproduced in R. E. Sherwood, *Roosevelt and Hopkins. An Intimate History* (New York: Harper and Bros., 1948), 893–94.

had caused concern to the Soviet Government. If the refusal to continue lend-lease was designed as pressure on the Russians in order to soften them up, then it was a fundamental mistake."

In this episode involving lend-lease, as well as in additional examples reported by Truman, Byrnes, and other American leaders, Molotov emerges as the leader and spokesman of the militant wing of the Soviet hierarchy. It should be remembered in this connection that Molotov caught the full impact of Truman's vehement anti-Soviet attitude in a face-to-face meeting on April 23, 1945, that followed the crucial discussion of that policy among American leaders on the same day. There is considerable and convincing evidence, furthermore, that Molotov often took and persisted in a very tough line with the United States until Stalin intervened to modify and soften the Russian position. This interpretation of the disagreements among Soviet leaders is further and dramatically reinforced by events after Stalin's death, and particularly by the continued agitation by Molotov against Premier Nikita S. Khrushchev's efforts to establish the policy of co-existence and peaceful transition to socialism and communism.

In 1945, as in later situations of a similar nature, the position of Molotov and his supporters was unquestionably strengthened by the actions of the United States. Stalin was broadly justified in his fears expressed to Hopkins about the developing American attitude concerning the importance of Russia after the defeat of Germany. Truman and his advisors did not immediately and drastically downgrade Russian help. They continued to seek Soviet assistance against the Japanese until they learned that the atom bomb was a success. At that point, their attitude changed drastically: they clearly wanted to defeat Japan before the Russians entered the war. Even before that, however, at the end of April 1945, the change had begun to occur. Following the meeting of April 23, for example, the United States stopped pressing for air bases in Siberia, and ceased worrying about clearing the North Pacific shipping lanes to Russia's far eastern ports. In a similar way, American position papers prepared for the forthcoming meeting with Stalin at Potsdam revealed a determination to push for the open door in eastern Europe.

III. A NEW VISION OF OMNIPOTENCE AND A MISREADING OF HISTORY PROMPT THE UNITED STATES TO OVERPLAY ITS HAND

Following upon President Roosevelt's clear expression of a desire to retain "complete freedom of action," the United States Government under President Truman initiated and sustained a vigorous drive to undercut the Stalin-Churchill agreement of October 1944, concerning eastern Europe, and to replace it with the Open Door Policy. Churchill supported that determined effort to subvert the understanding which he himself had originally and voluntarily written out and pushed across the table to Stalin. Truman and Churchill undertook that course, moreover, in the full knowledge and open acknowledgement that Stalin had honored his part of the bargain in Greece.

This insistence upon applying the Open Door Policy to eastern Europe (and, of course, to Asia) was decided upon before anyone knew for sure that the atom bomb would work.* Along with the feeling among American policy-makers that Russia's war-caused weakness would enable them to secure major concessions from Moscow, that consideration must be kept constantly in mind when following the sequence of events after the defeat of Germany. The success of the bomb strengthened an existing attitude and a traditional strategy—it did not call forth a new approach.

Stimson's diary entry covering a conversation with Truman on June 6, 1945, indicates that American leaders were con-

---

* This account of the Potsdam and London conferences, which took place betwen July and November 1945, is based upon a wide selection of primary and secondary materials. The reader without recourse to manuscript collections can find the main elements of the story, and most of the quotations used here, in these published volumes: J. F. Byrnes, *Speaking Frankly,* and *All In One Lifetime* (New York: Harper and Bros., 1947 and 1958); W. S. Churchill, *Triumph and Tragedy* (Boston: Houghton Mifflin, 1953); H. L. Stimson and M. Bundy, *On Active Service In Peace and War* (New York: Harper and Bros., 1948); *Memoirs by Harry S. Truman;* and the most illuminating volumes, *Foreign Relations. The Conference of Berlin (The Potsdam Conference), 1945. Two Volumes* (Washington: Gvt. Printing Office, 1960), which also print revealing excerpts from Stimson's Diary.

scious of the relationship between the bomb and their general strategy at an early date. Truman "said that he had been thinking of that," Stimson noted, "and mentioned the same things that I was thinking of, namely the settlement of the Polish, Rumanian, Yugoslavian, and Manchurian problems." By the end of the month, in preparation for the Potsdam Conference, the American position concerning the countries of eastern Europe had become clear and firm. The United States planned "to insist on the reorganization of the present governments or the holding of free general elections." The broad objective was phrased in the classic terms of the Open Door Policy: "To permit American nationals to enter, move about freely and carry on commercial and government operations unmolested in the countries in question."

The goal was "access, on equal terms, to such trade, raw materials and industry" as existed and developed. In the meantime, such access was sought "to modify existing arrangements." As part of that general effort, American officials planned to demand unrestricted movement for American newspapermen so that "the spotlight [can be] trained on these areas." And finally, the United States emphasized the specific objective of internationalizing the commercial waterways of the Danube River system with a Western majority on the board of control.

Similar stress was laid on guaranteeing the Open Door Policy in Asia. American leaders seem to have entertained a particularly vivid hope that the defeat of Japan would turn the clock back to 1903–1904; a maneuver that would enable the United States to step back on the mainland of Asia at the moment of its greatest success in Manchuria with the expectation that this time it would not be frustrated as before. The Russians posed the only danger to this idyllic picture. On the eve of the first general session at Potsdam, for example, Stimson seems to have set himself the role of special tutor to Truman and Byrnes on the importance of the Open Door Policy in the Far East. Even though the lessons had apparently been going on for some time, Stimson saw Truman again on July 14, 1945. "[I] went over [it] with him carefully," Stimson wrote in his diary, "again and again warning him to be absolutely sure that the Russians did not block off our trade."

Still concerned, Stimson wrote the President a special letter on July 16. Concentrating on "our clear and growing interests in the Orient," the Secretary all but hammered the words through the page in the course of his pounding on the crucial importance of the Open Door Policy. Ideally, of course, Russia should not have anything to say about handling Japan or the general problems of the Far East. At most, and only if it became absolutely necessary in the face of Soviet complaints, some kind of "token occupation" would be arranged.

Stimson next had a briefing session with Byrnes on July 17. The subject had not changed. Neither had the dedication of the tutor. "I impressed on him," Stimson recorded, "the importance of the Open Door Policy." A series of special reports made the same point. Harriman, for example, prepared one which placed—even in that context—a noticeable emphasis on "the development of commerce and trade of the United States." Perhaps his service as an artillery officer in World War I had inured him to such bombardments, for Truman seemed never to blink at the hammering on the same point. Obviously pleased, Stimson reported on July 18, 1945, that the President "was confident of sustaining the Open Door Policy."

Stalin arrived in Potsdam with a noticeably different set of priorities. He was still concerned about Russia's frontiers in Europe, about preventing Germany from trying it all over in another 25 years, and about a major economic transfusion for the Soviet Union's battered economy. Apparently shrewd enough to realize that he had but little chance to obtain a large loan from the United States, and in any event unable to plan on that basis in the summer of 1945, Stalin laid immediate and heavy emphasis on being treated as an equal and upon obtaining massive reparations from Germany and its former allies.

"This Council," Stalin remarked in explaining the Soviet view of the conference at its first general session, "will deal with reparations and will give an indication of the day when the Peace Conference should meet." The primary political issue, he continued, was that of dealing with Germany and its former allies. That was "high policy. The purpose of such a policy was to separate these countries from Germany as a great force." Recurring often to the "many difficulties and sacrifices" brought upon Russia by those Axis partners, Stalin argued that the proper strategy was "to detach them once and for all from Germany." As for reparations, Russia would if necessary "compel" such deliveries.

The American response on reparations was crucial to the outcome of the Potsdam Conference, and also, very probably, to the whole course of subsequent events. "Reparations," Byrnes told Molotov on July 20, "do not seem to the United States to be an immediate problem." He then added that "the United States does not intend to make advances to any country in order that reparations may be paid by them." "We do not intend, as we did after the last war, to provide the money for the payment of reparations." The full significance of those remarks by Byrnes cannot be grasped without understanding both the background of each of them, and the interrelationship between them. It seems wise, therefore, to discuss them separately before putting them together.

First of all, and as revealed in Byrne's remark about loans, American policy-makers had misread the history of their experience with reparations after World War I. They concluded that American loans to Germany had simply ended up as reparations to England and France, who themselves had not repaid their debts to the United States. In the American view, therefore, the United States had been twice played the fool. The vigorous assertion by Byrnes reflected a determination not to fall into the same trap still another time.

That reaction was based on a seriously distorted interpretation of the World War I experience. It neglected, on the one hand, the creative role of American loans and the harmful effects of having actually collected money from England and France. On the other hand, and regardless of the estimate made of those and similar factors, the World War I situation blinded American leaders to the vastly different one that existed at the end of World War II. It was not so much that they had learned no lesson from history but rather that they had become almost obsessed with the wrong lesson.

The real point was that the capital for reconstruction at the end of World War II had to come from some place. Alternative sources were available. Either it could come from the United States under more relevant conditions and terms than had been arranged at the end of World War I, or it could come in the form of reparations taken by Russia—reparations which could be stopped only by recourse to another war. American policy-makers had used history to block their view of the present.

In order to avoid the second alternative, American leaders would obviously have had to negotiate a loan to Russia in conjunction with their discussion and settlement of other issues. But that approach was never even initiated, let alone put into sustained operation. The contradiction involved can be explained, however, by reference to the atom bomb. *Byrnes knew, when he told Molotov on July 20 that reparations were not "an immediate problem," that the atom bomb was a success.* The first news reached Potsdam on July 18. And as Stimson noted in his diary, Truman and other American leaders were "highly delighted" and "very greatly reinforced." It seems very likely, therefore, that the information on the bomb (even though the first dispatches were not complete accounts) served to convince the United States that it could hold the line on reparations and bargain from a position of formidable power.

But this reaction actually served, in a deeply ironic way, to close both the intellectual and the psychological jaws of the trap that American policy-makers had set for themselves. For in fact it left the United States with no moderate, flexible policy. It hardened both the feeling that the Russians would have to come to terms and the reading of history to the point that no loans should be granted if they would end up as reparations. That attitude left the United States with no choice but to acquiesce or use the bomb if the Russians refused to give way and accept American conditions for economic aid.

The extent to which this analysis explains American policy can be seen by the response to further news about the bomb test. Truman had already indicated, in a private conference with Churchill, that he was very favorably inclined toward the old Roosevelt idea of an Anglo-American entente. He was also aware of the understanding between Churchill and Roosevelt of September 18, 1944, concerning the bomb: "The suggestion that the world should be informed . . . with a view to an international agreement regarding its control and use," the two had agreed, "is not accepted."

Churchill seems to have insinuated in his masterful way

that the secret might be kept from Stalin. This was by no means a novel idea. It had, after all, been kept from him up to that point. And Stimson records that he and others were very "doubtful" about sharing the news of the test bomb. However it evolved, and Truman appears to have refused to consider saying nothing to the Russians, the final compromise was to tell Stalin in a brief, casual way that the United States had developed a new weapon. Much has been made of the fact that Stalin already knew about the bomb through espionage. That is of course true, but he probably learned more of direct importance in observing how the news of the successful test firing affected the attitude and manner of Truman and Byrnes at the next session of the Potsdam Conference.

Stimson reports that Truman was "immensely pleased" and "tremendously pepped up by it." The President "said it gave him an entirely new feeling of confidence." This change is apparent even in reading the third-person stenographic account of the meeting with Stalin on July 21, 1945. One of the first questions to arise concerned the governments in eastern Europe, and this is the official account.

> PRESIDENT TRUMAN: The American Government was unable to recognize the governments of the other satellite countries [besides Italy]. When these countries were established on a proper basis, the United States would recognize them and not before. The President stated that the meeting would proceed and that this question would be passed over.

After he returned to England, Churchill told the House of Commons that "we possessed powers which were irresistible." His comments to Stimson at the time, in Potsdam, are perhaps even more revealing. "He [Truman] stood up to the Russians in a most emphatic and decisive manner, telling them as to certain demands that they absolutely could not have and that the United States was entirely against them. . . . He told the Russians just where they got off and generally bossed the whole meeting."

Truman bossed the meeting but he did not change American policy on reparations. That oversight served to subvert the power of the bomb. An astute American observer warned on the next day, July 22, that the Russian position on reparations should not be discounted. It was backed by "intense popular feeling and fresh experience." But the old bloc against loans, when combined with the new vision of omnipotence, led the United States into a dead end. In order to avoid financing Russian reparations through loans to Germany, Italy, or other former Axis partners, and with the myopic confidence induced by the news of the bomb, Byrnes proposed to Molotov on July 23 that "each country tak[e] reparations from its own zone."

*Now the fascinating thing is that the Russians fought that proposal for one whole week—from July 23 to July 31—before Stalin finally agreed to it. Even then, he remarked very sharply that it was "the opposite of liberal."**

Those two sentences have been set apart, and even further emphasized, for two reasons. First: the Byrnes offer to Molotov of July 23 clearly meant that the Russians would have a free hand in their zone of Germany and throughout eastern Europe. The freedom to control economics implied—demanded—political control. Assistant Secretary of State Clayton understood this point and commented on it with great perception in a memorandum of August 16, 1945, after the offer had been accepted by the Soviets. Although he was formally denying the point he was raising, the tone of his remarks needs no comment. "There appears to be," he noted ruefully, "an unfortunate tendency to interpret the reparations operating agreement as an indication of complete abandonment of four power treatment of Germany. This is not stated in the texts and should not be accepted as a necessary conclusion. . . ." But whether accepted or not, that was the meaning of the final arrangement.

To argue that the Russians did not understand the implications of the Byrnes offer of July 23 even though Clayton did is to argue that they were fools. To argue that they did understand it and still acted as they did is to argue that they played Byrnes and Truman and Stimson along for one entire week as a matter of private amusement. Those positions can be held and defended as viable explanations of Russian behavior. But

* Italics added to the material quoted, as well as to my words.

the evidence indicates that the Russians very deeply wanted a firm commitment on reparations in the form of heavy industrial equipment from the restored production of the Ruhr Valley more than they wanted anything else. Such reparations would not only provide crucial help at home, but the agreement providing for them would be based on an Allied control of German industry that would in turn limit Germany's ability to start another war. Clayton himself, certainly as conservative and hard-headed an operator as the United States had produced, concluded in a memorandum of July 27, 1945, that this was the correct analysis. Molotov's behavior between July 23 and July 31 further supports that interpretation.

Molotov connected the issues of reparations and German war potential very simply: "The question of reparations was even more urgent because unless this was settled there could be no progress on economic matters" involving the future strength of German industry. Hence the Soviets wanted "clear replies to the questions." Byrnes gave them one by suddenly remarking that the United States now considered the Yalta figure of 10 billions for Russia to be "impractical." Molotov then shot back that the Soviets were "entitled to a clear answer" on what figure the United States did find acceptable. Failing to obtain one, Molotov then raised—very directly and without any frills—the central implication of the proposal that Byrnes had offered on July 23.

> MR. MOLOTOV: My understanding, Secretary Byrnes, is that you have in mind the proposal that each country should take reparations from its own zone. If we fail to reach an agreement the result will be the same. . . .
> THE SECRETARY [BYRNES]: Yes. . . .
> MR. MOLOTOV: said would not the Secretary's suggestion mean that each country would have a free hand in their own zone and would act entirely independently of the others?
> THE SECRETARY [BYRNES]: said that was true in substance. . . .

In spite of those candid and revealing remarks by Byrnes, the Soviet Union nevertheless continued its efforts to reach an agreement involving all of Germany. Molotov was still "anxious" about the issue on June 29 and 30. He wanted "a fixed sum or quantity agreed upon," including materials from the Ruhr, because the Soviets feared "they would be left with very little equipment as reparations in spite of the fact that the Germans had destroyed Soviet industries. They needed agricultural machinery and [goods] to rehabilitate their railroads." They also wanted to settle what Stalin had on the first day of the conference referred to as the issue of "high policy"— preventing Germany from attacking Russia in another 25 years.

Finally, in the face of continued American refusal to discuss the issues in that related way, Stalin accepted the Byrnes proposal of July 23, 1945. He then extended it in a way that clearly foreshadowed the division of Europe. The specific issue involved the assignment of German assets in other European countries, but the discussion immediately picked up overtones of a far broader nature.

> PREMIER STALIN: . . . with regard to shares and foreign investments, perhaps the demarcation lines between the Soviet and Western zones of occupation should be taken as the dividing lines and everything west of that line would go to the Allies and everything east of that line to the Russians.
>
> THE PRESIDENT [TRUMAN] inquired if he meant a line running from the Baltic to the Adriatic.
>
> PREMIER STALIN replied in the affirmative. . . .
>
> [BRITISH FOREIGN SECRETARY] BEVIN said he agreed and asked if Greece would belong to Britain. . . .
>
> PREMIER STALIN suggested that the Allies take Yugoslavia and Austria would be divided into zones. . . .
>
> MR. BYRNES said he thought it was important to have a meeting of minds. Mr. Bevin's question was whether the Russians' claim was limited to the zone occupied by the Russian Army. To that he understood Mr. Stalin to say 'yes.' If that were so he was prepared to agree.
>
> PREMIER STALIN replied in the affirmative. . . .
>
> THE PRESIDENT [TRUMAN] said that he agreed with the Soviet proposal.

The American decision to give the Russians a free hand on reparations throughout eastern Europe can in the end be explained only in one of three ways. The first would be to assert that the United States knowingly handed eastern Europe over to the Soviet Union. This is absurd on the face of it. It is also belied by Truman's actions during the conference, and by his blunt public remarks after the meeting was over. The eastern European countries, he announced on August 9, 1945, were "not to be spheres of influence of any one power." The Open Door Policy was thereby reaffirmed. A second explanation would be based on the idea that the United States made the reparations deal without understanding its political implications. But that interpretation is undercut by the analyses prepared by Clayton and other American officials who did see those possibilities.

The third explanation is supported by direct and indirect evidence. It is, simply, that the United States—confident in its vast economic and military superiority over Russia—made the reparations agreement to avoid any indirect financing of Soviet recovery. American leaders were certain that the bomb, and Russia's great recovery needs, provided them with the leverage to re-establish the Open Door, and pro-Western governments, in eastern Europe.

This vision of omnipotence was apparent in Truman's remarks of August 11, 1945. "We must constitute ourselves," he explained, "trustees of this new force to prevent its misuse." As for the possibility that the Soviets would construct their own bomb, Byrnes recalled that "no one seemed too alarmed at the prospect." But perhaps the best evidence of the American attitude came in connection with the use of the bomb against Japan. Byrnes later remarked that American leaders had eastern Europe as well as Asia in mind when they reached the decision to use the weapon as soon as possible.

That recollection is borne out by the evidence of the time. The decision to bomb Japan as quickly as possible was made during the Potsdam Conference, and at the very time of the toughest discussions about eastern Europe. In a very candid meeting on July 23, 1945, Truman, General George C. Marshall, Stimson and others generally agreed that the Russians were no longer needed in the war against Japan. They also talked very directly of using the bomb before the Russians could enter that conflict. Actually, however, that was not a new approach. Stimson had recommended as early as July 2, 1945, that the bomb should be dropped at a time when "the Russian attack, if actual, must not have progressed too far." And once it had proved out in the test, Truman was "intensely pleased" with the chance of using it before the Russians even entered the war.

This sense of urgency about using the bomb makes it possible to advance beyond the question of whether the United States dropped the bomb to end the war against Japan, or whether it did so in order to check the Russians. The evidence provided by the government archives and private American leaders converges on one explanation: The United States dropped the bomb to end the war against Japan *and thereby stop the Russians in Asia, and to give them sober pause in eastern Europe.*

Once it was known to work, the atomic offensive against Japan could have been delayed as much as a month or six weeks—if all that had been at stake was the saving of American lives which might be lost in the invasion of Kyushu that was projected for the fall. By that time, for example, the United States would have had a small arsenal of the weapons, so that it would have made little difference if the first drop during a demonstration had misfired, or otherwise failed. As for the saving of lives, they would still have been spared by using the weapon in September. But the bomb had to be used quickly, and if necessary repeatedly, if the war was to be ended before the Russians honored their promise to attack within three months after Germany was defeated.

Secretary of State Byrnes has offered this very explanation of the dropping of the bomb—and with equal directness. Indeed, he has done so twice. He was asked in 1960, on the fifteenth anniversary of the bomb, whether there was "any urgency to end the war in the Pacific before the Russians became too deeply involved?" "There certainly was on my part," Byrnes replied. "We wanted to get through with the Japanese phase of the war before the Russians came in."* Even earlier,

---

* J. F. Byrnes, "We Were Anxious to Get the War Over," *U.S. News and World Report* (August 15, 1960). See also the remarks of Leo Szilard in the same issue for further evidence on the point.

in 1958, Byrnes revealed how the United States encouraged Chiang Kai-shek to drag out his negotiations with Stalin over their arrangements in Manchuria.* Referring to an American dispatch to Chiang of July 23, 1945, Byrnes explained the meaning and importance of a particular sentence. "The second sentence was to encourage the Chinese to continue negotiations after the adjournment of the Potsdam Conference. . . . If Stalin and Chiang were still negotiating, it might delay Soviet entrance and the Japanese might surrender. The President was in accord with that view."

American leaders were becoming so enthusiastic and confident over the power of the bomb that Secretary of War Stimson undertook a very courageous and searching review of the existing attitude. Even before Roosevelt died, Stimson was somewhat disturbed over the way various members of the government were reacting to the progress reports on the weapon. True enough, he felt that the bomb should be used against Japan, and kept from the Russians until safeguards had been established; but he also fretted that the attitude of the majority of American leaders would lead neither to peace nor prosperity. During the next five months, Stimson grew progressively more convinced that the American attitude and policy concerning the bomb was leading into another armament race, and perhaps even to a horrible war with Russia. On the eve of the Potsdam Conference, for example, he cautioned Truman that war would become inevitable if the United States took the position that all differences with the Soviet Union were irreconcilable. The Secretary's increasing concern was very probably caused by the interaction of four factors: the strong line taken by Truman and Byrnes at Potsdam; the awful destruction caused by the bombs at Hiroshima and Nagasaki; the clear evidence that Byrnes and the President had been encouraged by the bomb to maintain and even increase their pressure on Russia at the upcoming foreign ministers' conference scheduled for September in London; and his own searching thought and reflection on the problem, which was certainly provoked

---

* J. F. Byrnes, *All in One Lieftime*, 291–99; Truman's Memoirs, 315–19, 423–25; and *Foreign Relations. The Conference at Potsdam, Volume II*, 276.

in part by his own great responsibility in recommending the use of the weapon.

The evidence suggests very strongly that Stimson devoted most of his intellectual and moral energy to the problem of the bomb from the end of the Potsdam Conference through the time when he received reports on the havoc caused in Japan. The result was a performance very similar, though of course more courageous and dramatic, to the one resulting from his experience in the late 1920's with armed intervention in Latin America. In that instance he concluded he had been wrong and set about to bring the Marines home from Nicaragua and to change the basic policy.

Stimson decided in the late summer of 1945 that the United States "was on the wrong path" in handling Russia in connection with the bomb. Having made that judgment, he undertook a brave, serious effort to persuade Truman and Byrnes to change their policy. He saw Byrnes on September 4, 1945, only to discover that the Secretary of State "was very much against any attempt to co-operate with Russia." Stimson noted that Byrnes was "full of his problems with the coming meeting of the foreign ministers and he looks to having the presence of the bomb in his pocket, so to speak, as a great weapon."

Byrnes left for London on September 5, unmoved by Stimson's arguments. Deeply concerned, and aware that his long government service was coming to an end, Stimson took his case directly to the President. His formal letter and memorandum to Truman dated September 11, 1945, made two crucial points. The first involved his conclusion, based on a careful evaluation and analysis of all the evidence he could obtain, that American efforts to force the pace, or determine the nature, of internal relaxation or liberalization in Russia by applying pressure "would be so resented that it would make the objective we have in view less probable." It followed from that estimate that the most vital issue of American foreign affairs concerned the way that the United States dealt with Russia in connection with the bomb. Stimson outlined the consequences of the then existing attitude and policy of Truman and Byrnes with a degree of accuracy that seems almost eerie in view of subsequent developments. "Unless the Soviets are voluntarily invited into the [nuclear] partnership upon a basis of co-operation and trust, we are going to maintain the Anglo-Saxon bloc over against the Soviet in the possession of this weapon. Such a condition will almost certainly stimulate feverish activity on the part of the Soviet toward the development of this bomb in what will in effect be a secret armament race of a rather desperate character. There is evidence to indicate that such activity may have already commenced."

He continued in a passage so important that he italicized it when making the document public in 1948. *"Those relations may be perhaps irretrievably embittered by the way in which we approach the solution of the bomb with Russia. For if we fail to approach them now and merely continue to negotiate with them, having this weapon rather ostentatiously on our hip, their suspicions and their distrust of our purposes and motives will increase."*

In conclusion, Stimson stressed the need for a direct approach *"to Russia." "I emphasize perhaps beyond all other considerations,"* he wrote, *"the importance of taking this action with Russia as . . . peculiarly the proposal of the United States. Action of any international group of nations, including many small nations who have not demonstrated their potential power or responsibility in this war would not, in my opinion, be taken seriously by the Soviets."*

Stimson's powerful argument may have caused Truman to pause, and perhaps momentarily to reconsider the militant anti-Soviet policy he had laid down on April 23, 1945. If so, the second thoughts were quickly set aside. Byrnes arrived in London determined to apply the strategy of the Open Door Policy in every area of the world. On the question of Axis colonies, for example, the American proposal was to place them under a trusteeship guaranteeing the open-door principle. And as far as Japan and the Asia settlement were concerned, the United States took its control so much for granted that Byrnes was truly and literally "surprised" when the Russians asked for some share in making the decisions.

The clash in London was most fully revealed in connection with the two issues that had dogged American-Soviet relations ever since 1944. The first involved the continued efforts of the United States to abrogate the Churchill-Stalin bargain of October 1944, which had underwritten Soviet predominance in eastern Europe. The second was defined by the refusal of the United States to commit itself on the reparations issue, which for their part the Russians stressed above all else. On both questions, furthermore, Byrnes had in Labor Foreign Secretary Ernest Bevin an ally whose militance measured up to the standard set by Churchill.

As it happened in London, moreover, the United States used its power to attempt to displace an existing agreement. As Byrnes later explained to the Congress, the American objective was "the maintenance of the open door in the Balkans." Specifically, Byrnes was "disturbed" by, and sought to limit or stop completely, the Soviet moves to establish close economic partnerships with eastern European nations. In the positive sense, he sustained Truman's drive launched during the Potsdam meeting to internationalize the entire Danubian waterway system.

That move of Truman and Byrnes in 1945 was in many respects similar and comparable to Secretary of State Knox's attempt in 1909 to internationalize the Manchurian railway system. The analogy is illuminating. The American objective was the same in both cases: as the London *Times* described the postwar maneuver, to establish the conditions under which there would be "free entry into the Danube Valley and Eastern Europe for the goods and capital of the Western countries." And just as it had been assumed in Manchuria, so it was also assumed in eastern Europe in 1945 that such free access for American economic power would in turn help to create and sustain political predominance. The American demand for free elections in eastern Europe was considered by American policy-makers as much a means to such economic and political ends as a philosophic or moral end in and of itself.*

But as Knox had failed in 1909, so did Byrnes fail in 1945. As they had done in 1909, the Russians in 1945 evaluated the American proposal for exactly what it was. And as in the earlier episode, so also in the later one—the Russians resisted. One exchange between Byrnes and Molotov summarized not only the impasse at London in 1945, but much of the diplomacy of the succeeding 15 years. The Secretary of State tried to

---

* On this point see: H. J. Morgenthau, "The End of An Illusion," *Commentary* (November 1961).

persuade Molotov that the United States, despite its demands for the Open Door and its refusal to come to terms on reparations, was not trying to weaken or close out Soviet influence in eastern Europe. "I must tell you," Molotov replied, "I have my doubts as to this."

IV. THE DIPLOMACY OF THE VICIOUS CIRCLE

The New York *Times* correspondent Herbert L. Matthews wrote from London on September 25, 1945, what probably remains the best short analysis of what happened between the spring and the early fall of that fateful year. "France, Britain, and the United States, in seeking to absorb eastern Europe into a unified continental system, are aiming to weaken the Eastern bloc, and at the same time they are being forced with varying degrees of reluctance into the formation of that very Western block that Russia dreads.

"It is a vicious circle. . . ."

Soviet Russia's initial response to the American outlook and action was ambivalent. On the one hand, and by necessity, it launched a major program of reconstruction based on labor and capital extracted from a war-weary and weakened populace, supplemented where possible by reparations from Germany and eastern Europe. On the other hand, and as feared by former Secretary of State Hull as early as April 1945, it sought to "establish outposts, bases, and warm-water harbors in many areas and add buffer territory and otherwise prepare her own outward defenses just as fully as if the United Nations were not in existence." Yet in every case but one, that involving eastern Europe, Russia retreated from these efforts in the face of America's vigorous and militant opposition.

Thus Russia withdrew from Iran, leaving the Western powers in a predominant strategic and economic position. Thus it also retreated from its efforts to modify Western supremacy at the entrance (and exit) of the Black Sea. And thus it acquiesced, though under vigorous protest, when on May 3, 1946, the United States abruptly and unilaterally announced that it was terminating reparations to Russia from the Western zones of occupied Germany. These reparations, never large, had been arranged as part of interzone economic rehabilitation after the Potsdam Conference.

This decision, apparently taken on his own responsibility by General Lucius Clay, the Military Governor of the American zone, very probably had a crucial effect on the deteriorating relations between the United States and the Soviet Union.* It can of course be debated whether any single action can or should be called decisive when the general situation already exhibited such momentum toward sustained and embittered antagonism. On the other hand, Soviet officials stationed in Germany who later came to the West testified that it was "one of the pivotal events." And it provoked the first all-out postwar propaganda attack by the Russians upon American policy. Those considerations make it useful to examine the episode more fully.

It is essential first of all to realize the issue was economic. Given that, the importance and the impact of the action can best be understood by placing it in its general and specific context. At the beginning of the year, on January 5, 1946, Truman had declared that World War III was inevitable unless Russia was "faced with an iron fist and strong language." By the end of January, Byrnes had discontinued "the practice of having private meetings with the Russians," even though "they were always eager to do so." Then, on March 5, Truman applauded from the platform as Churchill delivered his extremely violent and unrestrained anti-Soviet "Iron Curtain" speech at Fulton, Missouri.

Stalin promptly and bluntly called Churchill's performance "a dangerous act." He went on to speak of it as "something in the nature of an ultimatum: 'Accept our rule voluntarily and then all will be well; otherwise war is inevitable'." A bit later, on April 4, 1946, Stalin told the American Ambassador to Russia that in his opinion the United States had "definitely aligned itself with Great Britain against the U.S.S.R."

Clay's action on reparations was intimately bound up with American conditions for a loan to Russia. American repre-

---

* W. H. McNeill, in his excellent volume, *America, Britain, and Russia. Their Co-operation and Conflict, 1941–46* (London: Oxford University Press, 1953), was perhaps the first to sense the importance of Clay's action.

sentatives persistently tied such aid to the question of the Open Door Policy in eastern Europe. Secretary of Commerce Wallace warned Truman on March 14, 1946, that such an approach was increasing the tension. He suggested that it would be more fruitful "to talk with them in an understanding way" about "their dire economic needs and of their disturbed sense of security." Contrary to the impression created by all the vicious attacks on Wallace, he was not proposing anything that could be called appeasement. He wanted a calm and less adamant approach to economic discussions as a means of persuading the Russians to modify "many of their assumptions and conclusions which stand in the way of peaceful world cooperation." Wallace wanted neither to demand or to surrender, but only to bargain in a mature fashion. But quite in keeping with his support for Churchill, Truman reports that he "ignored this letter of Wallace's." Note that the President does not say merely that he considered but finally rejected Wallace's analysis and proposal. He "ignored" it. In that difference lies considerable insight into the state of the cold war as of March 1946.

By cutting off reparations so soon thereafter from the western, industrial zones of Germany, Clay in effect put real and positive, as well as verbal and negative, pressure on the Russians. The Soviets no doubt interpreted Clay's actions as proof of America's double standard of judgment. For at the very outset of the four-power occupation of Germany, long before the Russians took any such steps, the French had refused to be bound by any joint Allied decisions. They handled their zone as they pleased. To the Russians, at any rate, the conclusion was obvious. Not only could they not negotiate a loan, as the French had been able to do, but they were being punished in a very vital area for the kind of behavior that, when taken by the French, was tolerated by the United States.

Clay's action was also important as background for a subsequent and very significant move by the United States. His termination of reparations came less than six weeks before the United States offered its long-heralded plan to control and ultimately share the secrets of atomic energy. The point here is not only that Clay's clamp-down on reparations squeezed a very tender Russian nerve, and thereby increased the general tension; but that it was an economic nerve that was very quickly pinched again and even harder by the American proposal on nuclear energy.

The American approach to the atom appeared first as the so-called Acheson-Lilienthal Report of March 1946. During the next three months it was transformed, under the general direction of Bernard Baruch, from a general analysis and report into a proposal involving sanctions against violators. Then, on June 14, it was presented to the United Nations. The final policy proposal is usually considered to be proof positive of American statesmanship and generosity, and its rejection by the Russians as the final evidence of their intransigence. While that matched set of conclusions can be, and has been, advanced with great power and persuasion, it nevertheless seems worthwhile to review the essential elements of the episode.

The strongest part of the generally accepted favorable interpretation concerns the point that the United States offered the proposal even though it enjoyed a monopoly of nuclear power. It is usually implied, furthermore, that America did this without any prompting or pressure. Let there be no misunderstanding on two points. It was a positive move, and there is no reason to question either the sincerity or the good intentions of American leaders. In a similar way, it can be argued that it is unrealistic and even unfair to criticize the United States on the grounds that it should have done more—or should have done differently what it did. This may be, even probably is, true in the sense of being highly improbable.

But it *is* fair to point out at the very beginning of any evaluation of the American plan that such criticism is *not* unrealistic or unfair in the sense of being made outside the context and obligations of direct governmental responsibility. For Stimson made exactly such criticism in September 1945, while he was Secretary of War.

Stimson's memorandum to Truman offers or suggests three crucial insights into the general nature of the American attitude and policy. The first stems from his blunt warning that the United States would not secure its objectives if it merely continued to negotiate with Russia *"having this weapon rather ostentatiously on our hip,"* or if it did so in a way that involved *"many small nations who have not demonstrated their* potential power or responsibility." The American proposal on atomic energy ignored and violated both those danger signals. Secondly, the rapid development of a tough American policy in the summer and fall of 1945 that prompted Stimson's memorandum also provoked serious concern and fears on the part of the British. Prime Minister Clement Attlee told Truman that the question uppermost in his mind was a fundamental one: "Am I to plan for a peaceful or a warlike world?" Attlee's subsequent visit to Washington in November 1946, was clearly undertaken to influence Truman to take the former course in connection with atomic energy, and did unquestionably have some effect. This British pressure has to be credited in any assessment of American action. Finally, Stimson's memorandum bears directly, and in two ways, on the whole question of American disarmament at the end of the war. The official and widely accepted view is that the United States disarmed almost completely. This conclusion seems to have stemmed from three things: the extremist rhetoric and rather frantic behavior of Secretary of Defense James V. Forrestal who replaced Stimson (and similar assertions by assorted newspaper columnists and other pundits); the annual scare campaigns conducted by the Army, Navy, and Air Force in connection with their budget requests; and various formal and pseudohistorical accounts of the immediate postwar period prepared by the State Department, other government agencies, and associated intellectuals as part of cold-war propaganda.

But the striking thing is that neither Stimson nor Truman thought that the United States stood disarmed and defenseless before the Russian bear. Neither did Churchill. The Stimson letter to Truman of September 1945, is based on the assumption that the possession of the bomb and the capacity to deliver it gave the United States a clear military advantage: it meant having "this weapon rather ostentatiously on our hip." Churchill stated the same thing very simply in March 1946: the bomb kept the Russians under control. And Truman, on July 10, 1946, in a letter to Baruch about the American control plan, phrased it with perfect candor. "We should not under any circumstances throw away our gun until we are sure the rest of the world can't arm against us."

The fact is that the United States had not disarmed just

because it had demobilized the mass army created to fight World War II. Nor did its leaders think it had disarmed. Men like Forrestal merely wanted more conventional weapons to exploit the basic advantage of nuclear supremacy. Granted their assumptions, it was an intelligent proposal, but it had nothing to do with a desperate need to provide a disarmed United States with the means of its survival. Indeed, Forrestal himself admitted during his own campaign—as in his diary entry for June 10, 1946—that "the Russians would not move this summer—in fact at any time."

Truman's remark about "our gun" brings into clear focus the first of three essential points concerning the Acheson-Lilienthal-Baruch plan for the atom. The American proposal not only failed to set any time for giving up the nuclear weapons monopoly held by the United States, but it never committed the United States to do so in any firm manner. "The plan," explained the joint committee, "does not require that the United States shall discontinue such manufacture [of the bomb] either upon the proposal of the plan or upon the inauguration of the international agency. At some stage in the development that is required."* But the United States never specified the conditions of that stage. Let the motivations of the United States be accepted as stated by its protagonists and defenders, that demand for an immediate *quid* from Russia without a clear commitment to supply the *quo* by America remains a gaping weakness in the plan.

This suggests very strongly that J. Robert Oppenheimer was being accurate and candid in his recounting of the proceedings of the Acheson-Lilienthal committee, of which he had been a member.† He makes the second principal point about the American proposal: it was conceived in the spirit of Truman's remarks in August and October 1945. "The prevalent view," he explained, "saw in the problems of atomic energy . . . an opportunity to cause a decisive change in the whole trend of Soviet policy." "There appears to be little doubt that we yearn for the notion of a trusteeship more or less as it was

---

* U.S. Congress: *Senate Report No. 1211* (19 April 1946).

† J. R. Oppenheimer, "The Control of Atomic Energy," *Foreign Affairs* (January 1948).

formulated by President Truman in his Navy Day Address of late 1945." At that time, on October 27, the President had invoked the "righteousness and justice" of American foreign policy, and had assured the public that he would refuse to participate in "any compromises with evil."

Finally, the American plan demanded even more of the Russians than that they trust the United States with a nuclear weapons monopoly for an indefinite period. It asked in the meantime that the international authority established to administer the program should be granted extensive control over the nuclear economic affairs, and by indirection all economic affairs, of the Soviet Union. This is clearly one of the points that Oppenheimer had in mind when he spoke of the committee's idea of changing Soviet policy.

This proposed international authority was to be one, according to Baruch, "to which should be entrusted all phases of the development and use of atomic energy, starting with raw materials and including: 1. Managerial control or ownership of all atomic energy activities potentially dangerous to world security. 2. Power to control, inspect and license all other atomic activities."

Baruch seems to have understood from the beginning what this meant as far as winning approval from the Russians. For this phase of the plan amounted to applying the traditional Open Door Policy to atomic energy, and backing it up with sanctions. If this seems at first glance to be an exaggerated or mistaken analysis, it appears that way only because of the matter of timing involved. Fundamentally, the plan proposed the same kind of internationalization of the atom that Secretary Knox advocated for the Manchurian railways in 1909, and that Truman demanded for the Danubian waterways in 1945.

The Baruch plan held out the prospect of an open door for the development and use of atomic energy. The only difference was that in this case the United States was going to retain the job of doorman for an indefinite period. It was as if the United States had enjoyed monopoly control of the Manchurian railroad system in 1909, and had proposed to admit other nations to participate in the venture on American terms and according to an American timetable. At some unspecified time, the

United States would remove all restrictions on share purchasing—assuming that it would retain 51 per cent of the voting stock. In the meantime, the new but still American-controlled board of directors was to have the power to prevent the construction of competing lines either across Siberia or in China proper.

That analogy should also help in understanding why the Russians refused to agree to the Baruch plan. Baruch himself explained it on June 16, 1946, as well as—if not better than—the Soviet spokesmen did in their own speeches. Russia, he commented, "has no intention of permitting a situation whereby the national economy of the Soviet Union or particular branches of that economy would be placed under foreign control." That was fair and accurate enough, but then neither did the United States have any such intention. The result was precisely what Stimson had predicted: "A secret armament race of a rather desperate character."

Secretary of Commerce Wallace had become, by September 1946, so disturbed by the tone and tempo of this race that he spoke out even more forcefully than Stimson had done exactly a year earlier. He bluntly told Truman and the American public that it was time to stop using a double standard in dealing with the Soviet Union. "We should be prepared to judge [Russia's] requirements against the background of what we ourselves and the British have insisted upon as essential to our respective security. We should be prepared, even at the expense of risking epithets of appeasement, to agree to reasonable Russian guarantees of security." He also reiterated his suggestion of March 1946, to make "a new approach along economic and trade lines."

Truman did not agree with Wallace. Neither did Secretary Byrnes, then engaged in being firm with the Russians during negotiations in Paris. Neither did Truman's other advisors, or the top men in the Department of State. And neither did the Congress. Wallace was dismissed from the Cabinet on September 20, 1946. The Russians no doubt interpreted the firing of Wallace for what it was—a resounding reassertion of the tough policy. And as if to make sure they got the point, Byrnes, on October 16, 1946, cancelled an existing Export-Import Bank loan to Czechoslovakia.

Most commentators make a great deal of Andrei A. Zhdanov's rise to power in setting and enforcing the Soviet interpretations of intellectual and political questions. He did win this authority, and he advocated a very tough and even vulgar anti-Americanism derived from his argument that the world was divided into two hostile camps. But Zhdanov did not reach his position as commissar of the party line until the same period that Wallace was fired for challenging Truman. Figuratively speaking, Wallace and Zhdanov passed each other going in opposite directions aboard their elevators in the respective power systems during the last week in September 1946. And as the Varga debates of May 1947 indicated, Zhdanov cannot really be said to have fully consolidated his position for at least six months.

In this, as in so many other aspects of the cold war, the timing of apparently disparate, incidental, and unrelated events is crucial to an understanding of what was going on inside and between the two countries. In a similar way, it is a grave error to evaluate or interpret the diplomatic moves of 1945 and 1946 in an economic vacuum. This is true in three respects. First, a good many of them were specifically economic in character. Second, all of them were intimately bound up with Russia's concern to obtain either a loan from the United States or extensive reparations from Germany and its former allies in eastern Europe. And finally, the determination to apply the Open Door Policy to eastern Europe, which led directly to the policies of "total diplomacy" and "negotiation from strength" later made famous by Secretary of State Acheson, evolved concurrently with a deep concern over economic affairs in the United States.*

This fear had never really disappeared after the Recession of 1937–38. It was even present, though in its most subdued forms, during the concentrated drive in 1942–43 to win the war by out-producing the Axis. It regained all its former vigor, and power over the thinking of American leaders, beginning with the congressional hearings of 1943 on postwar planning

---

* Perhaps the best single essay on these points is T. Balogh, "The Political Economy of the Cold War," in *Fabian International Essays* (ed. by T. E. M. McKitterick and K. Younger: New York, Praeger, 1957).

and economic policy. By March 1946, the *New York Times* reported that "in all groups there is the gnawing fear that after several years of high prosperity, the United States may run into something even graver than the depression of the Thirties." The Employment Act of 1946, designed to relieve such anxiety, did not seem to reassure very many people.

Perhaps an explanation was the growing feeling that the welfare state approach of the New and Fair deals had not changed the essential characteristics, or power structure, of America's corporate political economy. By the end of 1946, in any event, even government spokesmen warned that the United States might "produce itself into a bust" if it did not obtain more foreign markets and overseas investment opportunities. Complementing that fear was the increasing concern over America's "staggering" consumption and waste of raw materials. Open-door expansion, it appeared, was the answer to all problems—the Russians, markets, and raw materials.

That traditional outlook was given further support by two events early in 1947. First, the President's Council of Economic Advisors expressed concern about the probability of a serious economic slump. Second, western Europe failed to recover from the war and take its place in the American scheme of things. Hence the problem was to coerce the Russians, help western Europe, and thereby establish the reality of an open-door system throughout the world. These two themes converged during the spring of 1947 in George F. Kennan's famous policy of containment and Dean Acheson's proposal for solving the "hard task of building a successfully functioning system" at home by reinvigorating America's expansion. These and other American leaders shared John Foster Dulles' view of February 1947, that "peace lies not in compromising but in invigorating our historic policies."

Among the many ironies of Kennan's policy of containment, perhaps the greatest is the fact that he had so internalized the assumptions and principles of the Open Door Policy that he thought he was proposing a radically different program. This indeed is the final act in the transformation of a utopia into an ideology. As Kennan himself later acknowledged, containment and liberation are "the two sides of the same coin"; and it was Kennan—not Dulles—who first stressed the traditional open-door faith in America's overwhelming economic power to force the Soviet Union along a path preferred by the United States. Even in 1957, when he felt "at liberty" to admit that containment had not prevented Russian economic development, Kennan reasserted the traditional objectives of the Open Door Policy in Europe.

Kennan's condemnation of earlier exponents of the Open Door Policy who moralized about foreign policy (and other nations) provided another striking paradox. For, as a fellow foreign-service officer noted, Kennan was "constantly making moral judgments about the behavior of states." Thus, for example, he judged the Soviet system "wrong, deeply wrong," and ruled by a "conspiracy within a conspiracy." His blanket denial that the Soviets had ever considered that they could work with the United States was another such moral judgment, as well as being an error of fact.

Kennan's later remark that one of his objectives in 1947 was to counter the tendency of Americans "to take a despairing and dramatic view of Soviet relations" indicates still another facet of the ideological nature of the thought of American leaders. For he described the Soviets as moving "inexorably along the prescribed path, like a persistent toy automobile wound up and headed in a given direction, stopping only when it meets with some unanswerable force." Hence it was absolutely necessary, he warned, to "confront the Russians with unalterable counterforce at every point where they show signs of encroaching" and to block the Soviet Union with "superior force" and with "unassailable barriers in its path." This language was not only dramatic and despairing, but it had a very great deal to do with the "overmilitarization of our thinking about the Cold War," about which Kennan complained ten years later.

The policy of containment was supplemented in 1947 by the Truman Administration's stress on the necessity of economic expansion. Aware of the warning made by government economists that "without a new aid program there would be a sharp drop in American exports," the President explained and stressed that problem very candidly *before* he enunciated the Truman Doctrine. In two speeches prior to that dramatic performance, the President asserted the need to "act and act decisively" to sustain the Open Door Policy. "The pattern of international trade which is most conducive to freedom of enterprise,", he pointed out, "is one in which major decisions are made not by governments but by private buyers and sellers." On the assumption that America was "the giant of the economic world," Truman announced that "the choice is ours" to sustain and expand private enterprise.

Hence it is misleading to overemphasize the differences between the Truman Doctrine and the Marshall Plan. They were the two sides of the same coin of America's traditional program of open-door expansion. As the direct descendant of Winston Churchill's militantly anti-Russia "Iron Curtain" speech of March 1946, the Truman Doctrine blamed the Soviet Union for the troubles of the world and announced the determination of the United States to halt the spread of revolutionary radicalism. It was the ideological manifesto of American strategy, described by the head of *Time's* Washington bureau as a program to promote "trouble on the other side of the Iron Curtain." As Acheson revealed to the Congress, the American Government entered upon "no consultation and no inquiry" about the possibility of achieving the stated objectives either through negotiations with the Russians or within the framework of the United Nations. The approach proceeded from the assumption, openly avowed by Harriman in 1945, and by Truman in 1946, that the cold war was inevitable.

Considered in isolation, however, the Truman Doctrine provides a one-sided impression of American policy. Some of its crusading fervor seems clearly to have been the result of a conviction, most candidly expressed by Senator Vandenberg, that it would be necessary to "scare hell out of the American people." On the other hand, it contained no references to the economic difficulties that worried American leaders. It concentrated instead on the political dangers of communism.

For his part, however, Secretary of State George C. Marshall did not initially emphasize the Russian danger. In his speech at Harvard on June 5, 1947, he offered the aid program as an expression of America's warm humanitarianism. There can be no question but that it did represent America's generous urge to help the peoples of western Europe, and that it did play a vital role in the recovery of that region. Approached solely as a humanitarian gesture, however, the Marshall Plan raises several troubling questions. China and Latin America were excluded, for example, though their needs were certainly great from a humanitarian (or even a policy) point of view. Perhaps Marshall's own testimony before the Congress provides a broader understanding of the program.

Prior to Marshall's famous address at Harvard, moreover, the Congress and the Department of State had been preoccupied with the danger of another depression. Undersecretary of State for Economic Affairs Clayton redefined *the* problem as that of disposing of America's "great surplus." "The capitalistic system, whether internally or internationally," he explained in May 1947, "can only work by the continual creation of disequilibrium in comparative costs of production." Clayton was saying implicitly what Acheson had argued explicitly in 1944: the profitability of America's corporate system depended upon overseas economic expansion. Given this consensus among American leaders, it is not too surprising that Marshall took a similar approach before the Congress: "The paramount question before us, I think, can be stated in business terms." The consequences of failing to carry through on the plan, he explained, would be to confront America, "if not [with] a t~de barrier, certainly with a great detriment to our ordinary business, or commerce and trade."

Marshall and other advocates of the program also spoke openly of the parallel between their policy and America's earlier westward expansion across the continent. Marshall presented the program in those traditional terms as the way to avoid the loss of democracy at home. Assuming that it offered the only solution to America's economic difficulties, the Secretary argued that the nation faced an either-or situation. Unless the plan was adopted, he asserted, "the cumulative loss of foreign markets and sources of supply would unquestionably have a depressing influence on our domestic economy and would drive us to increased measures of government control." By thus defining America's expansion as the key to prosperity, Marshall defined foreign policy as the key to domestic problems and to the survival of democracy at home. The intellectual continuity of his thought with the frontier thesis and the policies of John Hay, Woodrow Wilson, Herbert Hoover, and Franklin D. Roosevelt was apparent.

Other Americans were even more explicit. Secretary of the Interior Julius A. Krug defended the plan as "essential to our own continued productivity and prosperity." Another enthusiastic supporter remarked that "it is as if we were building a TVA every Tuesday." Even in the most restrained temper of judgment, this might well be the biggest "as if" in American history; for whereas TVA qualified as one of what Alvin Hansen has described as "frontiers in our own backyard," the Marshall Plan was a concerted program to sustain and expand a frontier overseas.

The testimony of liberal and conservative leaders indicated that they viewed the frontier thesis as the answer to the theories and prophecies of Karl Marx. Chester Bowles, for example, warned specifically that it "was wholly possible that within the next ten years Karl Marx's judgment will have proved correct." Concretely, he thought the United States was "heading toward some sort of recession which can be eased by quick approval of the Marshall Plan." Nelson Rockefeller explained that "with the closing of our own frontier, there is hope that other frontiers still exist in the world." Spruille Braden also saw the program as a way to "repeat what had been done in the development of our own great west."

One of Truman's Cabinet members preferred to think of the whole operation as a "logical extension of the good-neighbor policy, that the Fair Deal for all cannot flourish in isolation." Another Cabinet official saw it as the "restoration of Europe as a paying market for United States goods." And such widely different men as William Henry Chamberlin and Marquis Childs pointed directly to the analysis and program advocated by Brooks Adams in 1900 as a wise guide for 1947. Writing in *The Wall Street Journal,* Chamberlain thought it was "high time to face the problem created by what Brooks Adams called 'America's vast and growing surplus.'" Childs republished Adams's recommendations for the deployment of "America's economic supremacy" in behalf of the open door, and pointedly remarked that Adams "would have . . . to alter scarcely anything to relate his views to the world of today." Perhaps Childs, along with others, was struck by Adams's praise for Britain's traditional policy of "containing" the Russians.

From the very beginning, for that matter, many American leaders stressed the desirability and possibility of making the countries of eastern Europe "independent of Soviet control" and the importance of the "struggle for the preservation of Western civilization." Even a casual reading of the *Congressional Record* makes it clear that John Foster Dulles was a latter-day missionary for the doctrine of liberation. Coupled with this thought was a general acceptance of the idea of ending Soviet rule in Russia. Hardly any American leader failed to contribute his insights to the "cheerful discussion of how America ought, and ought not, to try to remake Russia." Some thought it might be necessary, and certainly magnanimous, to allow the Russians to retain some features of socialism. Others proposed a Heavenly City of the American Century. All agreed on the morality and the practicality of the objective.

This emphasis on open-door expansion and the assumption of the inevitable downfall of the Soviet Union again indicated that American leaders were not motivated solely by fear of Russian military attack. When asked point blank, *even after the Russians had tested their first nuclear bombs and the Chinese communists had defeated Chiang Kai-shek,* whether or not "our position on foreign policy with respect to communism is not relative to Churchill's in 1940," Secretary Acheson replied in the negative. "I do not mean to infer at all that there is that desperate a situation. I said I was not discouraged and was not taking a pessimistic view at all." "The problem which confronts us," he explained, "can be stated very simply: To maintain the volume of American exports which the free world needs and which it is our national interest to supply as a necessary part of building a successfully functioning political and economic system, the free world must obtain the dollars to pay for these exports."

For their part, the Russians clearly interpreted the Marshall Plan as the over-all economic equivalent of Baruch's proposal on atomic energy. It was to them an American strategy for setting and maintaining conditions on economic development in eastern Europe and the Soviet Union. That estimate prompted them first to refuse to participate, and then to embark upon a series of actions which most Americans mistakenly think had already occurred. They initiated a program of general political repression in Rumania. They sharply curtailed freedom of the press in Bulgaria, Rumania, and eastern Germany. They shot the Peasant Party leader Patlov in Bulgaria. And within the year the Communist Party in Czechoslovakia seized a monopoly of political power.

These events typified the nature of the cold war as it continued on into the 1950's. In the United States, President Truman repeatedly blamed all the troubles of the world on the Soviet Union, and American leaders in and out of government "bombarded the American people with a 'hate the enemy' campaign rarely seen in our history; never, certainly, in peace time." This American propaganda barrage prompted analyses by two government figures that received little publicity. A congressional committee headed by Representative Forrest A. Harness concluded its long study of the problem with this estimate in 1947: "Government propaganda distorts facts with such authority that the person becomes prejudiced or biased in the direction which the Government propagandists wish to lead national thinking." Exactly ten years later, General Douglas MacArthur offered an even more biting commentary on the same pattern of distortion. "Our government has kept us in a perpetual state of fear—kept us in a continuous stampede of patriotic fervor—with the cry of a grave national emergency. . . . Yet, in retrospect, these disasters seem never to have happened, seem never to have been quite real."

Perhaps it was true that the community of American policymakers "fell in love with its Cold War plan." That was the considered conclusion of James P. Warburg, an eminent conservative student of foreign affairs. It was more likely, however, that the ideology of the Open Door Policy had come to be so firmly believed by American leaders that they never questioned either the freedom or the necessity of their program for America and the world.

Certainly the attitude of American leaders toward the underdeveloped societies of the world suggested that explanation. Kennan, for example, took an extreme position on China, discounting almost completely its immediate significance or its potential importance. Others defined the poorer areas in the traditional open-door manner, seeing them as markets for exports and as sources of raw materials. Even when they spoke of the need to help such regions—or provided such assistance —they did so from the point of view of developing them as part of America's corporate system. It was quite normal, given that conception of the world, for American leaders to consider such regions as dependent variables of the situation in western Europe. The problems and difficulties in the underdeveloped areas could be handled through their existing ties to European empire countries. Time after time, therefore, the United States endeavored to support the crumbling ruins of eighteenth- and nineteenth-century colonialism against the impact of nationalistic and radical onslaughts.

No American leader personified all aspects of the ideology of the Open Door Policy more dramatically than Secretary of State John Foster Dulles. In the 1920's, he supported the Hughes-Hoover policy of expansion based on a "community of ideals, interests, and purposes" with Germany and Japan, and specifically pushed American penetration of underdeveloped areas in line with his emphasis on the necessity of markets for surplus goods and capital. He followed the same policy throughout the 1930's. Arguing that it was necessary to accept changes in the world, and asserting the Christian way of compromise, he labored diligently as late as 1939 to work out a broad understanding with Nazi Germany and a militarized Japan.

Dulles continued to advocate and practice this approach after 1945. Understandably, he worked very well as an advisor and assistant to Secretary Acheson during the early years of the cold war. His definition of compromise did not include a fundamental rapprochement and accommodation with the Soviet Union, or the acceptance of fundamental changes in the underdeveloped regions. On the threshold of his lifelong ambition to be Secretary of State, Dulles provided in 1952 the definitive statement of the Open Door Policy. Synthesizing the moral imperialism of his missionary background with the necessity of economic expansion of his banking experience, Dulles announced that he would liberate the Russians and the

Chinese from "atheistic international communism" and usher in the American Century.

Perhaps Dulles himself provided the most accurate picture of the final failure of the Open Door Policy. Against the background of constant and record-breaking travels all over the world, Dulles undertook yet another mission to Latin America. He was greeted by his official host with the pleasant and gracious remark that it was "good to have you here, Mr. Secretary." "You shouldn't feel that way." Dulles replied, "for I go only where there is trouble." And trouble indeed there was for the policy of the open door.

A bit later, when it appeared that negotiations with Russia could no longer be avoided, Dulles inadvertently laid bare the basic flaw of the open-door conception of the world. He worried about such a meeting with the Soviet Union, he explained, because it might tempt Americans to turn their attention and energies away from the cold war. But only a view of the world which defined freedom and necessity in terms of expansion could lead to that response. For a growing number of Americans were beginning to join millions of others throughout the world in a reassertion of the elementary fact that man was born to achieve and exercise his self-knowledge in more fruitful endeavors than a cold war which persistently threatened to erupt in nuclear horror. Dulles apparently failed to realize that he felt anxiety for the wrong reasons and was pursuing a policy that had now become a denial of the spirit of man.

Though not as extreme as Dulles in their reactions, most other American leaders were slow to grasp the real meaning of the revolutions throughout the world—their ability to destroy a cherished American illusion in Asia, to manage the transfer of power in Russia, to initiate and carry through a major conference of underdeveloped societies without American leadership, and even to defy the United States to use its nuclear weapons in retaliation. But only such an understanding and acceptance of the revolutions, followed by the development of a program based upon their reality, would enable the United States to play its warranted role in the new society arising on the foundations of the old.

CHAPTER SEVEN

Despite the fact that they were simple people, the Russians should not be regarded as fools, which was a mistake the West frequently made, nor were they blind and could quite well see what was going on before their eyes.

JOSEPH STALIN

Revolution is not a dinner party, nor a literary composition, nor a painting, nor a piece of pretty embroidery; it cannot be carried out "softly, gradually, carefully, considerately, respectfully, politely, plainly, and modestly."

Our primary duty is, not to add flowers to the embroidery, but to send coal to the snowbound.

MAO TSE-TUNG

I want no freedom based upon the assumptions of the British. Such a freedom simply means exchanging a set of white masters for a set of black masters. If I'm against British rule, then I'm against the rule of her stooges.

BLACK MAN NUMBER ONE, IN WHITE MAN, LISTEN!
BY RICHARD WRIGHT

All day and all night they talk to us about "sound and solid

THE IMPOTENCE
OF NUCLEAR SUPREMACY

development, sound and solid education." . . . *I say to hell
with John Stuart Mill and John Locke. Let's make our own
philosophy, based upon our own needs.*

BLACK MAN NUMBER TWO, IN WHITE MAN, LISTEN!
BY RICHARD WRIGHT

*It is not yesterday, a tradition, the past, which is the decisive,
the determining force in a nation. Nations are made and go on
living by having a program for the future.*

JOSÉ ORTEGA Y GASSET

At the apex of its power, the United States found itself persistently thwarted in its efforts to inspire, lead, and reform the
world. This supreme paradox of American history becomes
comprehensible when viewed as a direct result of the nation's
conception of itself and the world in terms of open-door expansion. For America's weakness in strength was the product
of its ideological definition of the world. The United States
not only misunderstood the revolutions in economics, politics,

color, and anticolonial nationalism; it asserted that they were
wrong or wrong-headed and that they should be ignored and
opposed in favor of the emulation of the American example.

When this advice was not followed, the offenders were defined as conspirators in league with Russia. When it was followed, but failed to succeed, a variation of the same theme
was offered in explanation. Inherently exasperating because of
its less than satisfactory results, either in theory or practice,
America's definition of the world led to even deeper frustration when it was confronted by the continued vitality of the
revolutions. Having mocked America's nuclear supremacy,
the revolutions sustained their development outside the ideology and the empire of the open door.

These results of America's conception of itself and the
world can be seen and understood most clearly by reviewing
its explanation of the Soviet Union and other specific revolutions, and by examining the inability of the theory and the
practice of the Open Door Policy to promote either the balanced improvement of poor societies or the acceptance of
America as the leader of the world. For the Soviet Union did
not develop according to the pattern of Nazi Germany, and
the people of the underdeveloped regions of the world blamed
the American *system* of open-door political economy for their
troubles as much as, if not more than, the United States itself.

Though from time to time other estimates were offered,
George F. Kennan's 1946–1947 explanation of Soviet behavior established the framework and set the tone for all but
a tiny corner of the American discussion of Russian action.*
His analysis, and the more extreme interpretations derived
from it, concluded that continued outside pressure could and
would accelerate an inevitable process of dissolution. The
thesis held that Soviet behavior resulted primarily (if not exclusively) from the necessity of Marxian revolutionaries having to resort to force to maintain the domination of an alien
and evil ideology over Russian traditions and history. It asserted that the prime mover of Soviet action was a drive to

---

* For a different view see, beyond the works cited in earlier chapters,
G. A. Morgan, "Stalin on Revolution," *Foreign Affairs* (1949); J. Maynard,
Russia In Flux (New York: The Macmillan Co., 1948).

maintain centralized power in the face of fundamental and persistent hostility. The weakness of the analysis lies in the fact that it is a single-factor thesis which forces and limits one, in the first rather than the last resort, to a simplistic psychological interpretation of Soviet conduct. Such an approach lends superficial validity to the analogy with Nazi Germany and to the argument that Soviet Russia corresponds in reality to the sociological abstraction known as a totalitarian society.

On the one hand, therefore, Kennan's analysis spawned a vast literature which treated Stalin as no more than a psychotic and, on the other, an equally large body of comment which argued that the only effective way to deal with the Soviet Union was to apply the lessons learned from the experience with Hitler. When tested against known facts, rather than accepted on the basis of a syllogism, these interpretations and recommendations did not lack all validity. Even by their own logic, however, they pointed to ultimate failure. For, by creating in fact a real, avowed, and all-encompassing outside threat, action based upon such analysis and analogy lent substance to what Kennan originally defined as a hallucination in the minds of Soviet leaders. Having argued that they had to create imaginary foreign dangers in order to stay in power at home, Kennan concluded with a policy recommendation to create a very serious (and from the Soviet point of view, mortal) outside challenge to their authority.

Both in abstract theory and in practical fact, however, pressure of this kind on Soviet leaders served only to make them tougher at home and abroad and to spur them to redouble their efforts to match the West. The final result might indeed be the collapse of the Soviet Union, but only in the context of general nuclear war. Chester Bowles, one of the early supporters of the containment policy, ultimately recognized the consequences of that approach. "The harder the Soviet Union is pressed," he concluded in April 1957, "the more vigorously her people will rally behind their leaders. If the Kremlin is forced to the wall it will almost certainly strike out with all its very formidable nuclear capacity."

Bowles could point to a great deal of evidence in support of his observation, including such items as the speed of Rus-

sia's industrial recovery and improvement after the war, its
own program of economic aid to other countries, its ruthless
countercontainment in Hungary, and the Sputniks. But neither
Bowles nor the handful of other men who grasped the same
point made much impression on the majority of America's
corporate leadership. By and large, the policy-makers stressed
the urgency of regaining unquestioned supremacy over Russia.
But in view of the results of that approach, it may be helpful
to take a fresh look at Soviet behavior.

Startling as it may seem, in view of the constant emphasis
on Soviet military power, the central fact confronting any
past or present Russian leader is the imbalance of the economic and political development of the nation. Czarist and
Soviet history is the record of a continuous, all-pervading
struggle to reach a minimum level of material well-being, let
alone relative prosperity or actual wealth. Russia is big, but
much of its territory is inhospitable to organized society, and
other large sections are at best but marginally productive agri-
culturally and industrially. As in the case of China, the situation may be modified in the future, but at any given moment
in the past or present, no Russian leader has been able to escape the gnawing knowledge of poverty and the insistent
pressure to produce enough to save enough to produce more.
This essential fact of Russian history provides great insight,
for example, into Lenin's argument that revolution could
come first in the weakest link of world capitalism, or into the
long tradition of Gargantuan developmental plans—from
Peter the Great to Joseph Stalin.

At the same time it has been necessary for Russia to maintain strong armed forces, urgently needed to defend open
borders against the continuous threat and recurring actuality
of foreign attack. This military investment always drained off
a sizable segment of the savings which might have eased Russia's economic and cultural needs. The same circumstance gave
the Russians but little opportunity to practice and develop
the skills of self-government. It is not possible to maintain
seriously that Russia has no valid historical or present fears of
foreign attack. And to employ a metaphor from modern technology, the present actuality of nuclear bases around its
borders feeds back into, and reinforces, the historical memory

of the Tatars, of Napoleon, of World War I, of the intervention against the revolution itself, and of Japanese and German military attacks from the 1930's on through World War II.

Perhaps a game of "as if" would help Americans grasp the depth, scope, and meaning of this aspect of Russian experience. Imagine, for example, that instead of conquering the Indians and establishing them on reservations, Americans had been forced to concede a stalemate and accept several ethnically and culturally defined Indian states; that instead of defeating the Mexicans once and for all, America had suffered periodic and destructive counterinvasions (and a similar relationship with Canada); and that instead of having bases on the military frontiers of the Soviet Union, America was confronted by Soviet jets manned by Russian pilots deployed throughout the Western Hemisphere. The purpose of exercising one's historical imagination in this manner is not to work up a brief for Soviet action in the cold war, but rather to grasp and understand the basic economic, political, and social consequences of living in that kind of world for generation after generation.

There are still other important facets of the interrelationship between Russia's economic and political imbalance. For in order to close the gaps in the poverty-conditioned cycle of production, saving, and reinvestment for greater production, Russia constantly found it necessary to resort to borrowing abroad; yet that additional indebtedness further weakened the country's international security and so again increased the burdens upon its citizens at home. This not only *seems* like a vicious circle; it *was* a vicious circle. And, as with all human experiences, the memory lingers on to influence the future.

This interplay of fundamental economic and political hardship was reinforced by related problems. The necessity of sustaining a major effort to overcome poverty led to early, and ultimately successful, attempts to bind many diverse ethnic and cultural units into one centralized administrative organization. This not only intensified the existing pattern of localized coercion, but it demanded even greater investments of economic and political savings (money *and* brains) to sustain the central organization in the face of sporadic struggles by various subsumed units to break away on their own or attempts by outsiders to crack off one or more of the frontier provinces.

Moscow's problem has never been the loss of just a Poland or a Hungary. To czar and commissar alike, the real issue has concerned the Baltic States, White Russia, and the Ukraine. And the same may be said of the Asian provinces, whether the illustrations are drawn from the czar's difficulties with the Maritime Province, from the Soviet's troubles with the Far Eastern Republic and the new industrial centers east of the Urals, or from the abortive Japanese intrusions of 1918 to 1922 and 1937 to 1939.

It is within the setting of poverty and centralized power that the Russians have grappled with the eternal dilemma of freedom and power. Their search for freedom took several paradoxical forms. Localized, nongovernmental, collective action was at once a means of fighting back against the system itself and of holding on to a sense of humanity and community in the face of such institutionalized power. At the same time, however, the czar, though he stood at the apex of the entire apparatus of coercion, also became the symbol of whatever immediate rewards and ultimate hopes survived the grinding, enervating, never-ending effort to conquer poverty and win respite from foreign enemies. The czar's ambivalent role was strengthened by his position as the spokesman of the religious answer to the quest for freedom in the presence of poverty and power.

In addition, however, the search for meaning and freedom also turned inward in a deep and almost desperate reconnaissance of the secular self for valid insights and viable values. It is here, perhaps, that a paradoxical similarity with America is most noticeable. For the loss of identity in prosperity led Americans toward Freud, while the similar Russian experience in the context of poverty produced Dostoevski, Kuprin, and Gogol, to name but the obvious examples. The self-knighted robber baron and the anarchist-terrorist are not, after all, so far apart. Neither is the Calvinist with a calling very far removed from the secular revolutionary driven by a historical necessity. And both experiences produce their respective sense of mission toward the world. The Russian's search for self and emphasis on community in the face of poverty and power led him to conclude that man's essential goodness emerges as a phoenix from the pyre of degradation. Hence in his mind he is best qualified to lead a similar reconstruction of all humanity. For his part, the American concluded that his achievement of prosperity and military might elected him as trustee for the same responsibility.

This review of Russian experience suggests that the sources of Russian conduct are the drives to conquer poverty and achieve basic security in the world of nation states. From these efforts developed, on the one hand, the practices and traditions of centralized power to force saving, allocate investment, and maintain security, and, on the other, the heightened domestic tension between collective action and individual identity and the ambivalence of a foreign policy at once militantly and suspiciously defensive yet characterized by a missionary and benevolent desire to help other men save themselves.

By pouring this historical experience into a Marxian mold, the Bolshevik Revolution emphasized and highlighted these Russian traditions, offered solutions for the problems of poverty and security, and suggested a resolution between the individual and his society. Given the success of the revolution, the problem becomes one of assessing the direction and extent of the impact of a Marxian revolution on the sources of czarist Russian conduct.

At the outset, clearly enough, the Bolshevik Revolution accentuated the basic problems of poverty and security. It disrupted even more completely the war-caused derangement of the productive process while at the same time encouraging England, France, Japan, and the United States to join Germany in direct military intervention. Both individually and collectively, these powers sought far more than the mere overthrow of the revolution. Each of them, although in conflict with the others, had plans for the New Russia, plans which saw the country as an area for them to develop, each according to its own particular genius. Hence the central experiences of czarist Russia continued uninterrupted.

At the same time, moreover, the Marxian conception of the world jibed in essentials, if not in language and detail, with the prerevolutionary Russian outlook. It is all too easy, perhaps because it also is so convenient, to forget that the revolution attracted and inspired a great portion of Russian society from the end of the civil wars to the mid-1930's. It did so again, though to a lesser extent in all probability, at the end of World War II. But such forgetfulness is dangerous as well as self-indulgent, for it leads to a misunderstanding of present Soviet society.

Here it is essential to realize that Marx was four men, so to speak, and that each of them contributed a share to the final product known as Marxism. The four aspects of Marx may be described as follows: (1) Marx the romantic, who emphasized the freedom and the primacy of the individual; (2) Marx the brilliant, tough-minded economist, who not only analyzed capitalism but, even more importantly in the Russian context, also suggested the basis for policies that would effect the rapid and continuing production of wealth; (3) Marx the politician, who outlined strategy and tactics for a successful revolution; and (4) Marx the prophet, who came back from his researches in the British Museum and from his battles against poverty and carbuncles with the vision of a society in which men would live in comradely community blessed with plenty.

Each of these four aspects of Marxism paralleled and reinforced its counterpart in the existing Russian tradition. The romantic Marx offered inspiration to those Russians who emphasized the individual's central place in society. Yet he also made sense to those who stressed collective discipline and action for great domestic and international achievements. Most significantly of all, he offered theoretical and practical suggestions for solving the central problems of poverty and security. And his vision of a planned socialist society infused the Russian tradition of centralized, coercive power with meaning and promise. Whether by national accomplishment or by international revolution (or both), therefore, Marxism seemed to promise an end to Russia's perpetual struggle against poverty and insecurity, a resolution of the conflict between freedom and power, and a place in the vanguard of humanity.

For these reasons, it is dangerously misleading to stress the monolithic character and heritage of Marxism. It is in fact a most pluralistic tradition which can be described as totalitarian only by falsely isolating and dramatizing one of its particular facets. The most dangerous consequence of misconstruing Marxism in that fashion lies in the resulting conclusion that all Russian communists also follow such a single, narrow interpretation. For as the record reveals, the Russian communists have always been divided into the four groups which correspond to the four aspects of Marx. They also draw upon, identify with, and emphasize the corresponding Russian traditions. Thus Trotsky's commitment to international salvation through revolution. Thus Gorky's stubborn individualism. Thus Bukharin's emphasis on decentralization and consumer goods. Thus Stalin's single-minded concern with centralized, coercive power for saving and investment and for security. Thus Lenin's truly epic struggle to keep the Russo-Marxian traditions in dynamic balance so that the means would neither subvert the ends nor forestall forward movement toward the desired goal. And thus, too, the less poetic efforts of the present Soviet leaders to redress the Stalinist imbalance and sustain the evolution.

By their very success in establishing an industrial system, moreover, Soviet leaders reinforced and extended such competing forces within Russian society. Based as it is upon an extensive and complex division of function, responsibility, and labor, an industrial society develops within it different attitudes and ideas about what can be done, what should be done, and how to do whatever is finally agreed upon. There is, to be sure, a strong pressure exerted by the system itself in the direction of a general consensus on certain basic issues; but even on these questions there are various ideas as, for example, about how to increase the production and distribution of consumer goods while it is still necessary to increase capital investment. Just such questions were raised in Russia after the battle of Stalingrad (as they had been earlier), and they are still being debated at the present time.

Differences of function also lead to competing ideas and programs. At the broadest level, there is a conflict between those who produce and those who plan and direct the process itself. Similar disagreements arise within each of those groups. Such conflicts can never be resolved once and for all, and each time they are compromised the result is a change in the previous state of affairs. Given its traditions, it is very unlikely that such conflicts in the Soviet Union would ever lead to the development of Western-style democracy. But it is quite probable, given an era of peace, that they would promote the progressive loosening up of Russian political and intellectual life.

To miss or deny the existence of these competing traditions and groups, or to interpret the struggle between them as mere vulgar wrestling for power, is to substitute a creaky mechanistic model for the reality. And that, in turn, pyramids the probability that a policy based upon such an interpretation will fail of its objective. For the problems are poverty and security, not power per se. Stalin was not Hitler. Neither is the present leadership simply a conspiracy. Policy based on such analogies, however sophisticated their logic and presentation, is doomed to failure. The reason is clear. The composite Russo-Marxian tradition has arrived at the beginning of the end of poverty and has proved its ability to match foreign technology and military power.

It would be a serious error, therefore, to misintepret the present resurgence of the individualistic, local, and utopian traditions of Russo-Marxism as evidence of impending Soviet collapse. Their vigor is a sign of maturity and positive evolution, not an indication of decay and death. With such maturity comes an unshakable determination on the part of the people who brought it about to maintain the hard-won identity and to continue the process toward ever greater accomplishments. Such men will fight before they surrender. And they are armed with hydrogen bombs.

But America need not abandon all efforts to influence events because they cannot be controlled perfectly, or because one theory seems, in practice, to produce unfortunate results. By adopting the more modest aim of encouraging the positive forces, and undertaking the effort in line with a more subtle analysis, it would seem realistic to hope for a moderate degree of success. The key problems faced by Russia are those of poverty and security and the basic traditions are those of centralized power resisted by localized collective action and individual integrity. Hence the most fruitful approach would seem to be action designed to relieve the problems of poverty and security on the grounds that achievement in these areas would encourage the decline of centralized power—both by choice and necessity.

The effort of the United States to force more drastic changes in Russian affairs not only failed of direct success, but it subverted other phases of American policy. For unlike America, the rest of the world was not primarily interested in waging a cold war with Russia. Perhaps the majority, often criticized by American leaders as "neutralists," tried to ignore both Russia and America as much as they could in order to concentrate on developing their own societies in their own way. A sizable number of people, for example, were positively attracted to Marxism. Either they judged it relevant to their own problems, or they were impressed—despite the brutal and undemocratic aspects of the Bolshevik Revolution and the era of Stalin's terrorism—with the tremendous advances made by Russia in less than their own lifetime. Others throughout the world supported the Soviet Union, or at least did not side actively with the United States, as a check on the unrestrained expansion of America. And another group sought or accepted aid from Russia either because it was offered on good terms or because it was not available from other sources.

For their part, many Chinese were attracted by the Bolshevik Revolution and the accomplishments of the Soviet Union. Lenin's theory of imperialism provided them with an explanation of their weaknesses and backwardness which tallied with their own experience and flattered their capabilities: Western powers were to blame. The revolution in Russia renewed their confidence that the Chinese, too, could change their unhappy lot. This reaction was sustained by the help and advice provided by the Soviets, who did not seem to care very much about the color of a man's skin or his cultural and social eccentricities. It was further strengthened by the fact that the Chinese, like Sun Yat-sen and Mao Tse-tung, who turned to Marxism and the Soviet Union were more inspiring and appeared to be more effective leaders than the men like Chiang Kai-shek who followed Western—even American—ideas and advice. The Chinese communists not only had a program, they were willing and able to make it work.

These were the fundamental explanations of why the communists triumphed in China. They also were the basic reasons behind communist strength elsewhere in the world. The communists were harsh and ruthless, and during their agitation and revolutionary action against the old order they neglected or ignored many, if not most, of the more liberal traditions of Marxism as well as many of the more humane values of their own cultures. But as indicated by developments after 1952 in Russia, and by the events of 1956 in Poland and Hungary, communists began to return to, and reassert and act upon, those values.

It is crucially important to realize, and actually to integrate into one's thinking, that those changes were initiated by communists. For this means not only that they were demonstrating the pluralism of the Marxian tradition, and exhibiting great personal dedication and courage in doing so, but also that the communists were the most likely source of such improvements in communist countries short of war.* There is inherent in the American policy of containment, after all, a deep callousness and indifference to the very Western values that it asserts and proclaims as absolutes. Its logic rests on the proposition that the act of forcing hardships on people through outside pressure will ultimately provoke them to action in behalf of those Western values. It may or may not do so, and the evidence is that the communists hold those values as part of their own Marxism (which is, after all, a philosophical heresy born in the West), but in any event the means employed by the policy of containment can hardly be defended as being appropriate to the ends.

These considerations are also pragmatically significant because they are understood, and their implications appreciated, by men and women throughout the rest of the world. They realized that the communists worked hard, and progressively more effectively, to improve conditions in their own societies. To many, many people, who had known little beyond survival, cruelty, and ridicule, this dedication and the increasing suc-

---

* One of the best, short introductory surveys of the Polish and Hungarian revolutions is in Fleming, *The Cold War,* Vol. II. In addition to the materials he cites for further reading, no serious student can afford to neglect R. L. Garthoff, "The Tragedy of Hungary," *Problems of Communism* (Jan.–Feb., 1957). It is in many, many ways the single most important study.

cesses of the communists seemed more important than their
failure to operate according to the highest Western standards
of democracy. Indeed, the character and consequences of two
centuries of Western predominance and leadership had little
impressed those men and women.

Most American leaders failed to grasp the importance of
these considerations. Instead, they continued to think and act
according to their traditional assumption and belief that
Marxism, the Soviet Union, and communists in general were
wholly evil and incapable of maturing into something more
humane. In one form or another, therefore, Americans operated on the premise that most of the difficulties in the world
were caused by the Soviet Union or agents, fellow travelers,
and dupes of the Kremlin. This initial attitude was reinforced
and given emotional intensity by the victories of the communists in China, southeast Asia, and other parts of the world.
Perhaps it was understandable, under these conditions, that
Americans overlooked or neglected the important role of other
ideas and developments in producing such changes. They also
failed to consider whether or not their own Open Door Policy
had anything to do with the difficulties they encountered. It
was difficult to decide which of these consequences was the
most damaging, for they interacted upon each other in a way
that compounded the crisis.

By concentrating on the communists so much, for example,
Americans underestimated or discounted such realities as world
poverty, the fantastic increase in world population, Western
society's persistent discrimination against other races and ideas,
and the continued vigor of man's ancient urge toward self-
definition and creative activity. In a similar way, America's
stress on the communists amounted to a rather arrogant slap
in the face to the millions of people who were not communists
but who wanted and acted for a better life in the here-and-
now. Giving the communists most of the credit for such agitation had two unfortunate results. First, it encouraged others
to accept that misrepresentation of the facts. Second, it implicitly said that nobody else was capable of doing that kind
of work. This result of the American attitude was only heightened when the United States went on to assert—or imply—
that at least nobody else but Americans could do it.

Many people throughout the world might have forgotten that insult, or at least not let it rankle in their hearts and minds, if American diplomacy actually produced such highly favorable results. The trouble was that it did not. After fifty years of the Open Door Policy, twenty-five years of the Good Neighbor Policy, and more than a decade of a crusade against communism, conditions throughout most of the free world did not verify either the assumptions, arguments, or promises of the policy of the open door.

It is vital at this point to differentiate between the motives, the specific results, and the over-all consequences of American policy. The question is whether or not America has in fact translated its ideas and ideals into programs and policies which serve to realize its objectives. America's motives are not evil. Neither are all of its actions wrong or fruitless. Indeed, many of them have literally made the difference between life and death to hundreds of thousands of people throughout the world. The Marshall Plan in Europe and the Point Four Program and other assistance to less developed nations clearly benefited many human beings in those areas.

The difficulty arises from the general view of America and the world in which these specific policies are formulated and put into operation. America has defined assistance to other people far too much in terms of anti-Russian and counterrevolutionary objectives, and as a necessity for the continued functioning of the existing system in the United States. In the realm of ethics and politics this point of view has led America to define legitimate behavior almost solely as anti-Russian conduct. In practical affairs the result has been to define as acceptable those means which do not seriously challenge the American economic empire of raw materials and markets.

But neither of these definitions is valid. A nation can act in many ways and yet become neither a satellite nor a dupe of the Soviet Union. Nor would the United States stagnate or go bankrupt, for example, if Venezuela nationalized its oil reserves and then sold petroleum to American corporations in an open market. The tragedy of American diplomacy is not that it is evil, but that it denies and subverts American ideas and ideals. The result is a most realistic failure, as well as an ideological and a moral one; for in being unable to make the American system function satisfactorily without recourse to open-door expansion (and by no means perfectly, even then), American diplomacy suffers by comparison with its own claims and ideals, as well as with other approaches.

In this vital respect, at any rate, America's high standard of living is only part of the story. On the one hand, the United States relies, in its own thinking as well as in practice, upon a great imbalance in its economic relations with poorer and weaker countries to achieve that standard of living. Even then, moreover, there are great extremes of wealth and power within American society.* And, on the other hand, American foreign policy has not produced either the kind or the degree of military security that policy-makers have asserted to be desirable and necessary. The basic question raised by these failures is not, as so often is asserted, one of how to implement the existing policy more efficiently, but is instead whether or not the policy can—because of its inherent nature—ever produce its avowed objectives. The evidence indicates that it cannot.

The Open Door Policy has failed because, while it has built an American empire, it has not initiated and sustained the balanced and equitable development of the areas into which America expanded. When it increased the gross national product of an area, for example, it did so under conditions which immediately removed much of the added wealth of the United States. Little of what remained was invested in the development of the political economy, let alone distributed among the population. Finally, the basic change that occurred over the period of American penetration was an intensification of the tensions and conflicts within the other society. What the Catholic Archbishop of Caracas said of Venezuela on May 1, 1947, applied elsewhere with but minor modifications: "Nobody will dare affirm that wealth is distributed in a manner that reaches all the Venezuelans, since an immense mass of our people are living in conditions that cannot be qualified as human." Even in countries where conditions were better, the

---

* On this point see, as the two most recent studies, G. Kolko, *Wealth and Power in America. An Analysis of Social Class and Income Distribution* (New York: Praeger, 1962); and M. Harrington, *The Other America. Poverty in the United States* (New York: Macmillan Co., 1962).

Open Door Policy did not produce balanced and dynamic economic development. Neither did it contribute much to investing life in such areas with a sense of purpose. American action and intervention failed to initiate and sustain either kind of improvement on a broad and fundamental basis.*

Soviet and other communist leaders could be criticized far more severely. Their revolutions extracted a terrible price in terror and hardship. Many of their subsequent policies—Russian intervention in Hungary, for example—warrant harsh judgments. But to concentrate exclusively on these points is to neglect others of considerable importance. Most significant of all, perhaps, is the fact that life in the communist countries has improved. The picture is one of brutality *and* betterment, not simply one or the other. And it was that consideration which exercised a persuasive influence on men and women who had known little improvement under the American Open Door Policy or the imperialism of America's European allies. Pain and poverty they knew, but never as the price of progress in their own lifetime. Hence the communists, as examples and leaders of such development, gained stature and influence throughout much of the world.

A great deal has been said in America about the "revolution

---

* The literature on the nature and problems of underdeveloped countries, and their relations with the advanced nations, is so vast that any short list of recommended reading is almost certain to seem either biased or superficial. The following provide an introduction to the subject, and all have bibliographies. R. E. Asher, *Grants, Loans, and Local Currencies. Their Role in Foreign Aid* (Washington: Brookings Institution, 1961); P. A. Baran, "On the Political Economy of Backwardness," *Manchester School Economic and Social Studies* (1952); B. F. Hoselitz, *Sociological Aspects of Economic Growth* (Glencoe: The Free Press, 1960); B. F. Hoselitz, et. al., *Theories of Economic Growth* (Glencoe: The Free Press, 1960); J. L. Levin, *The Export Economies. Their Pattern of Development in Historical Perspective* (Cambridge: Harvard University Press, 1960); W. A. Lewis, *The Theory of Economic Growth* (London: Allen and Unwin, 1955); D. A. Morse, *Report of the Director-General, Seventh Conference of American States Members of the International Labour Office. Economic Growth and Social Policy* (Geneva: International Labour Office, 1961: in many ways the best single introduction for the general reader); and two volumes by G. Myrdal: *An International Economy* (New York: Harper & Bros., 1956), and *Rich Lands and Poor* (New York: Harper & Bros., 1957). My *Contours of American History* is an effort to reconstruct the way that early American leaders dealt with these problems.

of rising expectations" under way in the underdeveloped areas of the world, but it has often been overlooked that such a revolution is powered by a willingness to pay a high price for the realization of those aspirations. By appearing to be a nation which refused to let other peoples pay a price they thought justified, as well as a nation which did not extend itself to reduce that cost, the United States did more than merely forfeit leadership to the Soviet Union. Such action made it seem as though the United States was the major obstacle to the revolution of rising expectations. To many throughout the world, therefore, the Open Door Policy appeared to confront them with a door closed to their own progress.

As a result, America found itself impaled on the traditional dilemma of empire. It could resort to war or it could disengage, safeguarding its strategic position by formulating a new outlook which accepted the reality of a world in revolution and devising new policies calculated to assist those revolutions to move immediately and visibly toward their goal of a better human life.

The first way is to proceed with the final corruption of the American Dream. The second is to reassert and reinvigorate America's definition of its own national interest as that of tolerating, encouraging, and helping *all* men in their labors to realize their creative potential. This is not the definition of a crusade to save or remake the world; neither is it one which views the rest of the world as a mere contributing agent to America's self-realization. Rather is it a definition of the national interest which accepts the diversity of the good life and which derives from a society mature and confident enough to live and let live.

Having so returned to a viable definition of the national interest, Americans could comprehend and support the basic objective of the Bandung Conference of Asian and African nations: "No task is more urgent than that of preserving peace. Without peace our independence means little. . . . Our revolutions will not be allowed to run their course." In a similar way, Americans could also recognize the wisdom of their poet Robert Frost. "We ought to enjoy a standoff. Let it stand and deepen in meaning. Let's not be hasty about showdowns. Let's be patient and confident in our country."

CONCLUSION: THE WISDOM OF AN

The tradition of all past generations weighs like an Alp upon the brain of the living.

KARL MARX

It is not my duty as a historian to predict the future, only to observe and interpret the past. But its lesson is clear enough; we have lived too long out of contact with reality, and now the time has come to rebuild our lives.

CALLITRAX, HISTORIAN OF LYS, IN THE CITY AND THE STARS, BY ARTHUR C. CLARKE

Yes, strictly speaking, the question is not how to get cured, but how to live.

MARLOW TO STEIN, IN LORD JIM, BY JOSEPH CONRAD

OPEN DOOR FOR REVOLUTIONS

Future historians are apt to conclude that America's "total diplomacy" of the cold war was governed by the principle of the boomerang. For in little more than a decade, the United States found itself confronted by a reality that was almost the opposite of the world it had confidently expected to emerge as the product of its program and policies. The Soviet Union neither surrendered nor collapsed nor embarked upon an effort to remodel itself in the image of Western liberalism. Instead, it continued its economic development and began to evolve and structure a Russo-Marxian system designed to institutionalize and regularize the politics of mature industrialism.

Throughout the rest of the world, America was confronted by revolutions which looked elsewhere (and within themselves) for inspiration, help, and guidance. Even its conservative and liberal allies began to turn away from the example and the advice of the United States. At home, meanwhile, the spirit of the people, the substance and form of politics, and the functioning of the economy all denied that the diplomacy of the cold war could be defended on the grounds that it had at least improved the nature and the tone of life in America.

Perhaps the most hopeful sign was the existence of a general, though vague and unfocused, awareness that the program and policies of the past were insufficient unto the present and the future. But while a growing number of leaders recognized the fact of failure, and even specified numerous symptoms, almost none of them seemed to grasp the origins of the crisis. For that reason they did not offer much in the way of a new approach.

One of the most revealing examples of the underlying doubt and confusion, and consequent stress on symptoms, was provided by Harry Schwartz in the *New York Times* of April 6, 1958. Since Schwartz was the Russian expert of the *Times* (which had vigorously supported the cold war from its inception), a scholar whose books had emphasized the harshness, brutality, and weaknesses of Soviet society, and a political reporter and commentator who had exhibited little patience with critics of American policy, his article was particularly significant. It amounted, in more ways than one, to an admission that the failure of American policy had become news fit to print.

With considerable astuteness, Schwartz itemized the illusions upon which American policy was founded. He gave priority to the idea that the Soviet Union "will collapse," pointing out that it "has clearly been at the base of our postwar containment policy." His judgment was simple: it "seems unrealistic." Next he referred to the accepted idea that the conflict between America and Russia "is one between our absolute good and their absolute evil." He admitted that description was misleading because, "despite its evils and its demands, Communist rule in the Soviet Union has brought major advances in industrialization, in education and in health protection." As for the Soviet people, "they have made enough progress since the worst years of Stalin's rule to believe that the future will bring still more progress and will be more tolerable than the past."

In response to such harsh verities, some American leaders grasped fervently for Henry Wallace's old argument that the best way for America to recover lost ground—and come out on top—was to export an enlightened and updated version of the New Deal to India and other underdeveloped areas of the world. While certainly the most relevant program offered by any segment of American leadership, that proposal was nevertheless the product of a rather sophisticated naiveté which assumed that technicians, surplus food, and American machinery would convert wrong-headed revolutionaries into fine, upstanding liberals who turned their backs on false communist gods that failed.

Considered against the backdrop of American foreign policy

since 1890, such a proposal seemed impressively progressive. But when judged against the world scene, the result was startling: American leaders had reopened the great debate of the mid-1940's a decade too late. For Schwartz and others proposed little more than a liberalized and more effective version of the traditional Open Door Policy. They advised being more generous in extending economic aid and more intelligent in building "adequate communities of interest with other free nations." But the issues were neither generosity nor intelligence. America had exhibited and dispersed great quantities of both commodities.

The trouble was of a wholly different order. All segments of American leadership still shared the traditional objective of the 1890's: Stabilize the world in a pro-American equilibrium. Yet that conception of what could and should be done was precisely the cause of the continuing crisis. The scene recalled Alice in Looking-Glass Land running as fast as she could to stay under the same tree—with the vital difference that she was not succeeding in her effort. This image helped dramatize the point that America was not the victim of a simple case of failure, but rather was plagued by the infinitely more subtle paradox of the failure of success.

Though ridiculed and condemned by many experts and commentators (who nevertheless followed its essentials in their own policy recommendations and actions), the Open Door Policy had provided the strategy and tactics that enabled the United States to establish a new and persuasive empire during the era when the colonial empires of the eighteenth and nineteenth centuries were dying and being given the *coup de grâce* by the twentieth-century revolutions in economics and politics, in the relationship between the colored and the white peoples of the world, and of anticolonial nationalism. The very success of the Open Door Policy enabled America to exercise varying degres of economic, political, and military influence and authority in the very countries that were driving the British, French, and Dutch back to Europe. Such power also carried with it the spirit of American idealism and the vision of a better life for foreign peoples. And in many specific cases these ideals had to some extent been realized in the process of American expansion.

But the triumph of the Open Door Policy was subject to the

same process of cause and consequence—of change—which carried it to victory in fifty years. These results were inherent in the conception of the world which originally produced the policy and which translated it into concrete programs and actions. Central to the failure in success was the fact that the Open Door Policy defined America as an alien power in the eyes and the experience of most of the rest of the world. The Open Door Policy did not cease being a program of imperial expansion simply because it spurned territorial and administrative colonialism in favor of an empire of economics, ideology, and bases.

Attracted by its anticolonial character, foreign peoples initially welcomed it as a policy of assistance and friendship with no strings of absentee ownership attached. But within a generation they sensed that its minimum objective was to stabilize and freeze the status quo of Western supremacy and that its optimum goal was to institutionalize American expansion. At the end of a half-century they were rebelling against the subordination of their own cultural, political, and economic life that was implicit in, and was practiced under, the policy of open-door expansion. Hence it is clear that any effort to rehabilitate the Open Door Policy would only serve now to compound the existing failure and crisis—there are no better policies to accomplish the purpose. The goal of an open-door empire has been achieved. It is necessary to change the objective. First, because the traditional one is impossible to sustain and, second, because there are viable alternatives available to the opponents of America's open-door empire. If clung to much longer, the policy of open-door expansion will very probably end by producing either the literal isolation or the nuclear destruction of the United States.

Considerable intellectual and emotional discipline and courage are required if Americans are to change—not merely revise —their conception of themselves and the world. These demands and difficulties are dramatically illustrated by American policy during the Korean War.* Immediately after the North

---

* This discussion of the Korean war draws principally upon the materials in *Military Situation in the Far East. Hearings Before the Armed Services Committee and the Foreign Relations Committee, U.S. Senate.*

Korean forces crossed the 38th parallel, and the United States
had committed its forces in the battle, Secretary of State Acheson publicly defined American policy in unequivocal terms.
The United States was fighting, so he declared, "solely for the
purpose of restoring the Republic of Korea to its status prior
to the invasion from the north." This was a straightforward
indication that American leaders, at least at that time in that
situation, had reached the point of modifying their traditional
strategy of the Open Door Policy. The war was not to be used
to extend the policy, as had been done—or attempted—in
World Wars I and II.

Within three months, however, that apparent modification
had gone the way of Wallace. It had been dismissed. President
Truman approved military operations north of the 38th parallel on September 11, 1950, very probably on the assumption
that General MacArthur's landing at Inchon, scheduled for
September 15, would be a success. Orders translating the President's decision to MacArthur were sent on the day of the
invasion. When his brilliant and difficult operation at Inchon
did turn the tables on the North Koreans, MacArthur advised
Secretary of Defense Marshall of his proposed directive to
troops crossing the parallel. Marshall promptly ordered the
General to withhold the document. "We desire that you proceed with your operations without any further explanation
or announcement and let action determine the matter. Our
government desires to avoid having to make an issue of the
38th parallel until we have accomplished our mission."

The mission, as Acheson later revealed, was to realize one
of the earliest, turn-of-the-century objectives in the strategy
of the Open Door Policy. Put simply, it was to free Korea of
Russian as well as Japanese influence. World War II had accomplished the latter; the Korean conflict would finish the
job. Under American leadership, the United Nations General
Assembly on October 7, 1950, approved a resolution authoriz-

82nd Cong., 1st Sess. (5 Vols., 1951); Truman's *Memoirs;* and C. Whitney,
MacArthur: His Rendezvous with History (New York: Knopf, 1956); but
also on J. W. Spanier, *The Truman-MacArthur Controversy and The
Korean War* (Cambridge: Harvard University Press, 1959), and the materials in his fine bibliography.

ing "all appropriate steps to be taken to ensure conditions of stability throughout Korea." As Ambassador Warren Austin explained in supporting the resolution, the United States considered "the political aspect of the problem identified with the 38th parallel" to be "a matter of major concern."

Secretary Acheson was later asked the key question during a congressional investigation:

SENATOR HARRY CAIN: What, may I ask, were our United States forces doing on the shores of the Yalu River last November if it was not in an attempt to crush the aggressor and to unify Korea by force?

ACHESON: General MacArthur's military mission was to pursue them and round them up . . . and, as I said many times, we had the highest hopes that when you did that the whole of Korea would be united. . . .

SENATOR CAIN: If, sir, the Red Chinese had not entered the war, and our allied forces would have rounded up all those who were a party to the aggression in Korea, we would then have unified Korea by force; would we not?

ACHESON: Well, force would have been used to round up those people who were putting on the aggression . . . unifying . . . it would be through elections, and that sort of thing.

Force would have played a part. . . .

Finally, it is clear that the attitude toward China that was an inherent part of the open door outlook served in a real sense to subvert the effort to apply the strategy of the Open Door Policy to Korea. The United States assumed that it could unify Korea by force because it did not believe, despite many indications to the contrary, that the Chinese Communists would intervene. And the explanation of that belief resides in one of the classic axioms upon which the Open Door Policy was based; namely, that China and Russia were natural enemies, and that China would therefore align itself with the United States.

The power and the momentum of the traditional outlook as revealed in the Korean episode do not justify any optimism about the magnitude of the effort involved in changing such established assumptions and habits of thought. Yet it is wiser to employ such courage and discipline for living than for dying. There is, indeed, no courage or discipline involved in following failure down the trail to disaster. Tragedy is a tool for the living to gain wisdom, not a guide by which to live. Joseph Conrad's penetrating advice for getting to the heart of a fundamental issue is more fruitful: "The way is to the destructive element submit yourself, and with the exertion of your hands and feet in the water make the deep, deep sea keep you up."

Applied to the issue of America's conception of itself and the world, that insight suggests that the first step is to deny the validity of the crucial assumptions which provide the foundation for that *Weltanschauung*. Thus a radically different concept replaces the accepted thesis that America's freedom and prosperity depend upon the continued expansion of its economic and ideological system through the policy of the open door. Instead, it appears that America's political and economic well-being depend upon the rational and equitable use of its own human and material resources at home and in interdependent co-operation with *all* other peoples of the world. America can neither take its place in nor make its contribution to the world community until it believes and demonstrates that it can sustain prosperity and democracy without recourse to open-door imperial expansion. The central issue of the mid-twentieth century is how to sustain democracy and prosperity without imperial expansion and the conflicts it engenders. The reason is obvious: the sparks from those collisions now fall into a nuclear tinderbox. It is all very well to converse bravely, seriously, and learnedly about surviving such a holocaust, but that is like sitting around the evening fire talking about what to do in the morning after the horse has been stolen instead of discussing ways and means of barring the barn door that night.

It is true that there are no completely foolproof locks, but it does not follow from that quite mundane observation that the risks of using the ones we have are greater than the risks and costs of getting along without the horse—or of buying another one. Yet this is precisely what we are doing when we give up on disarmament on the grounds that it cannot be 100 per cent guaranteed in advance, and turn instead to discussions of how to intimidate the Soviets with superweapons, or of how to rebuild the United States after a nuclear war.

One of the most disturbing features of international affairs between 1952 and 1962 was the extent to which it was the Russians, rather than the Americans, who sensed and appreciated this essential aspect of reality. For this is the real meaning of the Soviet doctrine of coexistence. They are proposing that the existing political and military balance be accepted as the foundation of world politics for an indefinite period. It is ironic, but in a deadly way, that it has been the United States and China which have refused to agree to this proposition.

The American nonrecognition of Mao Tse-tung's government has served in this sense to mask an unspoken entente between them on this crucial point of policy. There is not even any conscious thought—let alone any conspiracy—involved on the American side of this agreement. For that matter, American policy-makers seem wholly deaf and unconscious to the point despite the very broad hints that have been shouted from the Kremlin. As far as Washington is concerned, it could in this respect be called the best-kept secret treaty in the nation's entire history. The only way that the United States can break free of this entangling alliance with the Red Chinese is by accepting the Soviet doctrine of coexistence.

Americans must do this, not only to make it possible to slow down the dangerous momentum of the cold war toward thermonuclear war, not only to strengthen the advocates of coexistence in China, but even more in order that Americans themselves can apply their intelligence and humanitarianism to the very real and serious problems in the United States. This proposal has nothing to do with reviving and embracing either the theory or the practice of isolationism. There is no longer any question of whether or not we shall have relations with the rest of the world; there is the far more significant one of the kind of relations we shall have. That problem cannot be discussed intelligently to any relevant conclusions so long as it is defined in the narrow terms of the existing approach. We need to ask questions about the very *nature* of the traditional foreign policy of the United States, not questions concerning merely the *means* of putting it into operation. The right kind of questions are admittedly those that make us squirm. But isn't it time to find out whether we can still take that kind of question?

Isn't it time to stop defining trade as the control of markets for our surplus products and control of raw materials for our factories? Isn't it time to stop depending so narrowly—in our thinking as well as in our practice—upon an informal empire for our well-being and welfare?

Isn't it time to ask ourselves if we are really so unimaginative that we have to have a frontier in the form of an informal empire in order to have democracy and prosperity at home? Isn't it time to say that we can make American society function even better on the basis of equitable relationships with other people?

Isn't it time to stop defining trade as a weapon against other people with whom we have disagreements? Isn't it time to start thinking of trade as a means to moderate and alleviate those tensions—and to improve the life of the other people?

Isn't it time to stop trying to expand our exports on the grounds that such a campaign will make foreigners foot the bill for our military security? Isn't it time instead to concern ourselves with a concerted effort to halt and then cancel the armaments race?

Isn't it time to stop saying that all the evil in the world resides in the Soviet Union and other communist countries? Isn't it time to admit that there is good as well as evil in those societies, and set about to help increase the amount of good?

Isn't it time to admit that our own intelligence reports mean that the Russians have been following a defensive policy in nuclear weapons? Isn't it time to take advantage of that attitude on their part, break out of our neurosis about a Pearl Harbor attack, and go on to negotiate an arms control measure?

Isn't it time to admit, in short, that we can avoid living with communist countries only by embarking upon a program that will kill millions of human beings? Isn't it time, therefore, to evolve and adopt a program that will encourage and enable the communist countries to move in the direction of their own utopian vision of the good society as we endeavor to move in accordance with our own ideals?

For beyond acceptance of coexistence, the United States must

embark upon a patient and concerted effort to establish and
maintain by continued negotiation and development a *modus
vivendi* with the Soviet Union, the People's Republic of
China, and their allies. To this effort, economic agreements,
involving normal credits and loans and a continuing increase
of trade in consumer items and goods needed for general economic development, are basic. Such an approach will facilitate
two processes essential to continued peace. First, it will open
the way for continued reform within communist countries.
That will make it easier, secondly, for the United States to
allocate its aid and assistance to other nations through the
appropriate agencies of the United Nations. Future requests
to the United States for aid should be referred to such committees of the United Nations for mutual discussion and decision. If approved, such grants should be administered by the
United Nations. For if America's objective is the improvement
of life throughout the world, then there is no better way to
speed that process. Such a policy would also strengthen America's own position. For it is true, as Thucydides is reputed to
have remarked, that the greatest exercise of power lies in its
restraint.

Once freed from its myopic concentration on the cold war,
the United States could come to grips with the central problem of reordering its own society so that it functions through
such a balanced relationship with the rest of the world, and so
that the labor and leisure of its own citizens are invested with
creative meaning and purpose. A new debate over the first
principles and practices of government and economics is long
overdue, and a statement of a twentieth-century political economy comparable to *The Federalist* papers would do more to
enhance America's role in the world than any number of
rockets and satellites. The configuration of the world of outer
space will be decided on the cool green hills of earth long
before the first colonizing spaceships blast free of the atmosphere.

Having structured a creative response to the issue of democracy and prosperity at home, the United States could again
devote a greater share of its attention and energy to the world
scene. Its revamped foreign policy would be geared to helping
other peoples achieve their own aspirations in their own way.

The essence of such a foreign policy would be an open door for revolutions. Having come to terms with themselves—having achieved maturity—Americans could exhibit the self-discipline necessary to let other peoples come to terms with themselves. Having realized that "self-righteousness is the hallmark of inner guilt," Americans would no longer find it necessary to embark upon crusades to save others.

In this fashion, and through a policy of an open door for revolutions, Americans would be able to cope with the many as yet unknown revolutions that are dependent upon peace for their conception and maturation. Only in this way can either the general or the specific tragedy of American diplomacy be transcended in a creative, peaceful manner. Otherwise the next Cuba may very well be the last. For unless the existing attitudes and policies are changed, another Cuba will clearly be dealt with through military intervention involving American troops. And that—even without direct Soviet or Chinese retaliation in kind—could insure the final catastrophe.

Of course, such an American intervention would have profound and reactionary consequences in Russia and China, and hence upon the relationship between them. The result would be a further acceleration of the already very serious momentum toward thermonuclear war. It would very probably, and whatever the outcome of the specific intervention by the United States, produce an increasing loss of control on both sides.

The way to transcend tragedy is to reconcile the contrasting truths which define the tragedy. Left instead to run out the string of their own logic, as they were and did in Cuba, the clashing truths will sooner rather than later kindle a global nuclear fire. To transcend tragedy requires the nerve to fail. But a positive effort to transcend the cold war would very probably carry the United States and the world on into an era of peace and creative human endeavor.

For the nerve to fail has nothing at all to do with blustering and self-righteous crusades up to or past the edge of violence. It is instead the kind of quiet confidence that comes with and from accepting limits, and a concurrent understanding that accepting limits does not mean the end of existence itself or of the possibility of a creative life. For Americans, the nerve to fail is in a real sense the nerve to say—and mean—that we no longer need what Turner called "the gate of escape" provided by the frontier. It is only in adolescence or senility that human beings manifest a compulsive drive to play to win. The one does not yet know, and the other has forgotten, that what counts is how the game is played. It would actually be pathetic rather than tragic if the United States jumped from childhood to old age without ever having matured. Yet that is precisely what it will do unless it sloughs off the ideology of the Open Door Policy and steps forth to open the door to the revolutions that can transform the material world and the quality of human relationships.

Perhaps it is by now apparent to the reader that there is a basic irony involved in this conception and interpretation of American foreign policy as tragedy. This irony arises from, and is in that sense caused by, the truth that this essay is in two respects written from a radical point of view.

First, it is radical in that it seeks to uncover, describe, and analyze the character and logic of American foreign policy since the 1890's. It is therefore critical in the intellectual sense of not being content with rhetoric and other appearances, and of seeking instead to establish by research and analysis a fuller, more accurate picture of reality.

Second, it is radical in that it concludes from the research and reflection, that American foreign policy must be changed fundamentally in order to sustain the wealth and welfare of the United States on into the future. This essay recommends that the frontier-expansionist explanation of American democracy and prosperity, and the strategy of the Open Door Policy, be abandoned on the grounds that neither any longer bears any significant relation to reality.

This essay also points toward a radical but noncommunist reconstruction of American society in domestic affairs. And it is at this point that the irony appears: there is at the present time no radicalism in the United States strong enough to win power, or even a very significant influence, through the processes of representative government—and this essay rests on the axiom of representative government. Hence, ironically, the radical analysis leads finally to a conservative conclusion. The well-being of the United States depends—*in the short-run but only in the short-run*—upon the extent to which calm and confident and enlightened conservatives can see and bring themselves to act upon the validity of a radical analysis. In a very real sense, therefore, democracy and prosperity depend upon whether the New Frontier is defined in practice to mean merely a vigorous reassertion of the ideology and the policies of the past or to mean an acceptance of limits upon America's freedom of action.

The issue can be stated as a very direct proposition. If the United States cannot accept the existence of such limits without giving up democracy and cannot proceed to enhance and extend democracy within such limits, then the traditional effort to sustain democracy by expansion will lead to the destruction of democracy.